CATCHING SIGHT

THE WORLD OF THE BRITISH SPORTING PRINT

VIRGINIA MUSEUM OF FINE ARTS

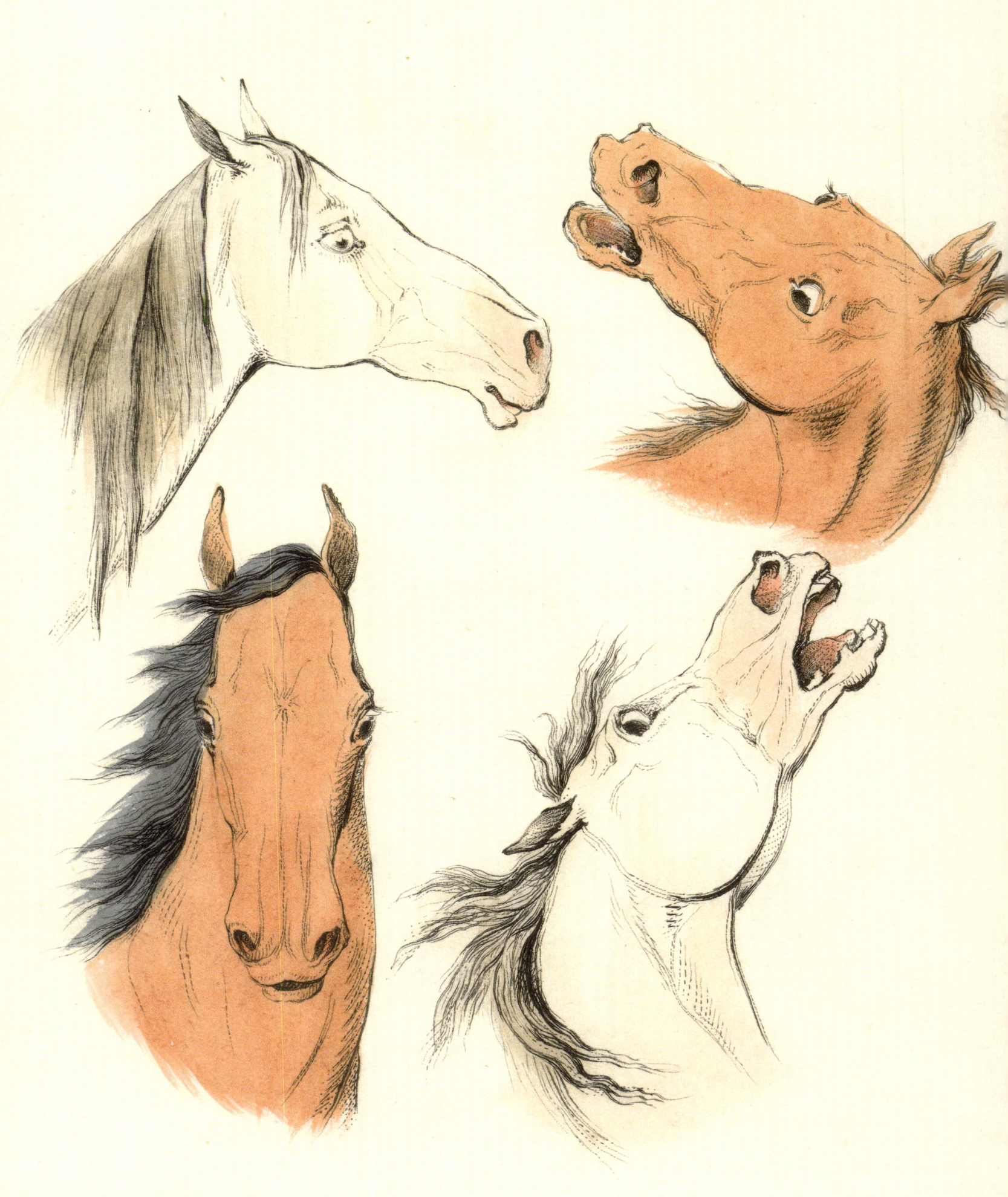

CATCHING SIGHT

THE WORLD OF THE BRITISH SPORTING PRINT

MITCHELL MERLING

with MALCOLM CORMACK and COREY PIPER

VIRGINIA MUSEUM OF FINE ARTS

This catalogue accompanies the exhibition
Catching Sight: The World of the British Sporting Print
at the Virginia Museum of Fine Arts,
August 31, 2013 through July 13, 2014.

Library of Congress Cataloging-in-Publication Data
Virginia Museum of Fine Arts.
Catching sight : the world of the British sporting print /
Mitchell Merling ; with Malcolm Cormack and Corey Piper.

pages cm

Issued in connection with an exhibition
held Aug. 31, 2013–Jul. 13, 2014,
Virginia Museum of Fine Arts, Richmond, Virginia.
Includes bibliographical references.

ISBN 978-1-934351-03-1 (alk. paper)

1. Sporting prints, British — Exhibitions. 2. Mellon, Paul —
Art collections — Exhibitions. 3. Prints — Private collections —
Virginia — Richmond — Exhibitions. 4. Virginia Museum of
Fine Arts — Exhibitions. I. Merling, Mitchell Frank. II.
Cormack, Malcolm. III. Piper, Corey. IV. Title.

NE960.3.G7 V57 2013

769.9755'451—dc23   2013019653

ISBN 978-1-934351-03-1

Produced by the Department of Publications,
Virginia Museum of Fine Arts
200 N. Boulevard, Richmond,
Virginia 23220-4007 USA

Rosalie West, Editor in Chief

Stacy Moore, Project Editor

John Hoar and Patrick Bell, Book Designers

Sarah Lavicka, Chief Graphic Designer

Composed and typeset in Minion Pro
Printed on Mohawk Superfine text by
Worth Higgins & Associates, Inc., Richmond, Virginia

All VMFA photographs by Travis Fullerton unless otherwise noted

COVER: *London Sportsmen Shooting Flying* (detail), ca. 1800, Isaac Cruikshank
(British, 1786–1811), hand-colored etching, 5 ⅜ x 8 ¹¹⁄₁₆ in., Paul Mellon Collection,
85.1282.2, cat. no. 34. FRONTISPIECE: *Six Heads of Horses Showing Expressions*
(detail), 1837, Henry Thomas Alken (after) (British, 1785–1851), hand-colored
etching, 9 ¼ x 12 in., Paul Mellon Collection, 85.1310.1, cat. no. 20.

Contents

Foreword

The Paul Mellon Collection of British Sporting Art is one of the great treasures of the Virginia Museum of Fine Arts. The Mellon galleries in our West Wing house the largest and most important dedicated permanent display of British sporting art in the world. Equally important, but less well known, is the vast collection of more than seven hundred sporting prints also donated by Paul Mellon. Together these works allow the museum to display fully the history of this rich and delightful movement in British art. This catalogue and accompanying exhibition, installed in the Mellon Focus Galleries, represent the Virginia Museum's commitment to studying and showcasing all of the Mellon collections for the enjoyment of art lovers everywhere.

Paul Mellon was both a great supporter and a leader throughout the history of the Virginia Museum of Fine Arts. He was the longest-serving trustee, devoting more than forty years to the post. The significant gifts of art from Mr. Mellon and his wife, Rachel Lambert Mellon, transformed the museum, adding vast collections of masterpieces in South Asian, British, American, and French art that have been treasured by generations of museum visitors. His financial assistance supported building campaigns over many decades and was especially crucial in establishing the performing arts and theater spaces at VMFA. In 1985, along with Richmond collectors Sydney and Frances Lewis, Mr. Mellon supported the construction of the museum's West Wing, which now houses both the Mellon and Lewis collections.

Paul Mellon was a great admirer of not only British art and culture but also the world of the turf and field sports. This exhibition takes a fresh look at the unique artistic contributions of those sporting artists working in print in the eighteenth and nineteenth centuries. The innovative approach of the catalogue examines the prints not from the perspective of sporting history but as serious works of art worthy of critical art historical attention. In the following essays, authors Mitchell Merling, Malcolm Cormack, and Corey Piper present three diverse but complementary interpretive discussions of the works exhibited. Following in the footsteps of *Country Pursuits*, Malcolm Cormack's catalogue of Mellon sporting paintings published in 2007, this book offers a serious and engaging study of the Mellon collection of sporting prints.

Thanks to the generosity of Paul Mellon, this significant aspect of British art history has been preserved, interpreted, and presented for the enjoyment of all.

ALEX NYERGES
Director

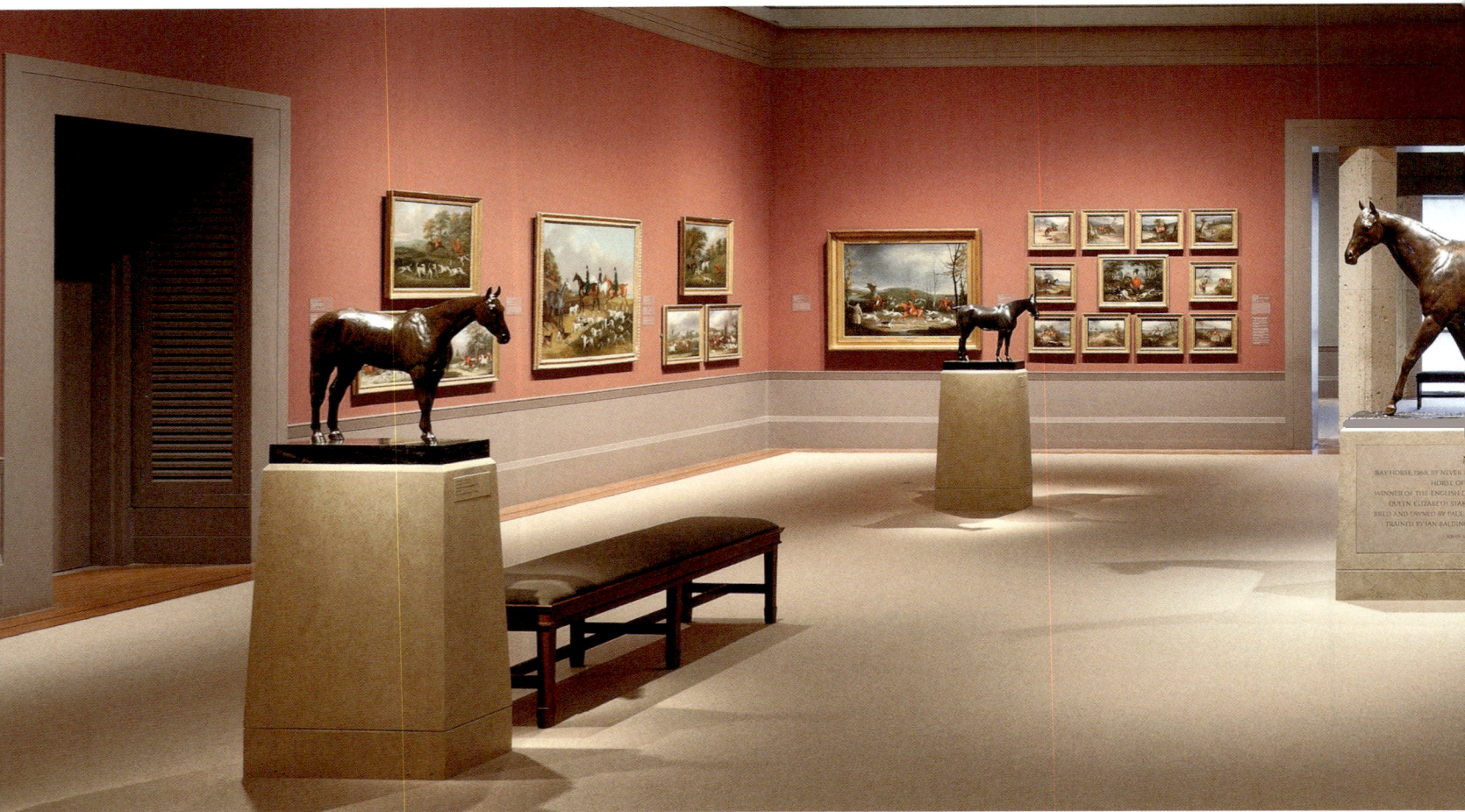

Preface and Acknowledgments

One day during my mastership [my wife] was following the hunt in a car. She stopped at the side of the road because the hunt had had a check, and I suppose we were milling around, with hounds trying to find again. As she sat there, a car drew up alongside, and its driver rolled down his window and asked, "What's going on over there?"

Bunny replied, "It's a foxhunt. The hounds are looking for a fox."

"Oh," the man said, apparently satisfied. Then he added, "I thought that only happened on lampshades."

PAUL MELLON, *Reflections in a Silver Spoon*

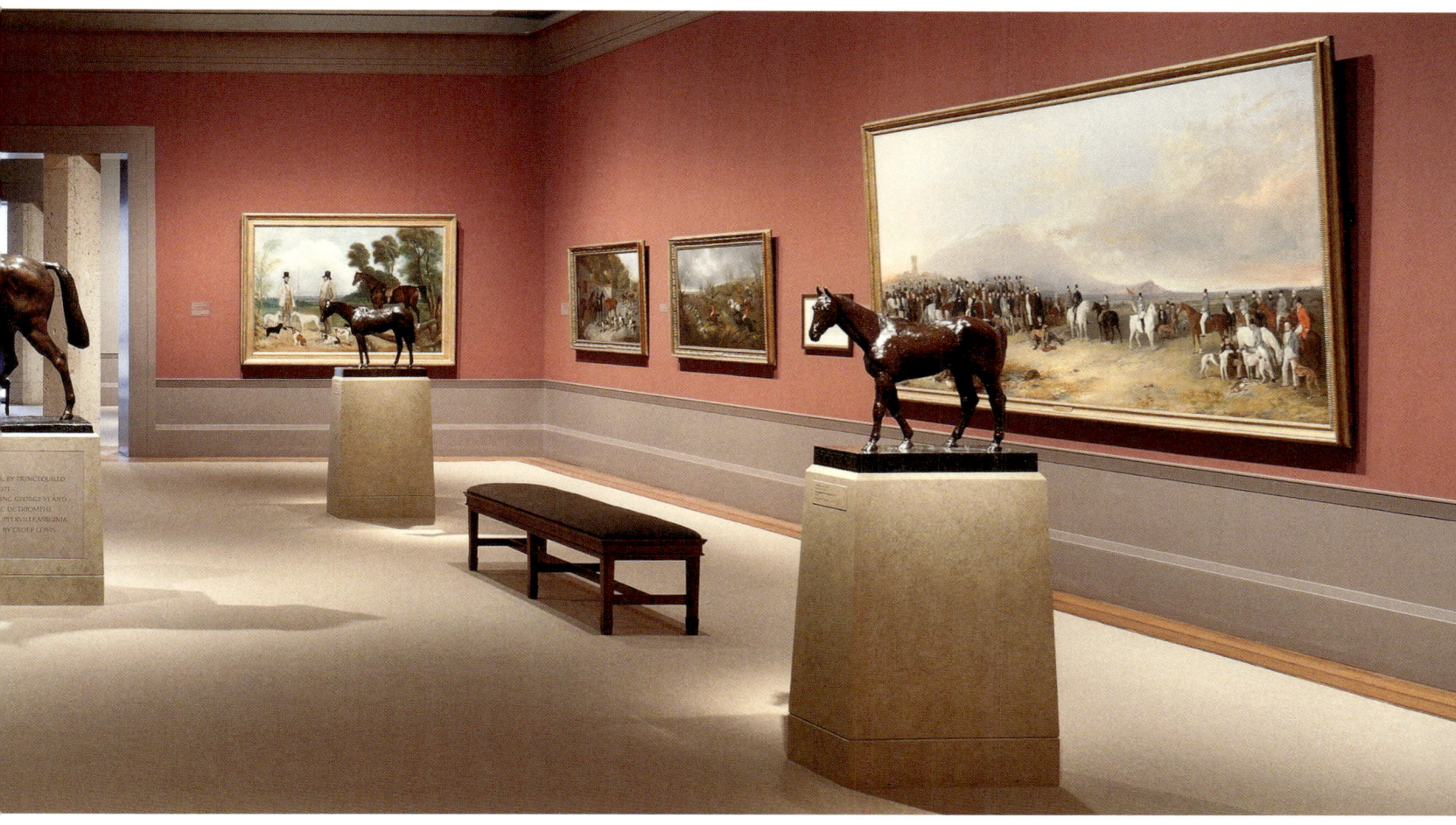

The Paul Mellon Collection of British Sporting Art at the Virginia Museum of Fine Arts

The Paul Mellon Collection of British Sporting Art at the Virginia Museum of Fine Arts is undoubtedly the most important dedicated public display of this material in the world. Its holdings, installed in galleries under the direction of Paul Mellon himself, constitute a celebration both of field sports and of British art. Furthermore, the collection includes important ensembles of paintings and sculptures by twentieth-century artists such as Sir Alfred Munnings, Herbert Haseltine, and John Skeaping (whose monumental sculpture of one of Mellon's most prized horses, Mill Reef, anchors the central gallery), thereby ensuring the continuity of the historical past and the sporting life Paul Mellon lived in Virginia — thoughtfully evoked in his autobiography, *Reflections in a Silver Spoon.*

The important paintings in the collection, including seven works by George Stubbs, have helped make the Mellon galleries a well-known destination for visitors who revel in the depth and range of British sporting art and the evocative gallery setting. Additionally, their renown has recently increased thanks to VMFA's 2007 publication of *Country Pursuits,* a scholarly catalogue by Malcolm Cormack, Paul Mellon Curator Emeritus.

The rich holdings of works on paper from Mellon's collection, however, are less well known, partly because their conservation requirements limit their display, and perhaps because there is a misconceived prejudice that they are preliminary, inferior, or merely reproductive of oil paintings. This was certainly not Paul Mellon's view, as proved by his sponsorship of the publication in 1978–81 of the monumental four-volume catalog of all the sporting material in his collection — including books, prints, drawings and paintings — now divided between Richmond, New Haven, and London. These massive tomes constitute an exemplary achievement in meticulous connoisseurship and empirical scholarship.

This publication and the accompanying exhibition

seek to supplement those volumes and Cormack's book by focusing critical attention specifically on the prints conserved in Richmond, which, thanks to Mellon's generous gift, may be considered a fair sample of the genre of British sporting prints both historically and typologically. The decision to focus our inquiry on sporting prints was based on many advances in recent scholarship of both prints as a medium of communication as well as of sporting art more generally. The studies of the place of sporting prints in social and intellectual history conducted by art historians such as Stephen Deuchar and Dianna Donald deserve particular attention. The authors of *Catching Sight* agree on the sporting prints' worthiness of research precisely because of their independence from the media of oil paintings and drawings, spectacular as those both may be in terms of "self-evident" "artistic" accomplishment and the general higher esteem in which they are held.

Thanks primarily to Deuchar and Donald, sporting art — traditionally considered a transparent record of deeds of animals and their owners in the field and thus generally denigrated by historians of art — is now better understood as a genre as purposeful (socially, historically, and intellectually) as any other art. Yet the study of sporting prints as a distinct category within sporting art has not progressed apace, and certain prejudices (as noted by Mellon in his autobiography, quoted above) are perhaps responsible for this.

On the occasion of VMFA's exhibition of his English painting collection in 1963, Paul Mellon advocated for both the study and appreciation of British art more generally, saying, "This is English Art, not just the *Duchess of Devonshire*, or *The Age of Innocence*; let's take it seriously, let's reevaluate it, let's look at it, let's enjoy it." The authors of *Catching Sight* seek to take Mr. Mellon at his word, and hope that this focused study of British sporting prints contribute to the broader study of prints, sporting art, and British art.

This exhibition and catalogue would not have been possible without the assistance and guidance of numerous friends and colleagues. The exhibition was supported by a generous gift from Frances Massie Dulaney. Many of the ideas for this project originated in a seminar taught in the Art History Department at Virginia Commonwealth University. Students Marisa Eileen Day, Denisse De Leon, Allison L. Frew, Heather Haney, Corinne McVeigh, Colleen Elizabeth Truax, Elizabeth Reilly-Brown, Janelle Sue Wilson, and Kimberly S. Wolfe contributed greatly to the project's success.

At VMFA, the authors would like acknowledge the leadership of Director Alex Nyerges, who guided this project, along with Deputy Director for Art and Education Robin Nicholson. Chief Curator Sylvia Yount provided invaluable counsel and input. Deputy Director for Facilities and Collections Management Stephen Bonadies oversaw the collections and conservation aspect of the exhibition. The conservation of the prints was carried out by Pamela Young and overseen by Bruce Suffield and Carol Sawyer. The prints were matted and framed by Daniel Brisbane. Lisa Hancock served as registrar for the exhibition. The prints were photographed by Travis Fullerton with assistance from Susie Rock. Heather Logue, Conservation Technician and Project Assistant in the VMFA's Frank Raysor Center for the Study of Works on Paper, also provided assistance.

The catalogue benefitted immeasurably from the insightful editing of Stacy Moore along with Rosalie West. It was beautifully designed by John Hoar and Patrick Bell, and overseen by Sarah Lavicka. Numerous interns and others, including Sara Moriarty, Jamie Staples, and Allison Frew, ably assisted with project research and coordination. In the VMFA Library, Lee Viverette and her staff helped with gathering often difficult-to-locate research materials. Research for Corey Piper's essay was supported by the John H. Daniels Fellowship at the National Sporting Library and Museum and was greatly assisted by the staff there, including Lisa Campbell, Librarian; Turner Reuter, Acting Curator; and Rick Stoutamyer, Acting Director. The authors would like to also thank the anonymous peer readers whose comments offered valuable perspectives.

MITCHELL MERLING
Paul Mellon Curator and
Head of the Department of European Art

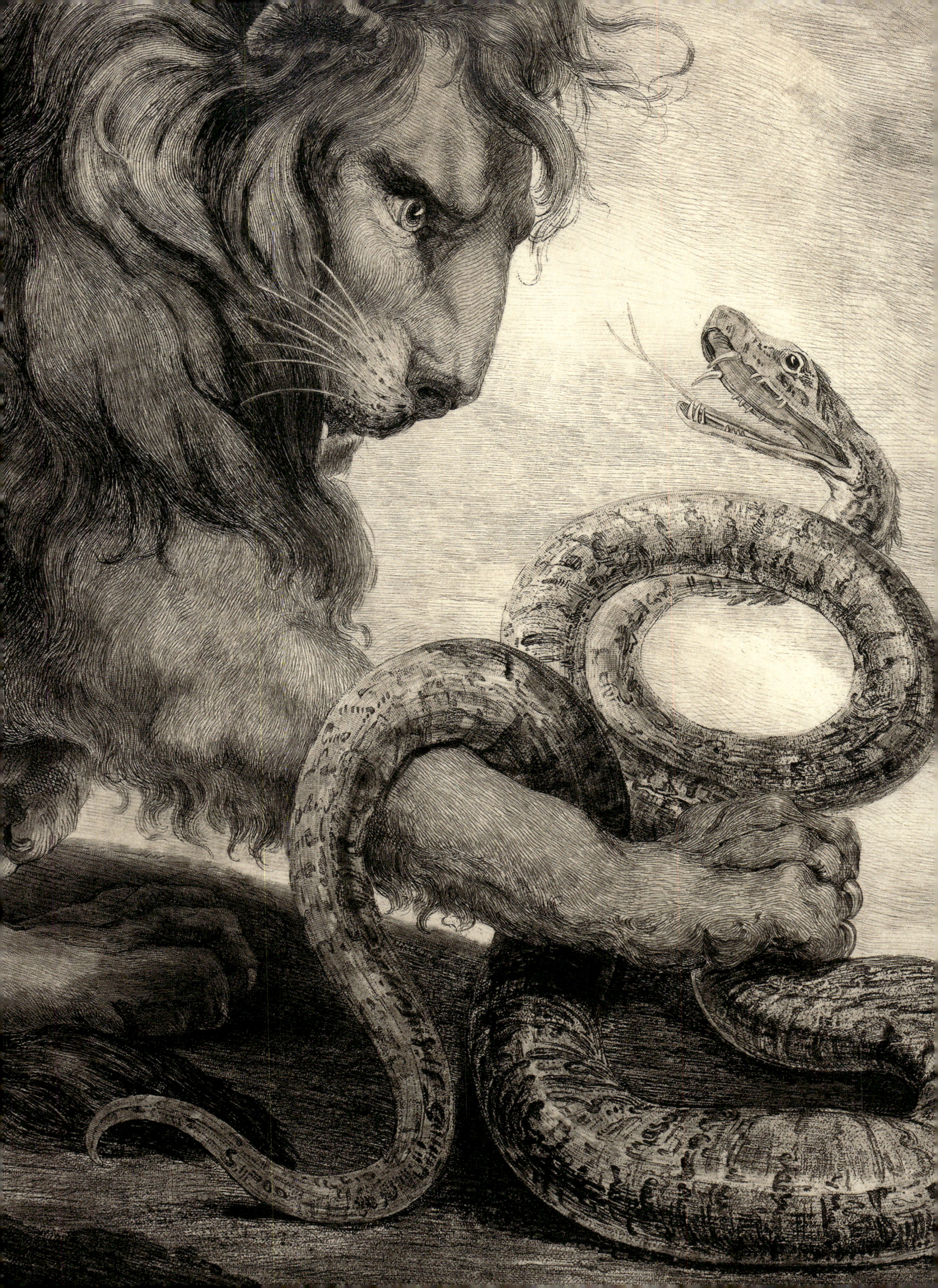

FIG. 1. James Northcote, *Lion and Snake* (detail), 1799, cat. no. 52

The Making and Marketing of the British Sporting Print

MALCOLM CORMACK

Images today — of people and events around the world — are summoned and distributed instantaneously. Any number of devices, some smaller than a pack of playing cards, allow one to see, hear, record, and transmit still or moving pictures of virtually any subject. Of course, this seemingly limitless visual record with immediate access has not always been available. In the more than five hundred years before the advent of photography, images intended for duplication and circulation were created from drawings and paintings through the medium of printmaking. During its first century, this process generated all manner of pictures on paper: a religious scene such as *Christ Crowned with Thorns,* one of the earliest wood engravings by the artist known as the Master of the Year 1446; Albrecht Dürer's portrait of *Albrecht of Brandenburg* (1519), or some other well-known person's likeness; a depiction of birds and beasts by the Master of the Playing Cards (ca. 1445); or even a set of those cards for play. Such printed images were included in books or framed and hung on walls. The production and distribution of any of these images in the premodern world was an important yet labor-intensive part of Western culture.

The most significant method of printmaking after the era of woodcuts was line engraving. Large numbers of people were involved in the process; there were reportedly ten thousand copperplate engravers in London alone at the end of the eighteenth century.[1] Once the plate was engraved, the demanding job of printing began, which required many additional workers to heat the copperplates over charcoal fires or, later, gas burners.[2] If the resulting prints were to be colored, a veritable army of pieceworkers was employed to add watercolor washes, in addition to performing the simple techniques of applying color to the plates themselves. These colorists were mostly women — some of whom worked at home from an acceptable example — each responsible for applying a single-colored wash and passing the print on to the next person.[3] When the prints were approved, they were ready for sale to the public through galleries, other dealers, or booksellers. In 1846 a series of prints based on paintings by John Frederick Herring was published in London by "Messrs. Fores at their Sporting & Fine Print Repository & Frame Manufactory," at 41 Piccadilly, and also abroad, in Paris, by Goupil and Vibert, at 15 Boulevard Montmartre.[4] Dudley Snelgrove, the cataloguer of the Paul Mellon collection of sporting prints, lists 264 engravers and 222 publishers for those produced between 1658 and 1874.[5]

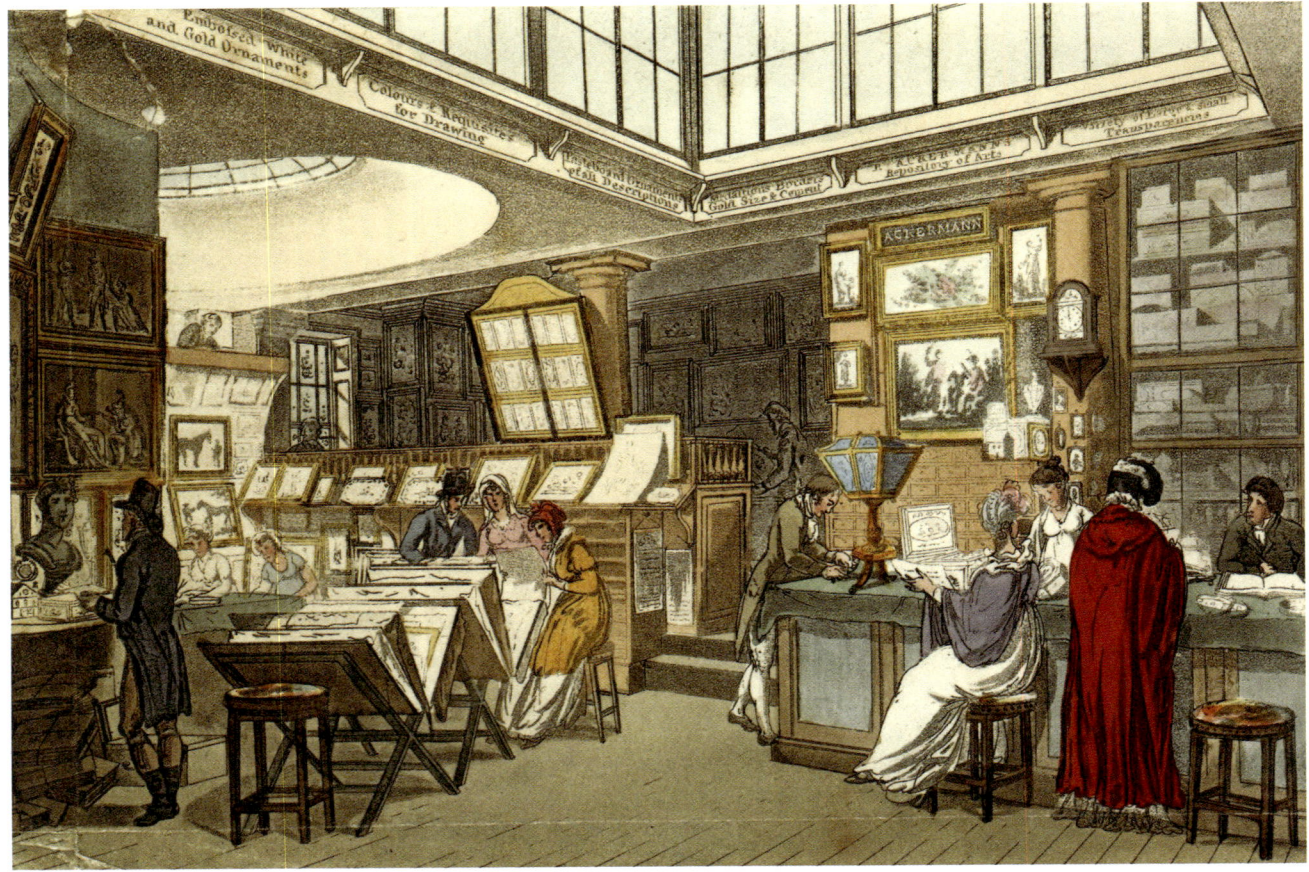

FIG. 2. *View of Rudolph Ackermann's Repository of Arts at 101 Strand, London,* hand-colored etching with aquatint, 1809, after Augustus Charles Pugin and Thomas Rowlandson. ©Trustees of the British Museum

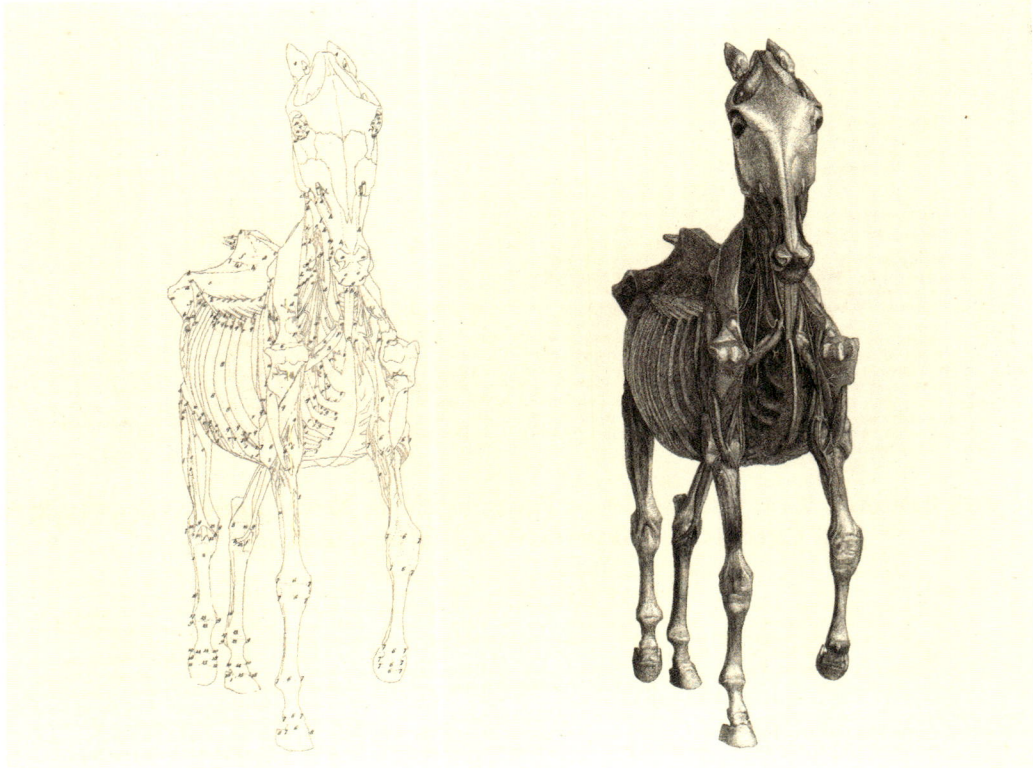

FIG. 3. George Stubbs, Plate IX from *Anatomy of the Horse,* 1766, cat. no. 70

Of the British publishers and retailers of prints, Rudolph Ackermann was perhaps the best known, though not wholly as a dealer in sporting art. He had arrived in England from his native Germany probably between 1783 and 1786 and began his career as a designer of carriages. His first business was at 96 Strand, but he later moved to 101 Strand and opened the Repository of the Arts (fig. 2). There, he operated a school for budding artists for whom he compiled a library of prints. Ackermann also published *Lessons for Beginners in the Fine Arts* and sold a wide range of drawing materials, including watercolors. His most important and earliest success was *The Microcosm of London* (1808–10), a handsome volume of large views of London drawn by Thomas Rowlandson and Augustus Pugin, and printed as aquatints. He followed that publication with similar histories of Oxford and Cambridge that were also well received.

In 1825 Ackermann set up his eldest son, Rudolph Jr., at 191 Regent Street, which became known in 1829 as the Eclipse Sporting Gallery. Although Rudolph Sr. had published sporting prints by Jacques Laurent Agasse, Richard Barrett Davis, and Dean Wolstenholme, the real boom in the genre developed at Rudolph Jr.'s gallery. After the elder Ackermann died in 1834, his younger sons continued to operate Ackermann and Company, competing with their brother at the Eclipse. In addition to sporting prints, Rudolph Jr. sold portraits of famous people, topographical views, "Drawings let out to copy," "genuine Cumberland lead pencils," (categorized as they still are today as *H, B, HB,* and *BB),* fine papers and "superfine watercolours."[6]

The Ackermanns were by no means Britain's only nor first dealers and publishers in sporting art. There were S. W. Fores, Sporting and Fine Art Repository at 41 Piccadilly; S. & J. Fuller's Temple of Fancy, renamed Sporting Gallery in 1819, at 34 Rathbone Place; Thomas McLean's Repository of Wit and Humour at 26 Haymarket; Thomas Palser on the "Surrey Side of Westminster Bridge," as he advertised himself; J. Moore's operation on Saint Martin's Lane; and, in the mid-eighteenth century, Carrington Bowles, map and print seller at 69 Saint Paul's Church Yard. During the nineteenth century, a number of workshops made prints from other men's designs: Thomas McQueen, at Tottenham Court Road and later 37 Great Marlborough Street with

twenty-five to thirty rolling printing presses; Dixon and Ross, on Hampstead Road from 1833 to 1966 and in business today as Thomas Ross Ltd. in Binfield, Berkshire; and others, such as Holdgate's. George Garrard, on the other hand, avoided such enterprises and published a print after his oil painting from the studio of his friend Sawrey Gilpin. Many other artists published from their own workshops dotted around Soho and Bloomsbury, where a few frame makers and craftsmen still survive today.

Despite this plethora of printmaking outlets, the production and distribution of images demanded time. For example, an illustration of the winning horse at the 1825 Saint Leger Stakes at Doncaster was not available until a week after the event. First, the initial drawing of the horse and rider was made, and then it was transported by stagecoach (there were no railroads yet) to London, more than a day's journey away. The woodcut was made next, and, finally, a print after J. F. Herring's painting of the winner, Queen of Trumps, was ready for illustration in a sporting magazine five days later, on September 25, 1825.[7] Even with the advent of photography, in about 1840, multiplying images was complicated, and reproductions could not immediately appear in a newspaper or magazine.

There is no doubt that the dissemination of sporting prints was very much a British phenomenon. During the heyday of the genre, from about 1750 to 1850, sporting prints were sold across the British Isles to countless households of all economic classes, and also abroad. In 1774 a visitor to Mount Airy, the Tayloe family estate in Richmond County, Virginia, noted in the dining room "twenty-four of the most celebrated among the English Race Horses . . . drawn masterly, and set in elegant gilt frames."[8] These must have been prints, as it would have been difficult to house that number of sporting paintings in a dining room. Later, Carle Vernet introduced prints after George Stubbs to fellow French painter Théodore Géricault, who then copied the British artist's *Anatomy of the Horse* (fig. 3). When Géricault was in England, he saw races as well as sporting prints, and made some of his own lithographs. In addition, the reestablishment of the French National Stud (Les Haras Nationaux) in 1806, after its thoroughbreds had been dispersed during the revolutionary period, depended to some extent on those English prints

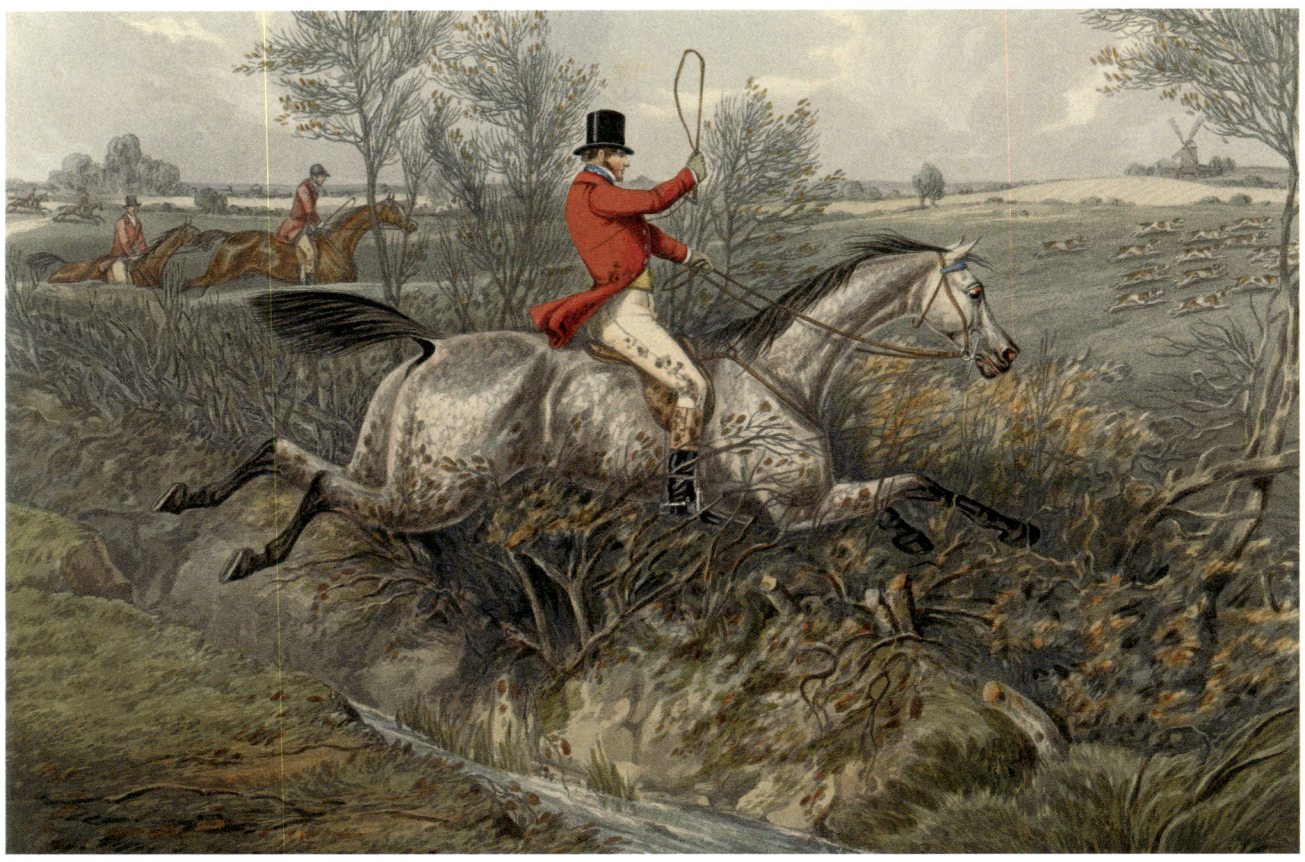

FIG. 4. Henry Thomas Alken, *Swishing a Rasper,* cat. no. 21

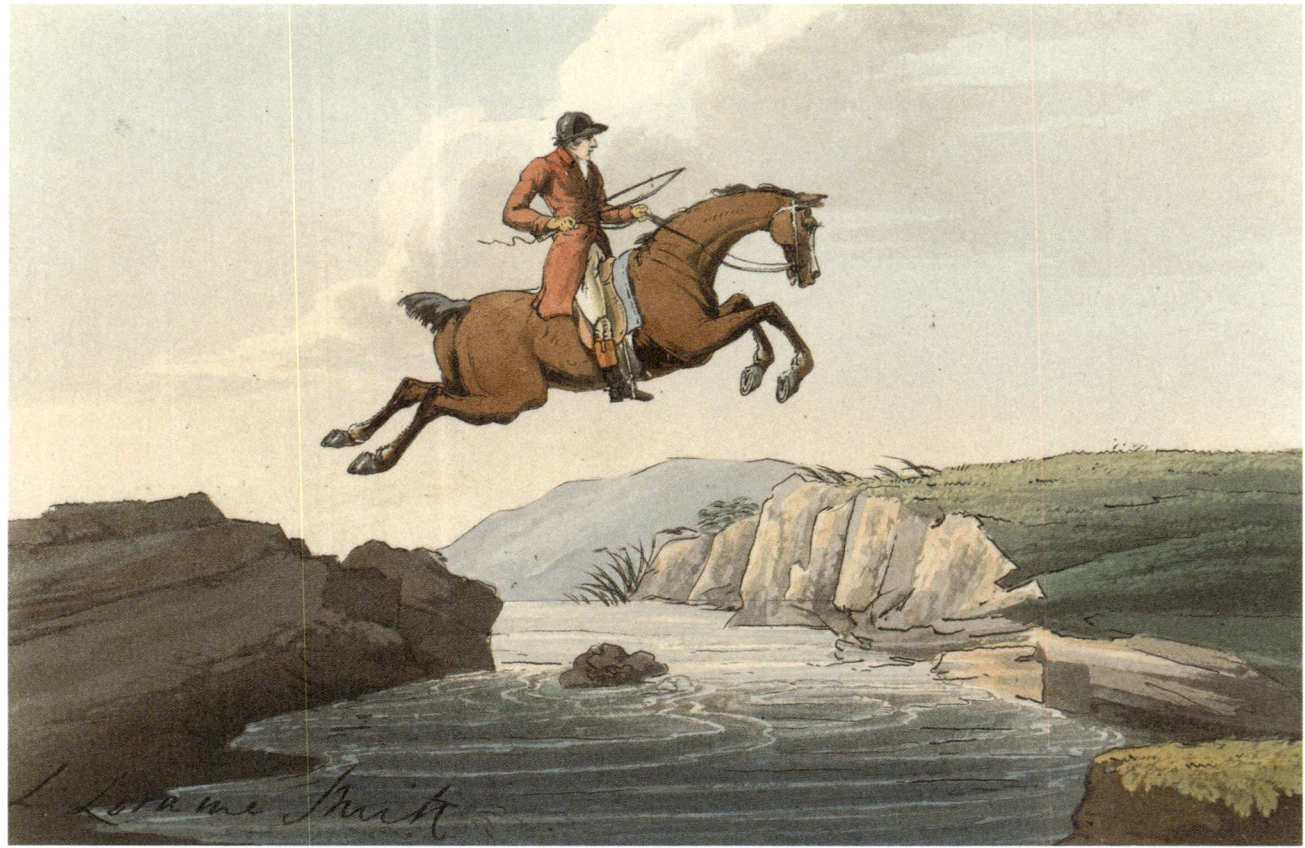

FIG. 5. Charles Lorraine Smith, *Sic Itur ad Catulos,* cat. no. 65

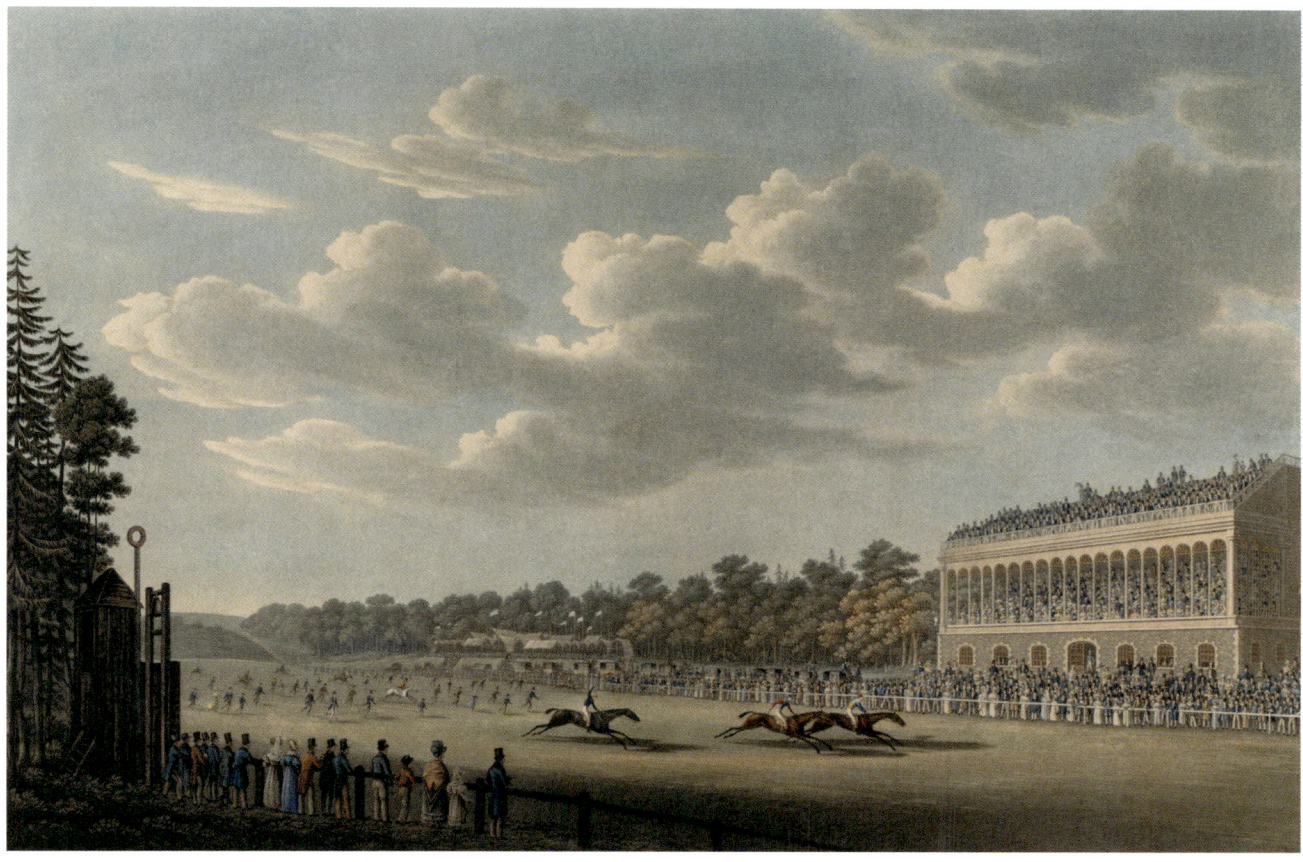

FIG. 6. Joseph Francis Gilbert, *Priam Winning the Gold Cup in 1831*, 1831, cat. no. 40

that listed their progeny, which were imported anew into France.

Sporting art prints covered a wide range of subjects, most of which are represented in the Mellon collection and illustrated in the Catalogue. Foxhunting, with all the thrills and spills of the chase, is a prominent theme. Scenes of derring-do and even the extreme foolhardiness that characterized the sport in the 1820s are many: Henry Thomas Alken's *Swishing a Rasper* (hunting parlance for jumping through a high hedge) and Charles Lorraine Smith's *"Sic Itur ad Catulos"* (So Do They Go to Hounds) are two examples (figs. 4 and 5). Both presented suitable subjects for a set of prints intended for Cambridge college rooms. The subtle snobbery of the hunter is well illustrated in Alken's *One of the Right Sort, Who Hunts Because He Likes It* and *One of the Wrong Sort, Who Goes Out with Hunters Because It Is the Fashion.* Among the various foxhunting episodes depicted in sporting prints, "The Death" is particularly popular.

Horse racing is also well represented. Featured subjects include views of famous racecourses (Joseph Francis Gilbert's *Priam Winning the Gold Cup in 1831,* fig. 6, for example) and famous racehorses (James Seymour's portrait of Flying Childers, the most successful horse of the early eighteenth century; Stubbs's Sharke; and Herring's Mango). Series depicting scenes from the life of a horse, from its triumphs to its eventual degradation, are also numerous; Sawrey Gilpin's *Characters of Horses* is one such series. Other animals frequently inhabit the sporting terrain: favorite dogs (*Spaniels* after a painting by George Arnald, 1803); prize livestock (a huge ram by John Boultbee); and the ever-present canine companions in any number of shooting and fishing pictures (Reinagle's *Fowling,* fig. 7).

Not all sporting prints are straightforward representations. Many incorporate lampoonery and mockery, ranging from the good-humored scene of *The Breakfast* by Rowlandson to the downright

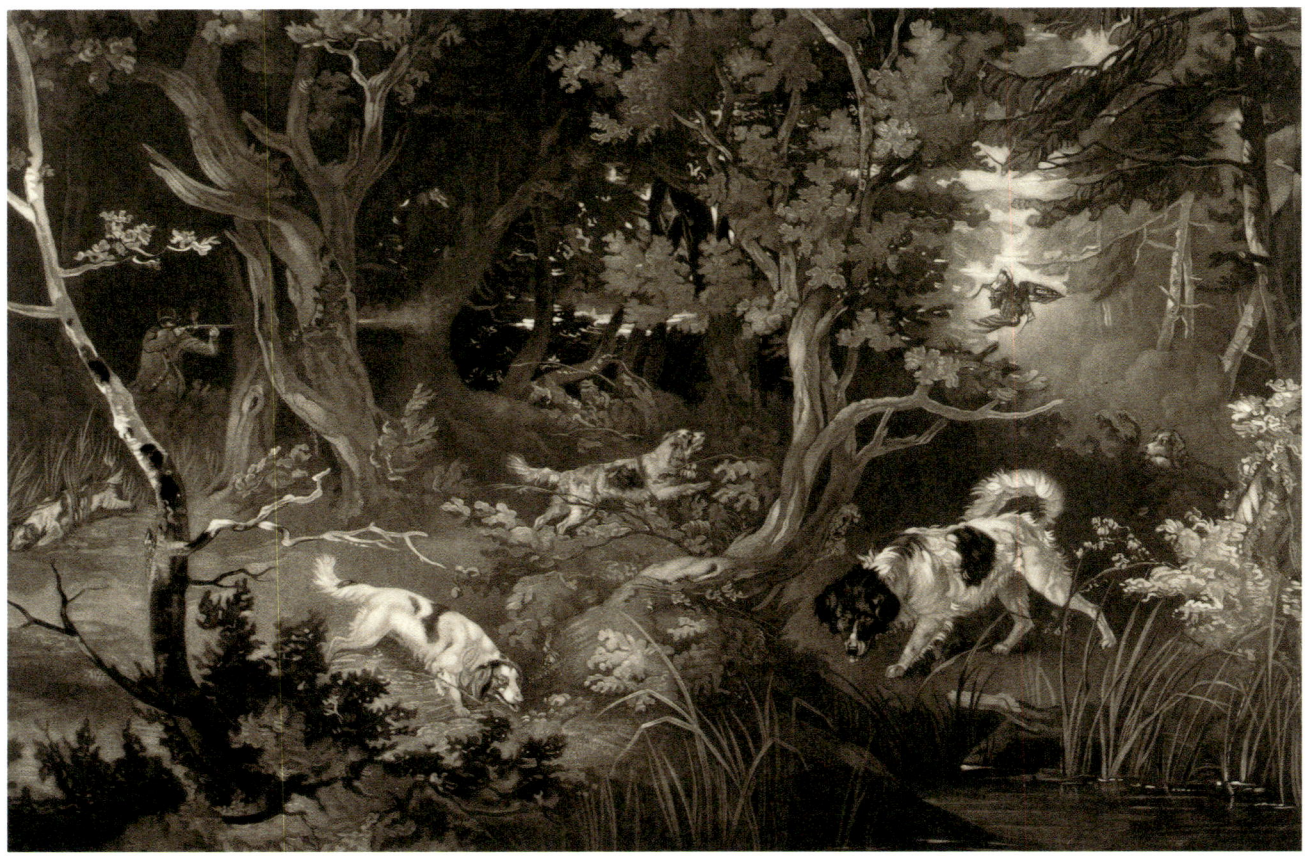

FIG. 7. Philip Reinagle, *Fowling*, 1810, cat. no. 57

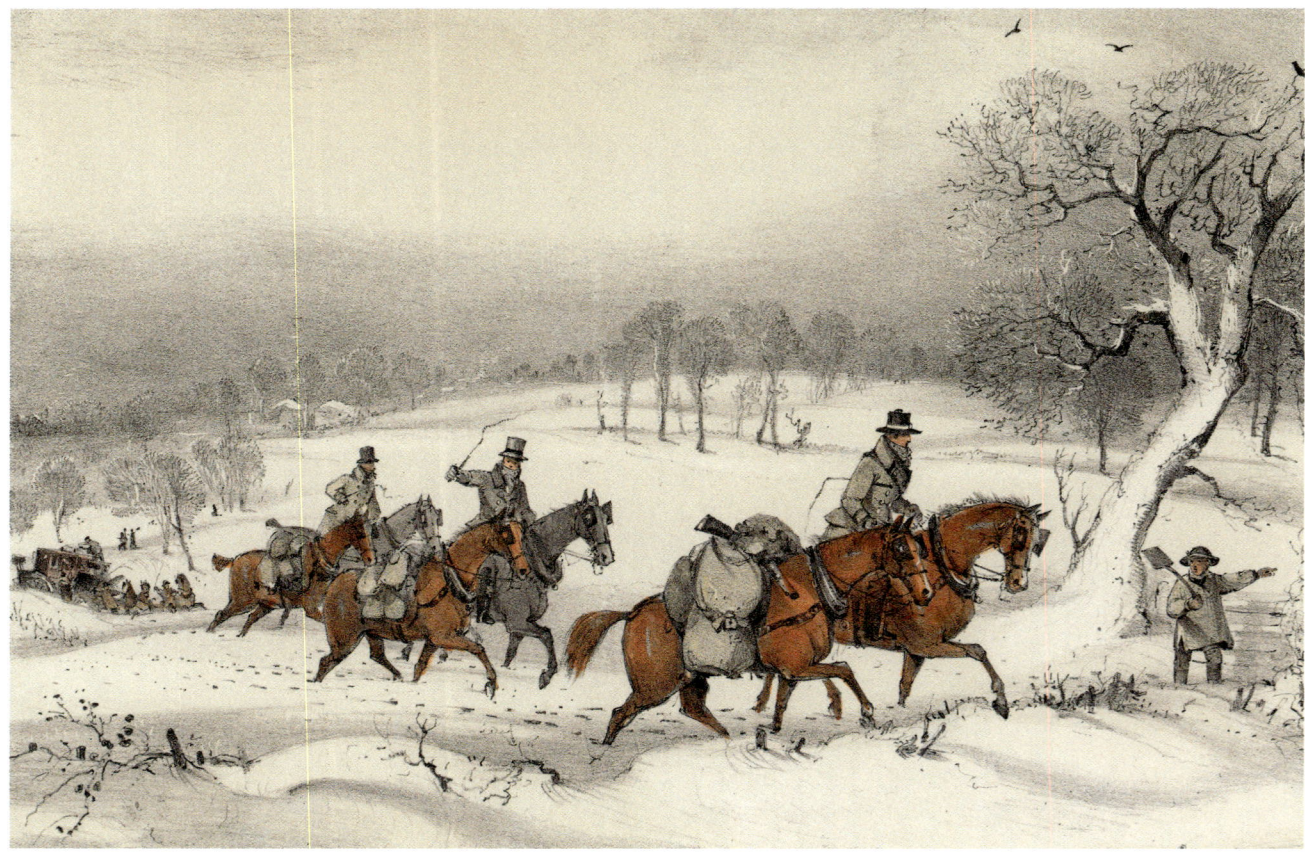

FIG. 8. James Pollard, *The Birmingham Mail Fast in the Snow*, 1837, cat. no. 56

coarse comedy of the Cockneys out shooting, as in the series *London Sportsmen* after paintings by Isaac Cruikshank. While reminiscent of the English tradition of harsh social and political satire produced by printmakers such as James Gillray, these caricatures might also be seen as early examples of the popular twentieth-century comic strip.

Against these satires could be balanced the sentimental genre of *The Amorous Sportsman* after Francis Wheatley and *Morning, or the Benevolent Sportsman* after George Morland. The quiet mood of these prints contrasts with the dramatic protoromanticism of *Horses Fighting* after Stubbs (1788), the violent entanglement of the *Lion and the Snake* after James Northcote (1799, fig. 1), or the staring racehorse Lop in a thunderstorm after Benjamin Marshall (1802). All of these can be seen as precursors of Théodore Géricault and Eugène Delacroix, and then, in other ways, of Alfred De Dreux and Edgar Degas.

If the drama and bustle that characterize the background landscapes of sporting prints have had some influence on French art, and the attitude toward animals some very faint effect on today's growing concern for animal rights, the resulting paradox is that they seem to have had no effect whatsoever on contemporary British landscape painting. It is true that they are straightforward and fairly literal without, on the whole, any of the eighteenth century's ideas of the Picturesque or, for that matter, a nod to any conventional traditions of landscape. These characteristics in themselves set them apart. Neither could they be accused in the realm of printmaking of subservience to the great masters of landscape prints, to Domenico Campagnola, to Claude, to Rembrandt, to Canaletto. It was as if these masters never existed. The English landscape *painters,* on the other hand, were very well aware of their Continental predecessors and spent the early parts of their careers trying to emulate them, J. M. W. Turner especially. But they also generated a realistic and atmospheric approach to landscape that, apart from Stubbs, Morland, and Marshall, and later John Ferneley, the sporting painters and the reproductive prints after them did not.

In particular, a whole history of transportation — and the opening up of the British Isles through the advance of technology, the movement of people and ideas, and the spread of images — is evident in the publications of Ackermann and his contemporary rivals, many of which feature coaching scenes. As the roads were improved, coaching benefitted, so that, as Thomas De Quincy wrote in his inspirational essay *The English Mail Coach:* "The Mail coach it was that distributed over the face of the land, like the opening of apocalyptic vials, the heart shaking news of Trafalgar, of Salamanca, of Vittoria, or Waterloo." In 1754, the traveling time between Manchester and London (187 miles) was four and a half days; by the beginning of the nineteenth century, it had been shortened to one. Public appreciation was long lived; later, after the introduction of rail travel, the coaching era became for some so nostalgic that prints were issued long after the coaches had ceased to run.

The heroic saga of horse-drawn vehicles delivering mail is the subject of James Pollard's print series based on the great snowstorm of 1836. In one, *The Birmingham Mail Fast in the Snow* (fig. 8), the passengers are left to fend for themselves while the guard rides on with the mail. Such topical series functioned much like later newsreels and up-to-the-minute journalism. In another print, *A View in Regent's Park, 1831,* from *The Progress of Steam,* Henry Alken foresees the triumph of steam power in a bizarre futuristic image of what might be. To Alken the steam age seemed likely to be a disaster. He, apparently, made his imaginary steam-coach drivers and steam-velocipede riders of the future into caricatures of Americans with Rip van Winkle hats and beards (van Winkle was well known in England after Washington Irving's tale appeared in 1819). Interestingly, this British artist saw Americans as the people of the future.

As it turned out, Alken's fanciful notions were not entirely wrong. London's traffic congestion became and remains a perennial problem. Furthermore, Sir Goldsworthy Gurney *had* invented a steam coach that carried passengers successfully between Gloucester and Cheltenham for three months without mishap in the decade before Alken's print and before George Stephenson's innovative railway line between Stockton and Darlington in 1825. Gurney's Steam Carriage Company, however, was forced out by the coaching interests who persuaded Parliament to impose intolerably high tolls.[9] Steam, though, had the last laugh through the triumph of the railways that moved society and goods quite efficiently for nearly one hundred years until the arrival of the internal combustion engine and the mass adoption of air travel.

During the time that saddle and carriage horses were the sole source of transport, and even into the twentieth century, they remained popular subjects for prints. Thomas Harcourt, in a scene painted by James Pollard in the late 1820s, was proud to be seen in Regent's Park in his handsome gig (a light, two-wheeled carriage) drawn by a favorite horse. The painting was later engraved in aquatint by William Callow, better known as a watercolorist, and published by R. Lamb at Gracechurch Street, London. Horses continued in common use at the beginning of the twentieth century for hansom cabs, drays, and all manner of work, including the demands of war. (In the First World War, in fact, British horse losses were 256,204, and French horse losses were 541,714 in France and Flanders alone.)[10]

Before further discussion of the printing process, it should be noted that sporting paintings, and the prints that were produced after them, on the continent of Europe had long preceded the British examples. Medieval illustrations of the seasons, such as *Les très riches heures* (The Very Rich Hours) of the Duc de Berry and the illuminations for Gaston Phébus's *Le livre de la chasse* (The Book of Hunting), ca. 1407,[11] set the way forward, and during the period of the spread of prints throughout Europe, from the Renaissance onward, sporting prints of some description were available. There were engravings after Paul Bril, Peter Paul Rubens, and Frans Snyders, and in the eighteenth century in France, Alexandre-François Desportes and Jean-Baptiste Oudry. These were scenes of autumnal hunts after the stag, violent and exotic hunts, and studies of animals both wild and domesticated. Nearly all were line engravings, and published widely. They had a great influence on Western painting, even on British sporting art, but not so much on British sporting prints, except for those dramatic renderings by Northcote and Ben Marshall already mentioned.

This is not to say that England had been completely out of the courtly business of hunting in the sixteenth century. Henry VIII was well known for his exploits with the horse. George Gascoigne's *The Noble Art of Venerie, or Hunting* (1575) has a woodcut of Queen Elizabeth I being handed the sword to dispatch the hunted deer. But it was not until the end of the seventeenth century that English sporting prints began to be published, and even those displayed a Netherlandish influence. The earliest with an English connection was actually printed in Antwerp in 1658 and was an impressive series of illustrations of the Duke of Newcastle's examples of manège, conducted at his riding school when he was in exile in Antwerp after the English Civil War. Racing had been banned during Oliver Cromwell's Puritan reign over the Commonwealth, but after the Restoration of Charles II, it began again. Scenes at Newmarket races were drawn by Jan Wyck, who also created prints of hunting.[12] The earliest English artist to produce sporting prints was Francis Barlow, whose *Severall Wayes of Hunting, Hawking, and Fishing, According to the English Manner* was published in book form in 1671 with etched plates by Wenceslaus Hollar. These, with Barlow's and Wyck's designs for the engraved plates in *The Gentleman's Recreation* of 1681, set the pattern for two hundred years of country pursuits and the attendant sporting prints in England. The folksy images appeared in groups — stag hunting, foxhunting, hawking, falconry, fishing, fowling with guns and setter dogs, and coursing with greyhounds — and their eighteenth- and nineteenth-century successors were often sold in similar groups, for which original wrappers still exist (see Appendix).

The notable technical link between prints after the giants of seventeenth-century animal painting, such as Rubens and Snyders, and the earliest sporting prints in England was the use of line engraving. Methods, however, changed during the eighteenth and nineteenth centuries in England, and it is useful to differentiate between these varied print techniques. The intaglio process (from the Italian *to engrave*) dominated printmaking from its earliest beginnings until the eighteenth century. Essentially, it required the engraver to cut into a copperplate using a burin, a handheld tool with a wooden, mushroom-shaped handle at one end and a chisel-like edge at the other, set at an angle and guided by the index finger. The edges of the copperplate, which was first highly polished on one side to eliminate all roughness, were also curved and smoothed to avoid cutting into the paper under the pressure of the printing press. Lines of varying depths, curves, and cross-hatchings created the hollows of the image, which may have been traced onto the plate beforehand. The plate was then inked and wiped, leaving the ink only in the hollows. Dampened paper was next laid over the plate and pulled into the depression by press. Thus, the intaglio method created a series of lines achieved by hollows rather than lines raised from the plate, as in relief printing, such as wood engraving and printing from typefaces. In the case of sporting prints, this latter method was almost never used, with the exception of woodblocks made for illustrations in early newspapers (for example, the aforementioned reproduction of J. F. Herring's design for the winner of the Saint Leger in 1825). Although the line-engraving process prevailed in France, English artist William Hogarth also found it eminently suitable for the reproduction of his "modern morale subjects," with their scathing details of expression and fashion. Hogarth was the first English artist to realize that the sale of prints after his paintings could bring him an income larger than the paintings themselves, particularly when his agitation against pirating brought about the passing of the Engravers' Copyright Act in 1735, whereby the copyright remained with the engraver's design for fourteen years.[13] This act required the details of those who were involved in the manufacture of the print and its date of publication to appear on all English prints, including sporting prints. The original designer's name was to be followed by *inv.* (for the Latin *invenit,* invented or conceived) or *pinx.* (for *pinxit,* painted). The name of the engraver or etcher was identified by *ext. (excudit,* executed). Any additional aquatinters or lithographers might also be named, as well as the publisher, his address, and the date of publication.

The most proficient line engravers in eighteenth-century England were, not surprisingly, French immigrants. Among the first was Nicholas Dorigny, who arrived in London in 1711, followed by a steady number of others, including Hubert Gravelot and S. F. Ravenet. Conversely, English engravers traveled to France to apprentice in well-established workshops with competent masters. At least two English engravers, Charles Grignion and Thomas Major, studied in the Paris studio of Jacques-Philippe Le Bas. The job was a demanding one: line engraving called for careful and dexterous application. British engraver

George Vertue explained that great assiduity was "required to become a master of that most manual profession which must be painfully practised when young, especially by those that use the graving tools." He continued, "for there is a constancy, a laborious & indefatigable temper necessary to be form'd for these operations, which by length of time, and practice can be attain'd & no other wayes. Wch is necessary to make a firm strong hand, and beautiful clean neat strokes wherin consists the foundation of the excellence of a Burinator."[14] Hogarth, himself a competent engraver of his own designs, also said as much: "fine engraving which requires vast patience, care and great practice is scarcely ever achieved but by men of a quiet turn of mind,"[15] though his art exhibits a livelier turn of mind than he proposed.

William Woollett came to fame with his engraving after Richard Wilson's *The Destruction of the Children of Niobe* (1761). Following that success, the production of prints after dramatic, history, and subject paintings achieved international sales in the hands of entrepreneurs such as John Boydell, who commissioned paintings by the leading English artists for his Shakespeare Gallery, which opened in 1786, and then engraved and sold them as prints. (Boydell and, incidentally, Carrington Bowles brought about the overlap between "fine art engraving" and sporting prints.) Thomas Macklin opened his very similar Poet's Gallery in 1787 for the same reason, and he also published his Macklin's Bible. Robert Bowyer's Historic Gallery had as its aim the sale of prints after patriotic episodes from English history. These line-engraving enterprises, together with the output of mezzotints after portraits by Sir Joshua Reynolds and other subject painters, mark the apogee of the more traditional methods of printmaking.

Mezzotint was particularly suited for tonal prints of works in the painterly manner that English artists developed and was therefore used to reproduce paintings by the greatest of English landscape and portrait artists. The process was actually invented in Germany by Ludwig von Siegen and later developed in England by Prince Rupert, nephew of Charles I. Prince Rupert met Siegen during his wanderings on the Continent during the English Civil War. After the Restoration of Charles II, the prince encouraged mezzotint engravers to relocate to England, where they were primarily employed making prints after Sir Peter Lely's portraits. This effort set the way for the development of mezzotints in England, so much so that they became known as works of "The English Manner." Though this was not an entirely accurate claim, the mezzotint had a profound influence on the eighteenth-century English print trade, dominated as it was by portraits after Sir Joshua Reynolds. By the end of the century, it had become almost entirely an English phenomenon. It is not surprising, therefore, that there are many sporting prints that were first executed in mezzotint.

With this method, the copperplate was first prepared with a rocker, a grooved tool that was used all over the plate to create complicated crisscross indentations that would produce a rich, black ground. The engraver then worked on the plate from the darkest parts to the lightest with a scraper to produce blank, smooth areas that would print as clear white with gradations of tones in between. The process was thus the reverse of line engraving and, apparently, quicker.[16] It had other advantages. The richness of tone and the varied highlights were eminently suitable for reproducing paintings, from Lely and Kneller,[17] to Reynolds, to those seen in the *Catching Sight* exhibition, Seymour, Stubbs, Zoffany, Wright of Derby, Morland, Wheatley, and Garrard. Mezzotint, however, was not without its disadvantages. Though the rocker raised burr on the plate that gave early proofs a deep richness of darks like velvet, the process quickly wore the plates down so that they were not adequate for extended editions. At the beginning of the nineteenth century, steel plates that greatly extended the life of the image were in use, notably by T. G. Lupton, who in 1823 received a medal from the Society of Arts for "engraving in mezzotint on steel," and, most prolifically, by Samuel Cousins, who reproduced in large numbers the works of Sir Edwin Landseer, particularly his animal paintings. John Martin generated his own steel-based mezzotints of his apocalyptic visions to enormous success. Thus began the period of mass-produced prints that were on every Victorian's walls. Photogravure changed the methods but thereby increased the spread of popular prints.

During the eighteenth century, however, other developments had infiltrated the sporting print trade. In much the same way that English painters (such as Reynolds and Gainsborough) cut corners technically and were not academically sound, the methods introduced for sporting prints were also mixed.[18] The amalgam of techniques — principally etching, soft-ground etching, aquatint, stipple engraving, and, in the nineteenth century, lithography — became inimitable. All of these methods had been imported from abroad but were then developed to suit the requirements of sporting prints, often used in complicated permutations.

Etching has a long history, from the sixteenth century in Italy to the Netherlands, France, and finally England. It was known for its fineness of line and individual character, making it suitable for individual artistic expression and thus almost like drawing. The haunting images of the Thirty Years' War by Jacques Callot display this expressiveness. Even more personal are the etchings of Rembrandt, for character studies, atmospheric landscapes, and sparkling detail. The small, intensely observed figures of Stefano Della Bella look forward in a way to the prolific series of figures from daily life in the original drawings of Henry Thomas Alken, who also etched some of his own sporting prints, occasionally using the pseudonym "Ben Tally Ho." The name makes his aim clear.

Print expert Richard Godfrey states that "pure etching was infrequently used for reproductive prints. . . . It was more usually the chosen medium of an artist wishing to make a print from his own design, since it permitted him to draw lines without restraint."[19] This, in fact, was generally what happened in the case of sporting prints produced by mixed methods. They may have begun as etchings but were further modified, often in the form of aquatint.

The etching process began with a polished and clean copperplate that was heated. A solid ball of the ground, made of various mixtures of wax and resin, was wrapped in muslin or silk and rubbed over the warmed plate, and then made into an even surface by a dabber, a tool that "dabs" at the warm wax. The plate was then held up over candles to darken the ground with smoke. This enabled the etcher to incise his line into the ground with a needle, so that he could see what he was doing. The etcher's needles were of varying thickness according to the job in hand. If the artist was inventing his own image, he

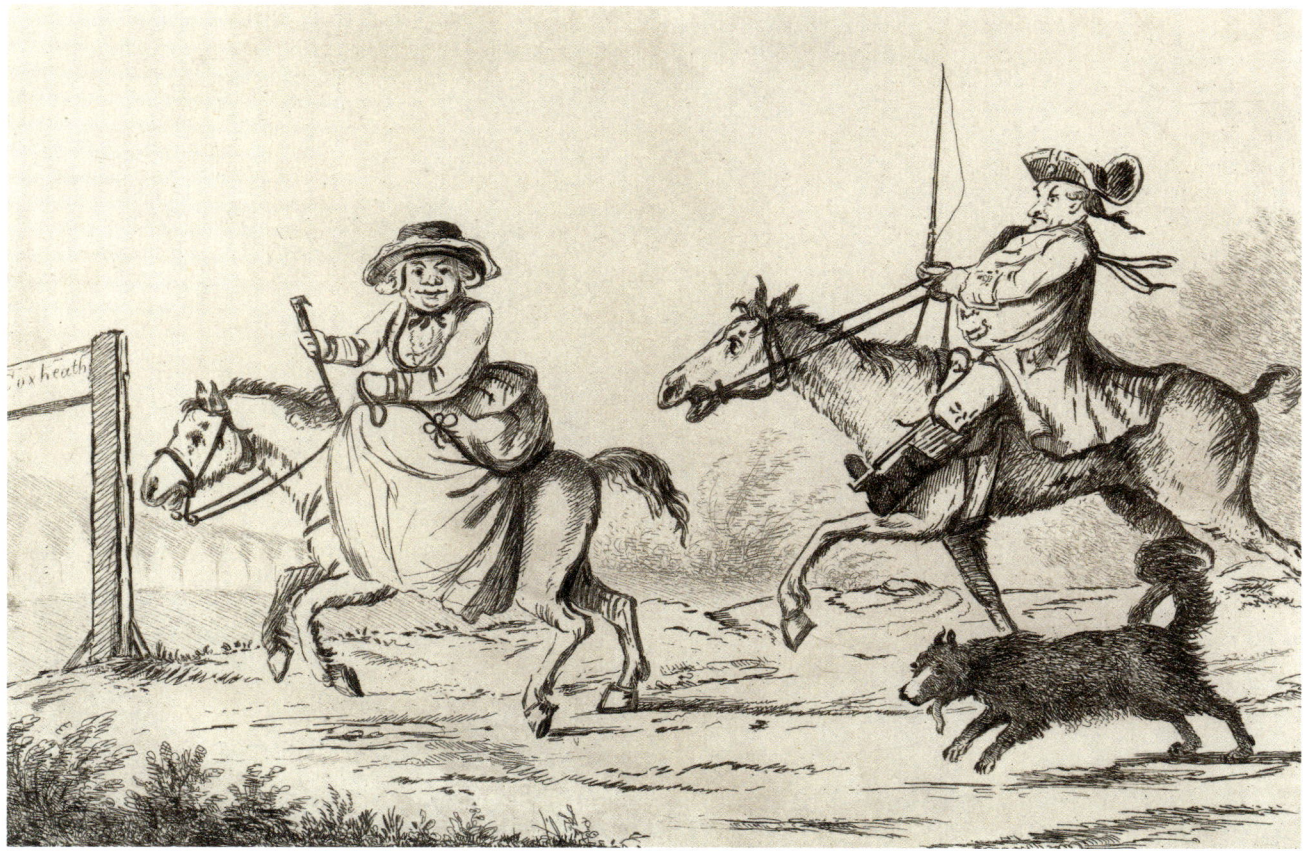

FIG. 9. Henry William Bunbury, *Coxheath Ho!*, 1779, cat. no. 31

could create his design and proceed for printing. The reverse side of the plate had to be covered with a stopping-out varnish so that it could be immersed into a bath of acid.

This was an important moment. In the eighteenth century the bath process began with forming a wall of wax around the edges of the plate. The liquid, known as mordant, was normally a solution of dilute nitric acid, but an alternative was a mixture of hydrochloric acid with chlorate of potash, known as the "Dutch Bath." This method did not bite so deeply, so finer lines could be produced. The plate was placed in the acid, which would bite into the copper through the incised lines. The duration of the bath was a matter of judgment, as the etcher watched for the bubbles with nitric acid or relied on experience with hydrochloric acid that produced no bubbles.

The final stage before printing involved cleaning the ground from the plate, heating it, and covering the surface with ink. The ink was then wiped off

with muslin and the palm of the hand, leaving it in the lines and the plate ready for printing. Dampened paper was applied to the plate and put through the heavy rollers of the printing press. The plate mark is often much more visible with etchings.

As mentioned, pure etching was not so common in sporting prints, though examples do exist. The simplest, and crudest, is by J. S. Bretherton after a drawing by the satirist Henry Bunbury, *Coxheath Ho!*, of 1789 (fig. 9). Coxheath was the site of an encampment for local militias and volunteers near Maidstone in Kent, in southeast England, roughly halfway between the Channel coast and London. Bunbury is poking fun at the middle-aged volunteers who hoped to gain glory in the militia without the inconvenience of having to fight. There are also some hand-colored etchings, such as the two satirical prints of London sportsmen by Isaac Cruikshank.

Generally, however, an etching was merely the first stage in the published print. Some artists — Thomas

Rowlandson outstanding among them — etched their own designs, passing them to the publisher's specialized aquatint engraver for the next stage of the print. The Rowlandson scenes included in this exhibition are early examples of sporting aquatint. They were published by S. W. Fores in 1789, before the establishment of Ackermann's, with whom Rowlandson later had such a long association. They reveal all the verve of his imagination and fluency of line that he could express by etching but probably found tedious to continue in aquatint.

Aquatint had been developed in France by J. B. Le Prince, and it was introduced in England by P. P. Burdett in 1771. It is basically a tonal process and needs an etched line for the basic design. Powdered resin was put into a box and blown over the plate. When the dust settled, it was fixed to the plate by heat. Another method was to dissolve the resin in spirits of wine and then spread the solution over the plate. After the spirit evaporated, the plate was ready for fixing. Any areas that were to be left white were brushed over with a stopping-out varnish. The plate was then immersed in the acid, which would bite through the tiny spaces between the grains. This process could be repeated according to the darkness of tone needed, again using the varnish to protect the lighter parts. Without the original etching that provided the lines, the print would be entirely an exercise in tones.

Aquatint quickly came to dominate English sporting prints. More than fourteen printmakers represented in this show worked in aquatint. It proved very suitable for reproducing watercolors, and often watercolor washes were added to it by that army of anonymous home workers. (Ackermann reportedly employed many exiled French noblemen and women during the Napoleonic Wars because of their genteel skills of painting in watercolors. Many, however, seemed to have returned to France at the Peace of Amiens in 1802.)[20] Because the tonal quality was close to that of watercolors and most of the preliminary designs took the form of watercolors and spirited drawings, a group of fresh, bright, hand-colored aquatints gave the effect of a connoisseur's cabinet of drawings. Luckily, most of the prints in the exhibition have never been shown, so they have retained their original freshness. Unfortunately, if printed in large

numbers, the plates quickly wore out, and as the prints were so popular for interior decoration, they are often encountered in a very faded state. (The problem of wear was later solved in the nineteenth century by facing the plates with steel by electrolysis.)

Another, closely allied technique in which color was frequently added late was soft-ground etching. Most often used to imitate the effects of drawing, soft-ground etching was, indeed, achieved by drawing on a piece of paper that had been laid on a plate prepared with more tallow in the ground to make it softer. When the paper was removed, the ground where the pencil had been pressed down adhered to the paper. The plate could then be immersed in its acid, etched with these softer lines, inked, and finally printed on the press. Gainsborough, ever eager for spontaneous effects, experimented with this method. There are soft-ground etchings by Alken in this exhibition.

One other eighteenth-century technique warrants discussion, and that is stipple engraving. It, too, was particularly suited for reproducing drawings and was imported from France. As in etching, the ground of the entire plate was covered in dots and marks with a roulette, a tool with a spiked revolving wheel. Often etching was employed to determine the main outlines or details. The roulette and other tools were also sometimes used to create a texture after the plate had been etched. In England colored plates were frequently produced with different colors applied to the plate with rags (or *à la poupée*). The finished prints were also hand colored. The most outstanding example in the exhibition of a stipple engraving in black and white is after Ben Marshall's portrait of the racehorse Lop. Some of the earlier prints by Stubbs are stipple engravings with additional color.

The great printmaking revolution of the nineteenth century, however, was the invention of lithography. This process had been discovered in Bavaria between 1796 and 1799 by Alois Senefelder, a playwright who was trying to find an easy way to reproduce the text of his plays. By 1799 he had refined his method to gain exclusive rights in Bavaria, and by 1801 he had obtained a patent in Great Britain. Senefelder called the process "chemical printing." Philip André, the brother of Senefelder's partner, Johann Anton André, produced the first works of lithography in England, where it was known as "polyautography," after drawings by the president of the Royal Academy, Benjamin West, and three other academicians, James Barry, Henry Fuseli, and Thomas Stothard.[21] Those prints, however, were not of sporting subjects, although H. B. Chalon produced a lithographic print of two horses in 1804.

Lithography flourished more vigorously in France, where easier contact with Germany during the Napoleonic Wars made cross developments more fruitful. Nevertheless, Henry Bankes had written the first English treatise on lithography in Bath in 1813. Thereafter, Rudolph Ackermann, a native of Germany, and Charles Joseph Hullmandel, an Englishman of German descent, eventually moved the process forward in England during the final years of the second decade. Hullmandel had met Senefelder in 1817, and Ackermann had long been aware of the new technique's potential. Indeed, Ackermann had tried to buy Senefelder's English patent in 1803[22] and published the playwright's original thesis in English in 1819. Though both Ackermann and Hullmandel set about to produce and publish prints by means of the new method, Ackermann eventually bowed out, realizing that the printing of Hullmandel was superior. Ackermann and his son, however, continued to sell the finished product.

This new process of lithography was essentially a "planographic," or surface manner, of printing. It did not involve gouging into metal with any sharp or blunt instrument. In fact, metal was not used at all in the beginning; zinc plates were employed only much later. What Senefelder had found in Solnhofen, Bavaria, was a porous limestone that turned out to be the best-suited material for lithography. The action of printing occured on the surface of these stones and depended on the basic principle that oil and water do not mix. The earliest lithographers drew on the stone with a pen of special greasy ink. The earliest English lithographs of 1802–3, in fact, look like pen-and-ink drawings. Later, during the first decade of the nineteenth century, a waxy crayon was introduced for this step. The drawing was fixed with gum and acid and then wetted. The oily, waxy image rejected the water. Next the stone was rolled with the greasy lithographic ink, also rejected by the wet parts of the stone. Paper was then laid down on the stone and both were rolled through the press, which had much less pressure than an engraving press.

The 1820s saw a growth of lithography throughout Europe, including among the leading artists of the Romantic movement: from Russia to Spain, where the aging Goya took up the new art; to Italy, where Ingres had already drawn some lithographic portraits in 1815; to France, where Géricault, Delacroix, Bonington, and many others were much involved; and to England, where Géricault on his visits of 1820 and 1821 drew on stone some horse subjects that were printed by Hullmandel. In the world of sporting prints, there was an interaction between the French and the English. James Ward, the animal painter, had begun his career as a printmaker along with his brother, William, who remained a printer in the trade. Between 1823 and 1826, James Ward published some lithographs illustrating various types of horses that are reminiscent of Géricault, and it could equally be said that Géricault's English lithographs are close to English sporting prints. The French artist had studied Stubbs, and the works of Morland, Sawrey Gilpin, and Ben Marshall are not without relevance, given his contacts with the English sporting world.[23]

The decade also witnessed the development of printing techniques that led to an increasingly commercial use of newer improved methods, eventually, all over the globe — changes in which even today's large-scale printing has its origins. One important introduction that had been foreseen by Senefelder was transfer lithography. In this process, the artist drew with the appropriate crayon on paper that was laid down onto the stone, which accordingly picked up the image. New paper was then applied to the stone and, when printed, the result was not a mirror image but one with the orientation of the original drawing. This made things a lot easier, and in turn led to off-set lithography and, after the invention of photography, photo-litho offsets and the whole commercial world of printing an image to a roller that could then churn out thousands of copies.[24]

Chromolithography was the next great advance in printmaking. In 1820 Joseph Lanzedelly had produced a color lithograph that required nine separate stones, but it was not until the end of the 1830s that the simpler manner of using three stones for the primary colors of red, yellow, and blue became feasible. Engelmann's *Album chromolithographique* was published in Paris and Leipzig in 1837, and two years later in England, Hullmandel used tinted stones to color print George Alexander Hoskins's *Travels in Ethiopia* and *Picturesque Architecture in Paris, Ghent, Antwerp, Rouen &c* for Thomas Shotter Boys. By the time of the Great Exhibition of 1851 in London, chromolithography was common.

None of the lithographic sporting prints in this exhibition were printed in color; they were all hand colored in the traditional way, having first been printed in black and white. Henry Pierce Bone, best known as a portrait and miniature painter, also drew on stone a lithographic version after his own painting *John Giffin, Under-Keeper of East-Hainault Walk in Waltham Forest* of 1825 and published it himself. The original picture was painted for Sir Thomas Tomkins, the steward of the Forest Courts, the group that looked after the former royal forests. Thus, Bone must have been hoping to sell further versions of his portrait.

The reproduction of paintings and sporting images by lithography proceeded rapidly during the next three decades. An 1831 painting of *The King's Harriers in Their Kennel* by Richard Barrett Davis, official animal painter to the king, was "drawn on stone" by John West Giles and published by J. Dickinson, a rival of Ackermann's. It was printed by Engelmann, Graf, and Coindet, "Lithographers to his Majesty." All of these printers had Continental connections, and Graf printed another lithograph after an 1826 painting by John Bryan. Bryan's portrait was of John Twemlow of Hatherton, Cheshire, shown with his hunter and groom. In the class of sporting images that commemorate famous sportsmen, it was not actually drawn until 1841, again by John West Giles, and printed by Graf, by that time risen to the status of "Printer to the Queen." The portrait likely commemorated some special event in Twemlow's life.

Graf was also the printer of two journalistic scenes by James Pollard picturing the Birmingham and the Liverpool mail coaches stuck in the snow during the bad winter of December 1836. The lithographs were drawn by George Bryant Campion and published by Ackermann and Company, at 96 Strand, on February 1, 1837, which was a fairly speedy turnaround for delivering a set of hand-colored prints to the market.

One notable lithograph that was produced during this early flourishing of lithography, when mechanical methods were already available and chromolithography was all the rage, is after H. T. Alken's *Sketches: The Stable, The Road, The Park, The Field,* originally from 1822. This work represents a pure exercise in nostalgia: a capriccio of coaching scenes together on one sheet printed in 1854, when long-distance coaching had come to an end (the last coach between Edinburgh and Newcastle halted operation in 1847). Since Alken himself had died in 1851, the publisher, no doubt, initiated the reprints.

The publisher of this lithographic print, Ernest Gambart, had already become the most important dealer in London, rivaling Agnew, who had newly arrived from Manchester. Gambart came from France and quickly dominated the Victorian art market, paying high prices, particularly for the leading Victorian artists, and quickly securing engraving rights that would bring in further income for the firm and the artist. An example is W. P. Frith, who in 1858 painted *Derby Day*, perhaps the most popular quasi-sporting picture of the nineteenth century. Gambart's biography is subtitled *Prince of the Victorian Art World.*[25] Dante Gabriel Rossetti, the Pre-Raphaelite painter called him "Gamble-Art."[26] Significantly, for all his power over the greater art world, Gambart, as with other dealers, would sell all levels of art, from high to low, to all classes of society and was not above reprinting an old Alken design if he thought it would make money. He was willing to have it hand colored to resemble conventional sporting prints even when more modern methods of coloring were already available.

The prints that have been selected here are just a small fraction of the Paul Mellon collection, which was possibly the largest ever assembled privately. He had acquired in 1956 the vast holdings of sporting prints then in the possession of Henry, Duke of Gloucester, fourth child of George V and thus the brother of the Duke of Windsor and George VI (fig. 10). Where Henry had acquired them is not known, but it is interesting to remember that his father was a great stamp collector, and there is something about the small size and bright colors of sporting prints and the concern about mint condition among collectors that is reminiscent of philately. Some of the prints or wrappers bear the Duke's bookplate, while others bear the bookplate of that other encyclopedic collector of

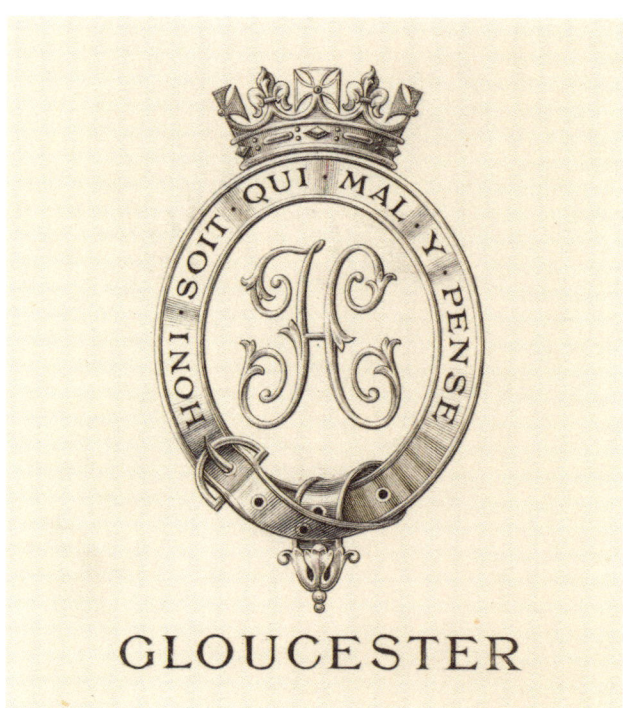

FIG. 10. Bookplate of Henry, Duke of Gloucester. Virginia Museum of Fine Arts, Paul Mellon Collection, 85.1268.1/41

sporting prints, C. F. G. R. Schwerdt (fig. 11). Because individual prints appear in Schwerdt's exhaustive catalogue of his own collection does not mean, however, that this or that individual print was part of his collection because, after all, they are all multiple images. Paul Mellon also bought prints from a wide range of dealers, such as Ackermann's, Frank Sabin, and the Parker Gallery.

Collecting prints, nevertheless, was more than a hobby like stamp collecting. Sir Kenneth Clark once remarked that when you asked an Englishman about art, he immediately talked about landscape. Sporting prints generally give a rosy picture of a prelapsarian world where the country and weather are always suitable for hunting, where the fisherman always catches his fish, where eager and loyal dogs are ever ready to retrieve the fallen game that had been carefully reared to be shot. Though this view of the world may be deeply conservative, the genre still communicates important aspects of a particular time in Britain's history.

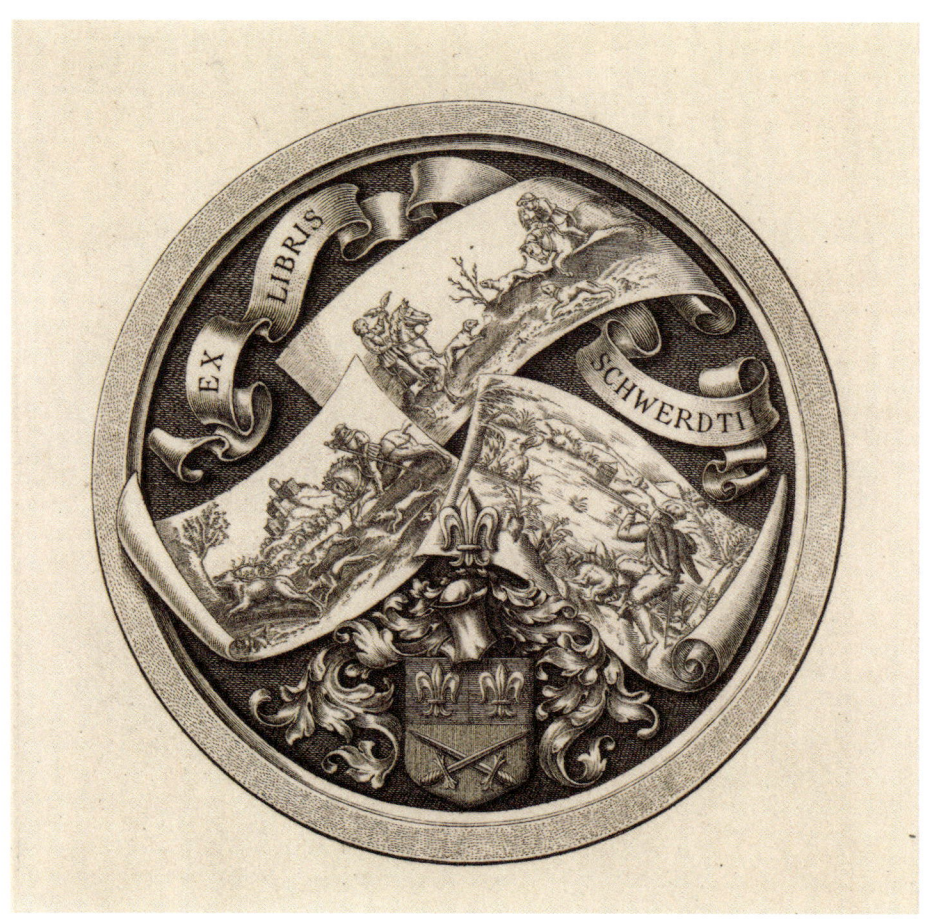

FIG. 11. Bookplate of C.F.G.R. Schwerdt. Virginia Museum of Fine Arts, Paul Mellon Collection, 85.1309.1/6

NOTES

1. A. D. Mackenzie, *The Bank of England Note: A History of Its Printing* (Cambridge: Cambridge University Press, 1953), 66, cited in Ford 1983, 65, 136n.

2. Ford 1983, 48.

3. Wilder 1974, 24.

4. Snelgrove 1981, 102.

5. Ibid., 221–26, 227–33.

6. For a detailed account of the history of Ackermann's, see Ford. Unfortunately after the book was published the archives were destroyed.

7. Cormack 2007, 51, 262n, following Egerton's description of the print of *Queen of Trumps* in Bell's *Life of London.*

8. Cormack 2007, 292, 17n.

9. See Snelgrove 1981, 6, pl. 104, for a description and illustration of Gurney's New Steam Carriage in an anonymous print dated there ca. 1810, but possibly later. Another similar print is in the British Museum, engraved by Pyall after G. Morton.

10. See Hyland 2003, 68–86, particularly 84. British and Empire human losses were 908,371, French losses were 1,357,800, U.S. losses were 53,000, Russian losses were 1,700,000, and German losses were 1,773,700.

11. Cormack 2007, 4, repr.

12. Snelgrove 1981, 211.

13. Paulson 1971, 489–90; Alexander and Godfrey 1980, 6.

14. Vertue, 59–60, cited in Alexander and Godfrey, 6.

15. Burke, cited in Alexander and Godfrey, 6.

16. Vertue, cited in Alexander and Godfrey, 7.

17. Bayard and D'Oench 1975, 1976.

18. For example, see M. Kirby Talley Jr., "'All good pictures crack': Sir Joshua Reynolds's practice and studio," in Penny 1986, 55–70; and for Gainsborough, see Cormack 1991, 23.

19. Alexander and Godfrey 1980, 7.

20. Ford 1983, 29, 238, 52n.

21. Man 1953, xii, pl. 1, 2, 3.

22. Ford 1983, 61, 240, 119n.

23. Lodge 1965, 616–27; Cormack 2007, 366.

24. At the end of the century, the English artist Walter Richard Sickert, who also made prints, including lithographs, was involved in a court case where he claimed that transfer lithography was not a "true" form of lithography. He lost.

25. Maas 1975.

26. Robertson 1978, 205.

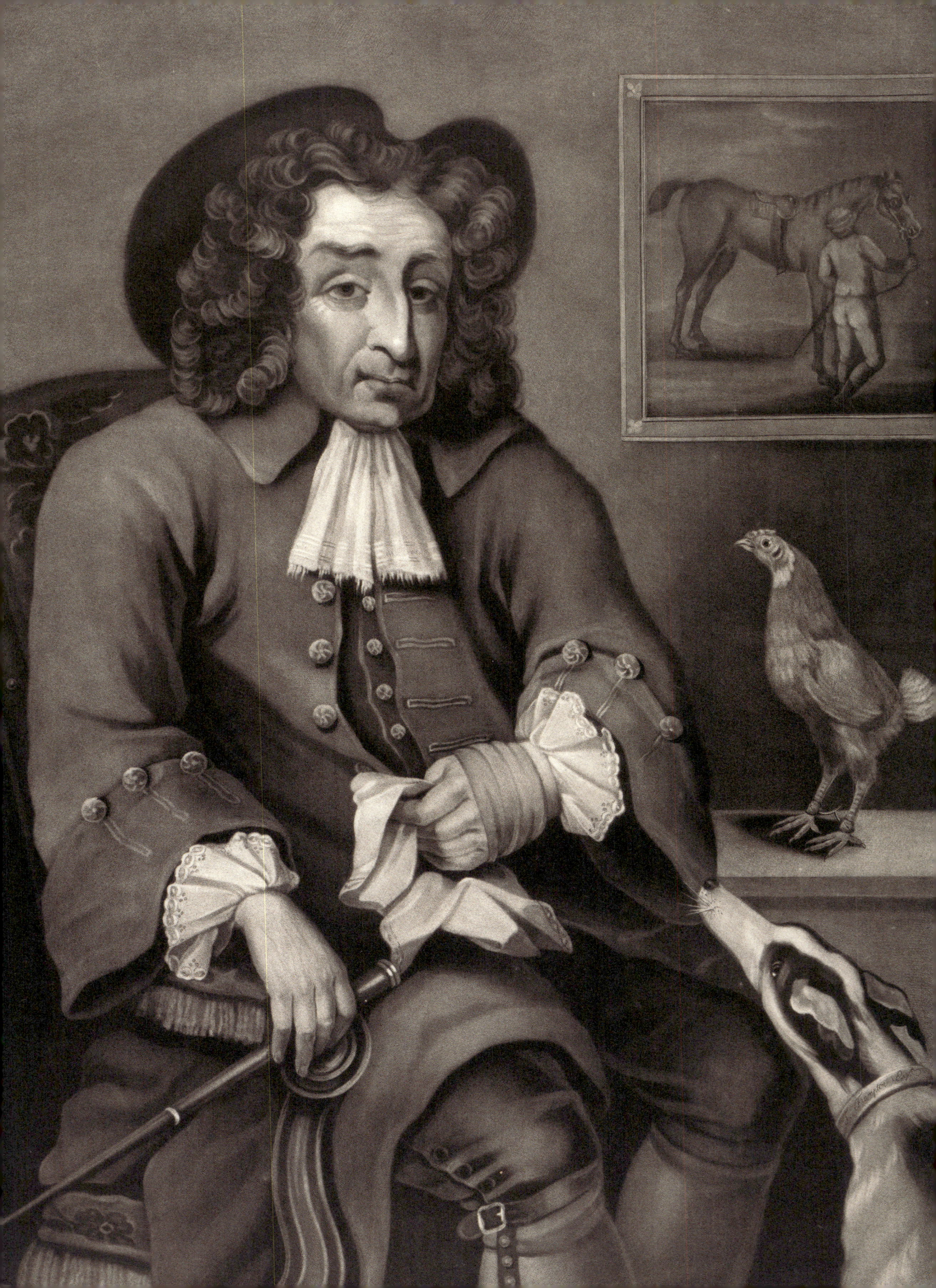

The Aesthetics of the British Sporting Print

MITCHELL MERLING

In 1968 the art historian Theodore Reff famously identified the artwork hanging on the back wall in Edgar Degas's particularly enigmatic image, *Sulking* (1869–71, fig. 13), as a British sporting print — John Frederick Herring's *Steeple Chase Cracks* of 1847. In his groundbreaking article, Reff wondered whether the interior depicted by Degas was inspired by an actual location such as a bank or the office of a bookmaker, where such prints might logically have been found. Reff then suggested that an increased interest in horse racing in France during the late 1860s might account for the print's presence in the painting, but then (positing "pictures within pictures" as a major device in Degas's work) segued into a discussion of the formal function of the print in the composition. He concluded that the painting, because of the less than rhetorical expressions of the main figures in the interior, is "more . . . characteristic of modern life."[1] By implication, then, the print by Herring must also be seen as an emblem of that "modern life," which Degas sought to capture in his compositions in the 1860s and 1870s.

For present-day viewers, it is likely puzzling that Degas would select a sporting print to exemplify modernity, as such images are now typically thought of as the visual and art historical embodiment of

"tradition"— a tradition not only of field sports and their role in British society but also of a kind of picture making particular to a certain time and place. However, British sporting prints underwent a remarkable aesthetic evolution during the eighteenth and nineteenth centuries, culminating in the work of Henry Alken, James Pollard, and John Frederick Herring in the early nineteenth century. During that time, artists moved away from models drawn from both classical and "high" art toward an independent style, unique to sporting prints, signifying modernity as an art free of influence and not dependent on other masters or traditions.

A close look at the development of the pictorial language of sporting prints (an often overlooked aspect of the history of British art, and visual culture more generally) not only offers a better understanding of how the artists arrived at the style that came to define the genre but also reveals an art form — now thought to be static and rooted in tradition — that was actually quite forward looking. Indeed, these works pushed aesthetic boundaries and exerted an influence outside of the narrowly defined genre of sporting art, inspiring such artists as Théodore Géricault and Degas, who appreciated them for their very modernity.[2]

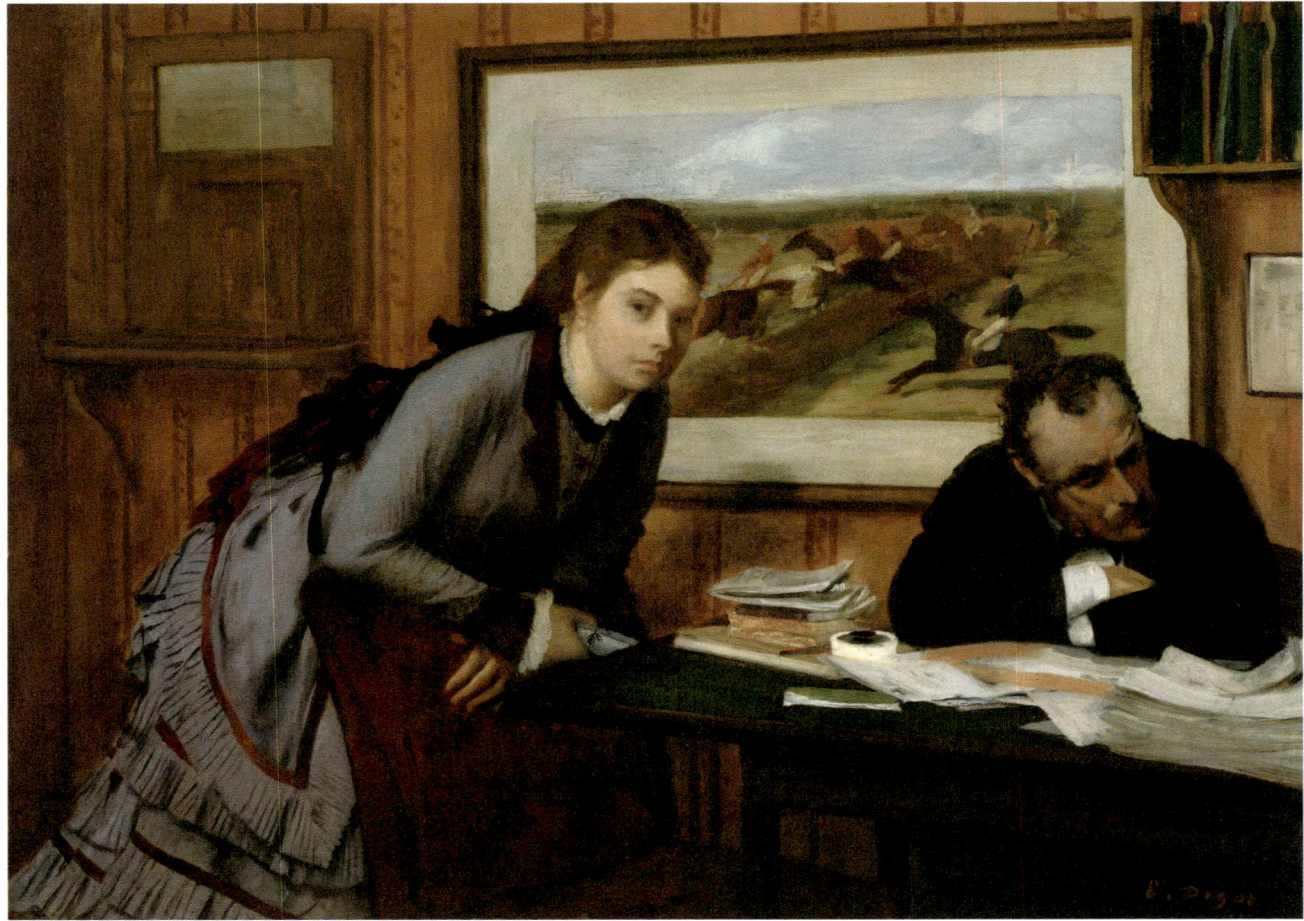

FIG. 13. Edgar Degas (French, 1834–1917), *Sulking,* oil on canvas, ca. 1870. The Metropolitan Museum of Art, H. O. Havemeyer Collection, Bequest of Mrs. H. O. Havemeyer, 1929, 29.100.43

A more complete understanding of the aesthetic contributions of the genre must take into account the visual mechanics of the British sporting print. These works, at once commonplace and invisible, have received considerable attention in terms of connoisseurship, most notably through Paul Mellon's patronage and Dudley Snelgrove's catalogue of the Mellon collection. They have also been explored through the lens of social and intellectual history (along with many other kinds of pictorial, literary, and historical evidence) in foundational volumes by Stephen Deuchar and Diana Donald.[3] However, an examination of sporting prints through visual analysis and an account of their modes of depicting the world of animals and sport, despite their often seemingly selective viewpoint, might be productive. Indeed, the figures and features left out of the microcosmic world of the sporting print were often as important as those the artist portrayed. In their

selectivity, artists were actively engaged in shaping a unique vocabulary inherent to this pervasive genre and in the process created the distinctive "world" of the British sporting print.

The most important early sporting prints produced in Britain are from the set entitled *Severall Wayes of Hunting, Hawking, and Fishing, According to the English Manner* (1671). This series, a fundamental document for the history of sport, was the result of collaboration between the Bohemian-born etcher Wenceslaus Hollar and the English animal painter and printmaker Frances Barlow.[4] Hollar, who arrived in England in 1636, was among the retinue of the sophisticated and intellectual Earl of Arundel and turned his highly developed skills of observation to creating an encyclopedic body of work — including landscapes and townscapes, portraits and costume studies, and prints after great masters such as Leonardo da Vinci. In keeping with his comprehensive

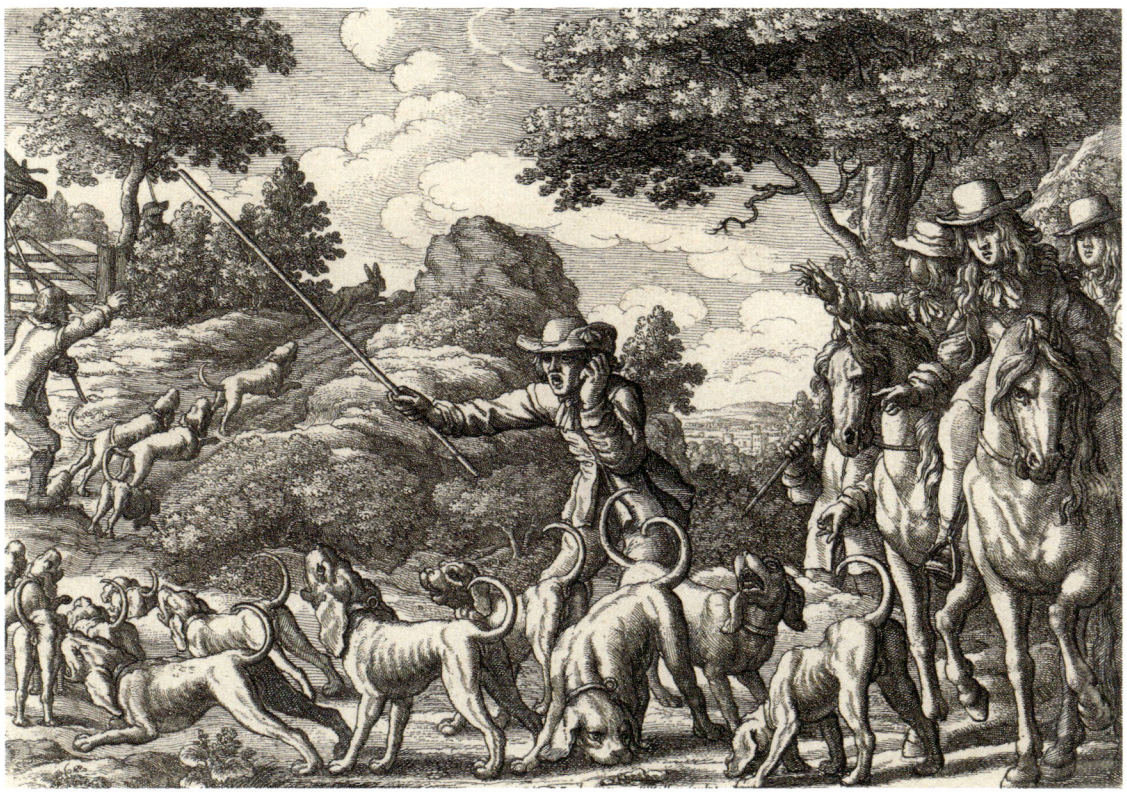

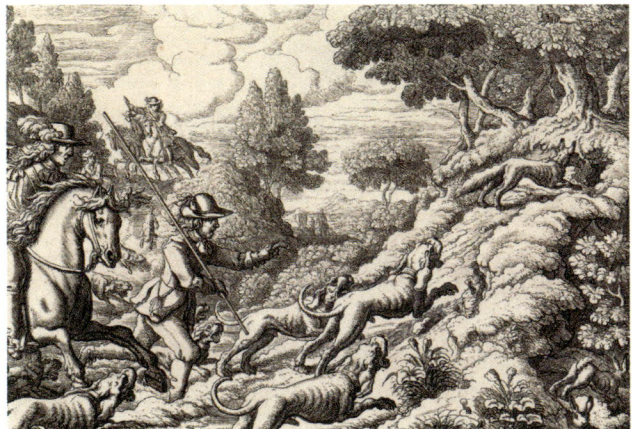

vision, Hollar here portrays the world of sport in a manner that recalls earlier compendia and treatises on various hunts, for instance those by the French count Gaston Phébus, known through numerous manuscripts, and Johannes Stradanus in Italy, who produced a series of engravings published by Philip Galle. But, unlike those other artists, the etchers delineate the various "national sports of Great Britain" such as otter and stag hunting and varieties of hawking rather than foreign and historical sports.[5] The two prints from that source chosen for VMFA's exhibition demonstrate the revolutionary clarity that Barlow and Hollar were able to bring to the subject

(figs. 14 and 15). In *Severall Wayes,* the charming, informal naturalism of illustrations in Phébus and the mannerist contortions of Stradanus are replaced by a rather static atmosphere that emphasizes the hunters' mastery of the chase. These etchings, with their wide but shallow perspective, give the viewer a maximum of information and contribute to an air of formality and organization, unlike the sometimes chaotic scenes rendered by other artists of the hunt.

However fecund the encyclopedic outlook and unaffected compositions of the series may have been for later artists such as Henry Alken, author of the 1824 *National Sports of Great Britain,* they made no immediate impression on the next generation of British sporting artists (including the genre's two most powerful forces: John Wootton and James Seymour), who sought their own styles according to their conceptions of the field.

John Wootton, as appropriate for a pupil of Flemish painter Jan Wyck, created paintings that were somewhat classicizing and derivative of the Flemish manner, characteristics that are also evident in the few prints after his hunting scenes — for example, the rare series of *Hare Hunting* prints, preserved at

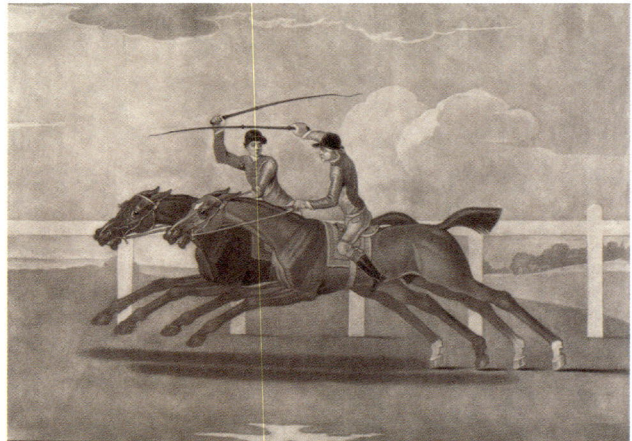

FIG. 16. James Seymour, *Two Jockeys Racing,* 1752, cat. no. 61

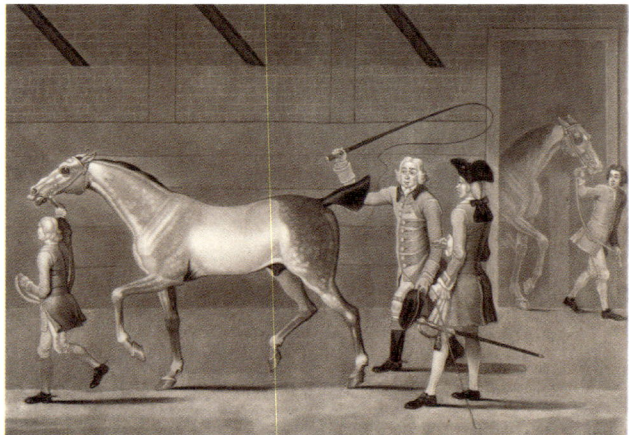

FIG. 17. James Seymour, *A Horse Courser Selling a Nag,* 1752, cat. no. 62

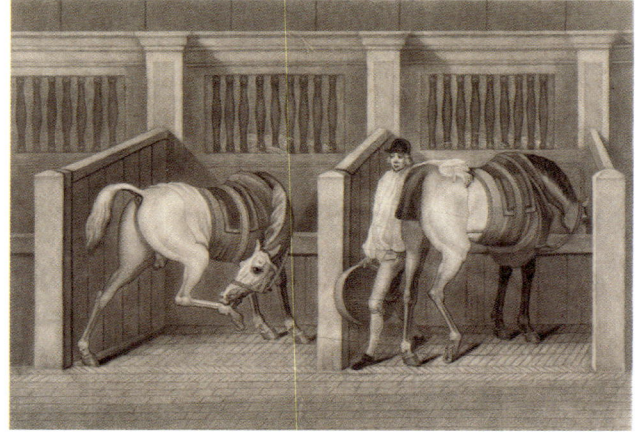

FIG. 18. James Seymour, *Two Horses, Rugged in Stalls,* 1752, cat. no. 60

Clandon Park in Surrey, England.[6] Here, deep perspectives of subjects like distant ports and mountains are framed by luxuriant trees and figures appear in heroic attitudes, revealing Wootton's reliance on classical models such as Claude Lorrain's grand landscapes.[7] Wootton rarely engraved his own plates, and in this exhibition he is represented by a reproductive print produced by Jonathan Jones in 1791 (fig. 12), itself a variant of a mezzotint by John Faber depicting Wootton's portrait of the famous trainer Tregonwell Frampton, who was called "The Father of the Turf." The only significant difference between the 1791 print and the earlier version is the addition in the background of a framed print (known to be a print because of its narrow, plain frame) of Frampton's famous horse Dragon (the horse's portrait is shown in a medallion below in the earlier example).[8] However, in both versions of the portrait, the depictions of Frampton and especially Dragon are notable for their utter bare-bones simplicity and eschewal of the heroic manner characteristic of his other works.

In the case of the 1791 mezzotint, the engraver Jones may have been looking at prints by Wootton's chief rival, James Seymour, who, unlike Wootton, was specialized only in sporting subjects and developed an art of stunning, unstudied simplicity different from the typically more monumental vision of Wootton.[9] Seymour's aesthetic tendency in both his paintings and his prints was to strip his subjects of every detail. A good example of this inclination is seen in *Two Jockeys Racing Neck and Neck to the Winning-Post* (fig. 16), one of a series of twelve prints that illustrate the daily lives of horses. The collection also anticipates the various and widely popular series featuring the life and death of horses (such as Henry Alken's *The High Mettled Racer* of 1821, also in this exhibition).

Other prints from Seymour's series display the same perfunctory naturalism. *A Horse Courser Selling a Nag* captures without irony the misleading transaction — only the legend "Caveat emptor" (Buyer beware) discloses the narrative (fig. 17). The straightforward print *Two Horses, Rugged in Stalls* simply depicts two horses in a stark interior (fig. 18). Although the treatment of the subject may seem artless, Seymour's typically original invention leads directly to the rich subject matter of stable and blacksmith interiors that later became more elaborately visualized in the hands of such artists as the distinguished Joseph Wright of Derby. In this and other prints, Seymour's art is constructed mainly of outline

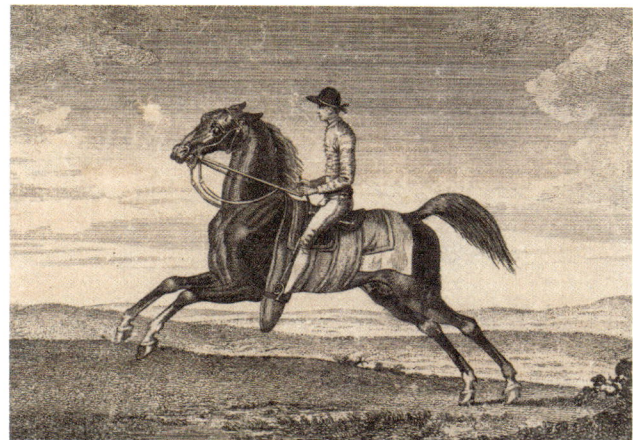

FIG. 19. James Seymour, *Childers,* 1773, cat. no. 63

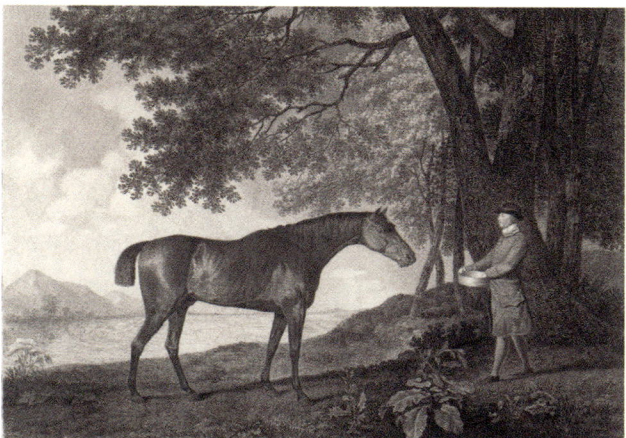

FIG. 21. George Stubbs, *Sharke,* 1794, cat. no. 74

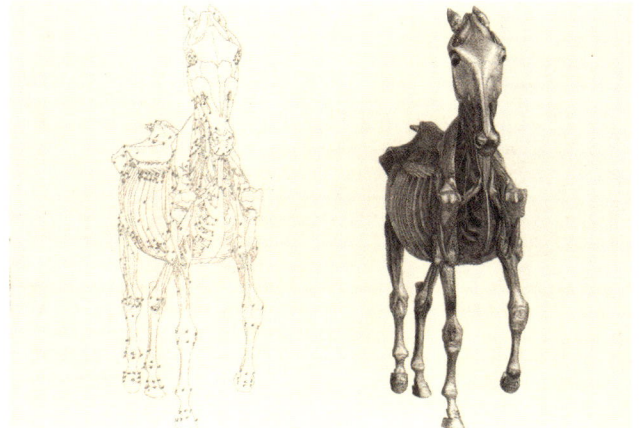

FIG. 20. George Stubbs, Plate IX from *Anatomy of the Horse,* 1766, cat. no. 70

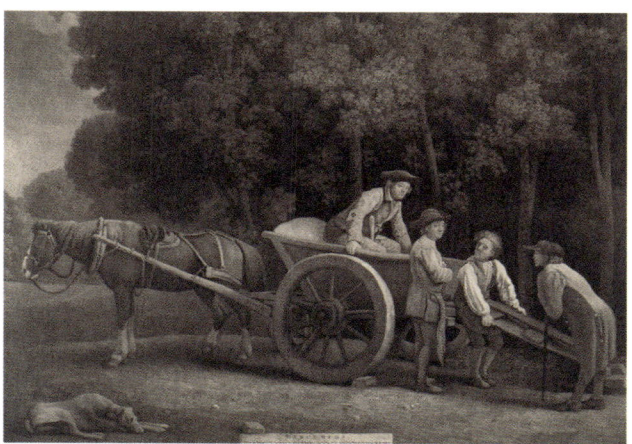

FIG. 22. George Stubbs, *Labourers,* 1789, cat. no. 71

and silhouette. For example, *Childers* shows only the rudimentary elements of anatomy (fig. 19)—an art literally of "skin and bones." Similarly, a plate by anatomist Jeremiah Bridge from about the same period delineates the horse exclusively in this way—as merely a system of bones connected by sinew and muscle.

It was up to George Stubbs to change the understanding of the equine body forever through the publication of his *Anatomy of the Horse* in 1766. Stubbs's subtitle — *a particular description of the Bones, Cartilages, Muscles, Fascias, Ligaments, Nerves, Arteries, Veins and Glands . . . all done from Nature* — underlines the painter's aspiration to move beyond the superficial naturalism of Bridges and Seymour. In these still-startling plates, Stubbs depicts the horse's physical elements not only separately but also miraculously intertwined, as well as in motion (fig. 20).[10] Stubbs's extensive knowledge of anatomy transformed sporting art altogether and furnished

a reference point for the genre's later development. His portrait *Sharke* shows the results of his hard-won understanding of anatomy, landscape, and human posture, which enabled him to speak to a very specialized audience (fig. 21).[11] Furthermore, the labor-intensive medium of stipple engraving contributes to the illusionism of the image, producing a veridical and highly nuanced print that warrants more careful notice than do similar horse portraits by the earlier Seymour.

Explanations for Stubbs's often surprising images have looked to intellectual and historical contexts of the period. His images of fighting animals, especially horses, have usually been seen in the framework of eighteenth-century sublime aesthetics — as forces of nature that exist outside the control of man.[12] At the same time, his *Labourers,* which depicts Lord Torrington's servants in the midst of a dispute, has usually and rightfully been understood in the particular social context of the nobleman's patronage

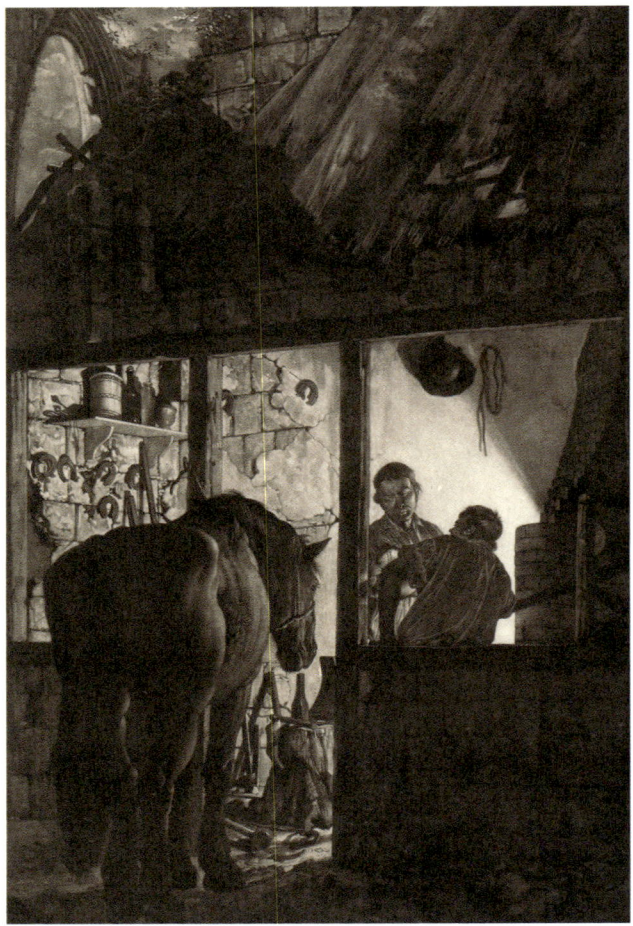

FIG. 23. Joseph Wright (of Derby), *A Farrier's Shop,* 1771, cat. no. 83

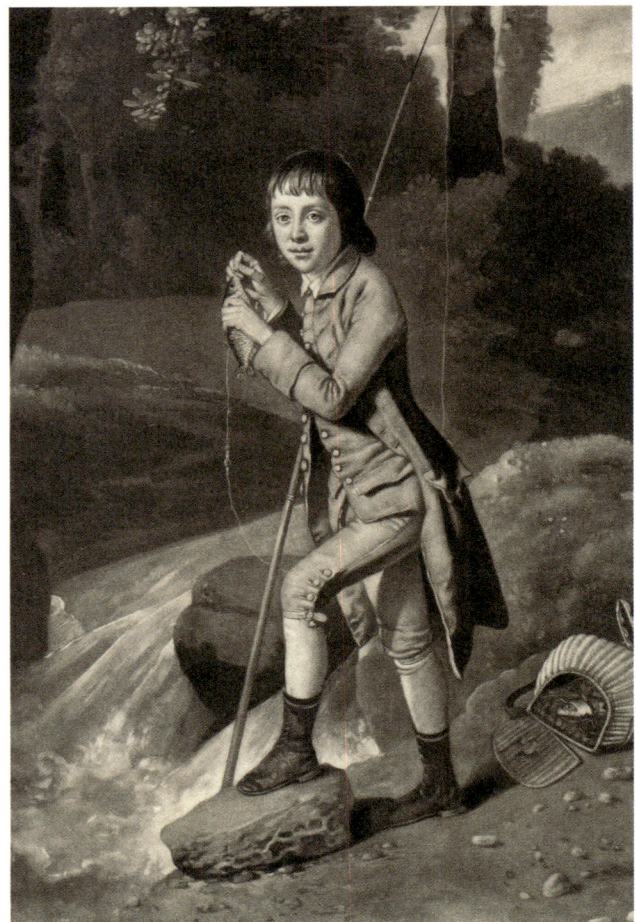

FIG. 24. Johann Zoffany, *Portrait of Master Sayer Fishing,* cat. no. 84

of Stubbs (fig. 22).[13] However, setting aside the common subject of the struggle for dominance, whether between horses or men, both of these prints share the idea that close observation of the minutiae of country life are suitable subjects for an artist.

Contemporary artists such as Joseph Wright of Derby and Johann Zoffany, though painters of predominantly nonsporting pictures, employed a similar strategy in their images of rural subjects. Wright of Derby's *A Farrier's Shop* shows the artist's singular and spectacular investigation of light while seeking inspiration from Dutch naturalism — Paulus Potter for the figure of the horse itself and perhaps Essias Boursse for the humble setting (fig. 23). Zoffany, in his portrait of a print seller's young son out fishing, characteristically tones down the English Grand Manner style to produce a relaxed "natural" portrait set in an idyllic rustic landscape. Zoffany's unique image is replete with the idealization of fishing as a pleasant and thoughtful sport (fig. 24).

The glorification of country life at a time when urbanism was draining the countryside of its inhabitants was one purpose of the sporting print (the comedic possibilities of sport being the other). Above all other artists, George Morland explored the ideal of country life in greatest depth in his large oeuvre of paintings and prints. Though the prints soften some of the mordancy of Morland's painted work, as noted by art historian John Barrell, they were presumably produced under the supervision of Morland himself (fig. 25) and thus adequately reflect his views.[14] Therefore, rather than condemning the prints as inaccurate to Morland's social project as Barrell does, they are better understood as a unique vision of a contented, well-fed nation motivated by the spirit of class reconciliation.

Francis Wheatley and Morland together are responsible for another important contribution to the further development of the sporting print — the easy transition to color that marks the works of the late

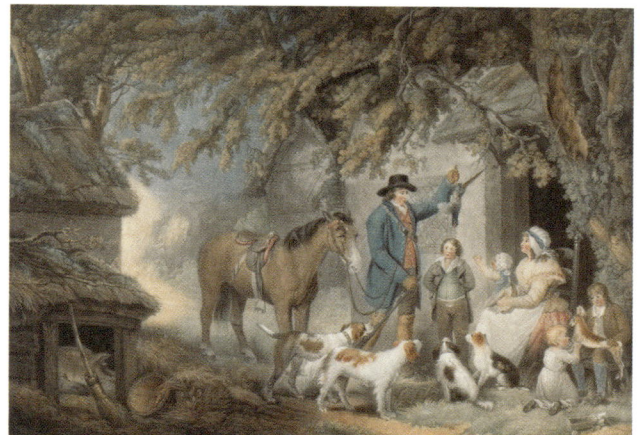

FIG. 25. George Morland, *Evening,* 1795, cat. no. 51

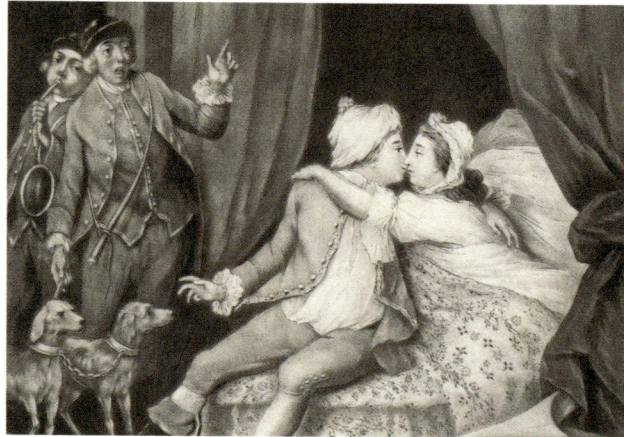

FIG. 27. Unknown artist, *The Old Free Method of Rouzing a Brother Sportsman* (detail), ca. 1780, cat. no. 78

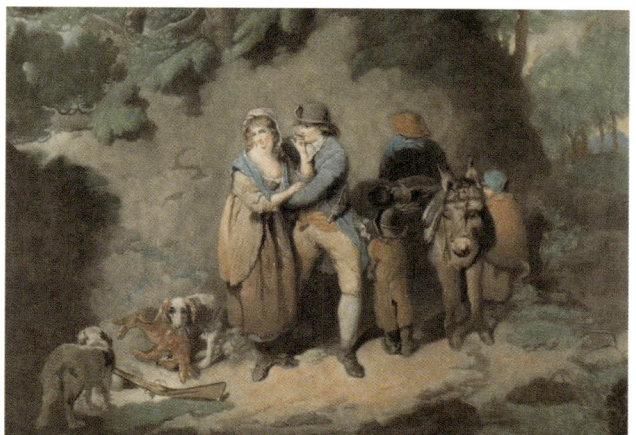

FIG. 26. Francis Wheatley, *The Amorous Sportsman,* 1786, cat. no. 79

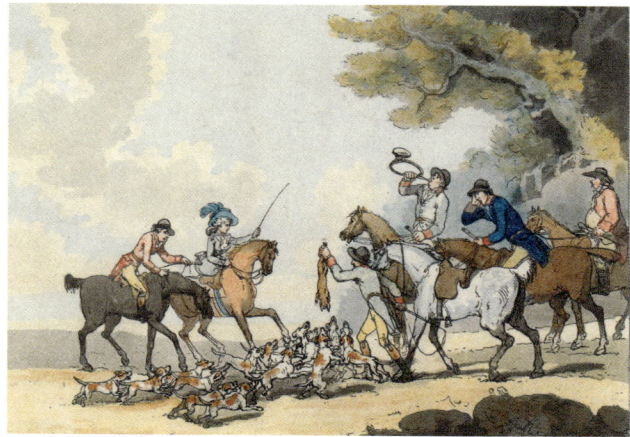

FIG. 28. Thomas Rowlandson, *The Death,* 1789, cat. no. 58

eighteenth century. Although certainly tinted images were made before that time, coloring became a regular and expected feature of sporting prints, especially by the time of Thomas Rowlandson and Henry Alken. A comparison of Wheatley's *The Amorous Sportsman* (fig. 26) and the anonymous *The Old Free Method of Rouzing a Brother Sportsman* (fig. 27), of almost identical subject matter, exemplifies the potential of color in sporting prints: the expressive qualities of color in Wheatley's create much greater visual impact. In the work of Wheatley and Morland, both painter-printmakers, subtle hand coloring is combined with mezzotint to produce painterly effects. Other sporting printmakers such as Thomas Rowlandson and Henry Alken (Alken's few paintings are most likely preliminary to his prints) joined the more planar qualities of aquatint with coloring to compose in large areas of flat color.[15]

Rowlandson's two prints in this exhibition, *The Death* and *The Breakfast,* also represent the stylistically

diverse modes in which the artist was able to move with ease (figs. 28 and 29). *The Death,* derived from the earlier traditions of Seymour and Barlow, depicts a characteristic moment of hunts (with *Meeting at Cover, Setting Off, and Streaming Off*). In *The Death,* Rowlandson emphasizes with great skill the easy attitudes of the riders in an idealized view of country life set in a landscape that could easily have issued from the brush of Gainsborough (though Gainsborough, unlike Morland, has never been embraced as a sporting artist). But in *The Breakfast,* Rowlandson employs caricature much as William Hogarth in the earlier print *The Cock Pit* (fig. 30). Like Hogarth, Rowlandson utilizes references to the "high" art of antiquity and the Renaissance to add bite to the satire as well as visual gravitas to the images. Hogarth achieved this by basing the overall composition on da Vinci's *Last Supper,* while Rowlandson makes a direct reference to the ancient statue known as Cincinnatus in the pose of the foreground figure putting on his boots.

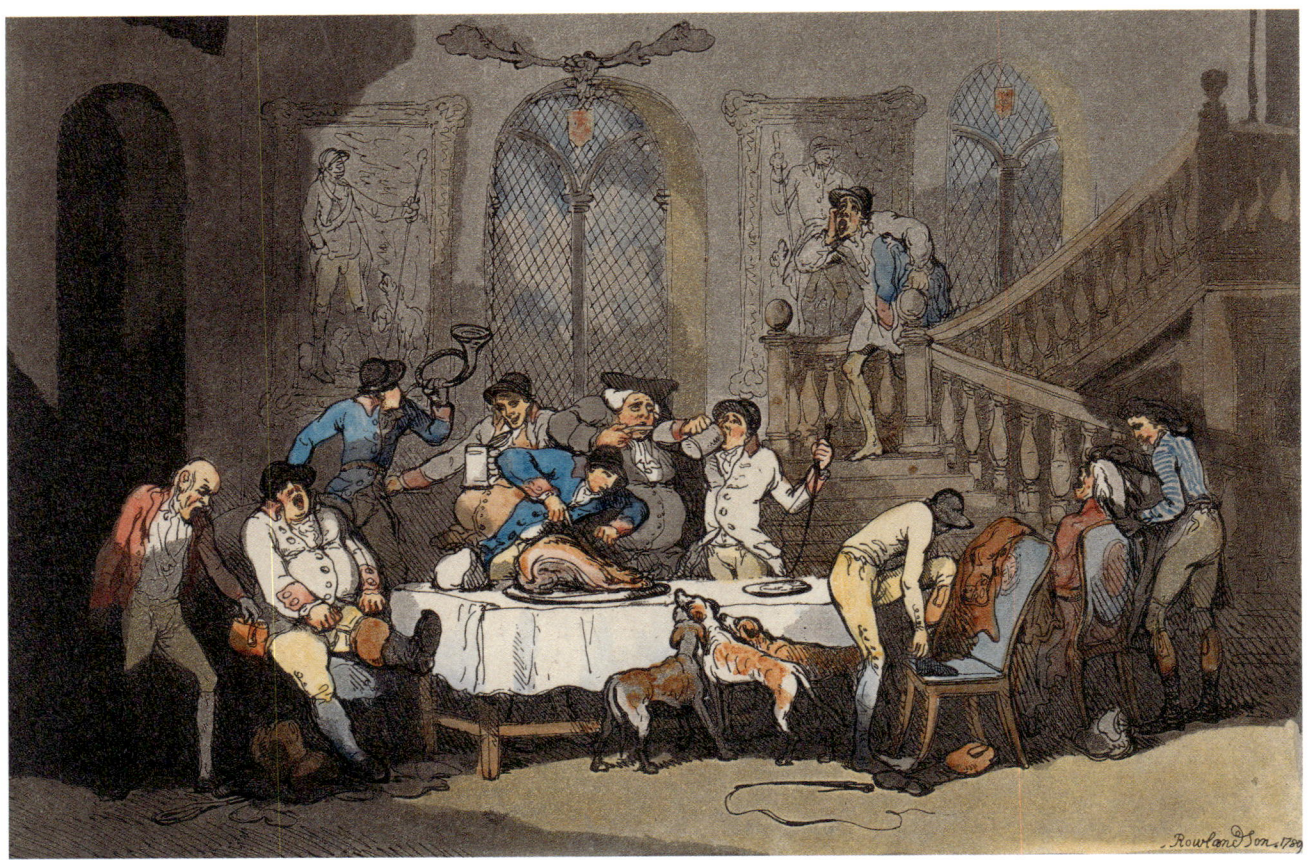

FIG. 29: Thomas Rowlandson, *The Breakfast*, 1789, cat. no. 59

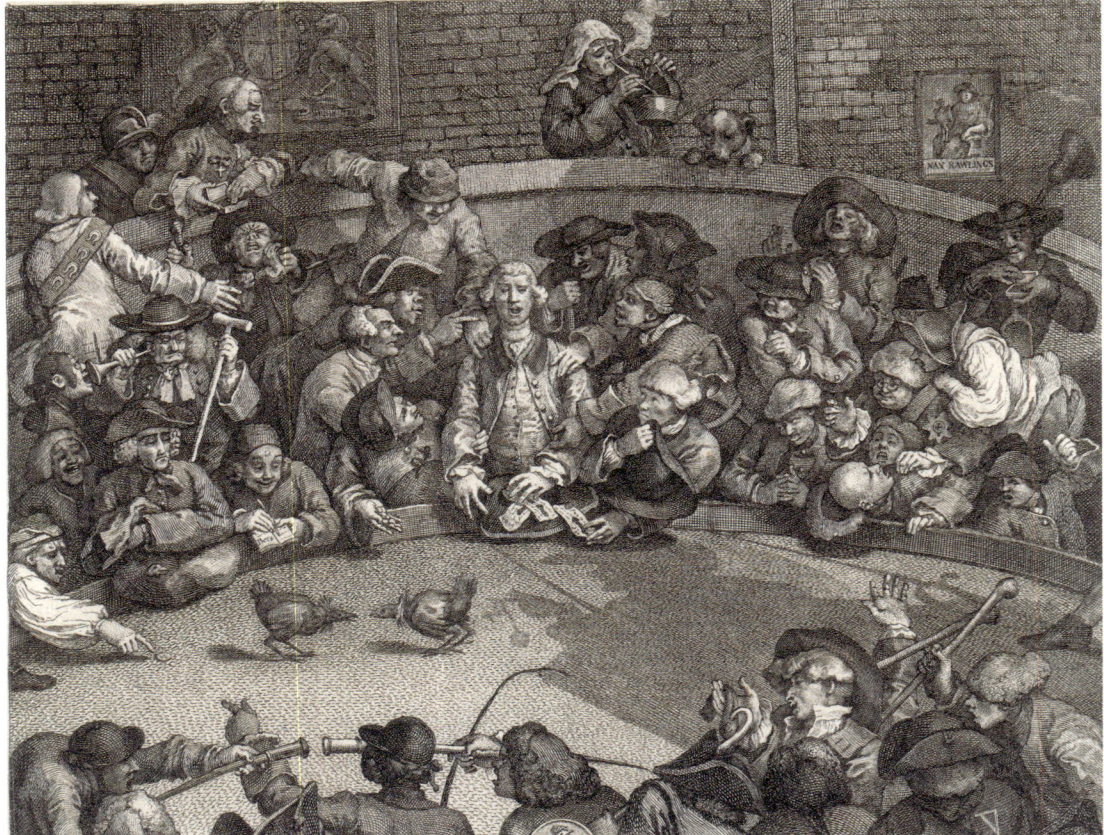

FIG. 30. William Hogarth, *The Cock Pit*, 1759, cat. no. 46

In such prints, accomplished sportsmen are gently mocked by artists for rather modest failings, such as voracious appetites, as in Rowlandson's *The Breakfast,* or the somewhat more acceptable vice of excessive amorousness (usually directed against servants or peasants) as in works by Wheatley.[16] True satire rather than jocularity was better rendered in a coarse style derived from popular prints and caricatures, as in Henry William Bunbury's *Coxheath Ho!* (fig. 31). An even more deliberate artistic primitivism is evident in the prints of Charles Ansell and Isaac Cruikshank (figs. 32 and 33). These images satirize "London" sportsmen — townspeople pathetically engaged in rural pursuits for which they are ill suited. While the townsman is never portrayed as truly at home within the sporting world, other artists, following Morland's example, depicted sport as an ideal place for the mixing of classes. In Jacques Laurent Agasse's *Peasants Coming to the Race* and *Race Ground,* country folk appear orderly and well behaved (figs. 34 and 35).

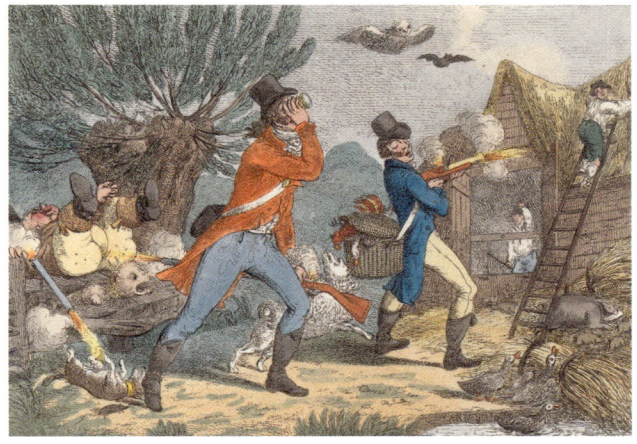

FIG. 31. Henry William Bunbury, *Coxheath Ho!,* 1779, cat. no. 31

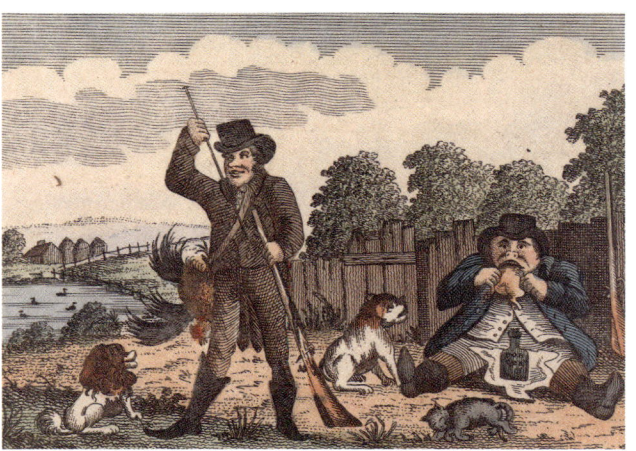

FIG. 32. Charles Ansell, *Cockney Sportsmen Spying Game,* ca. 1805, cat. no. 23

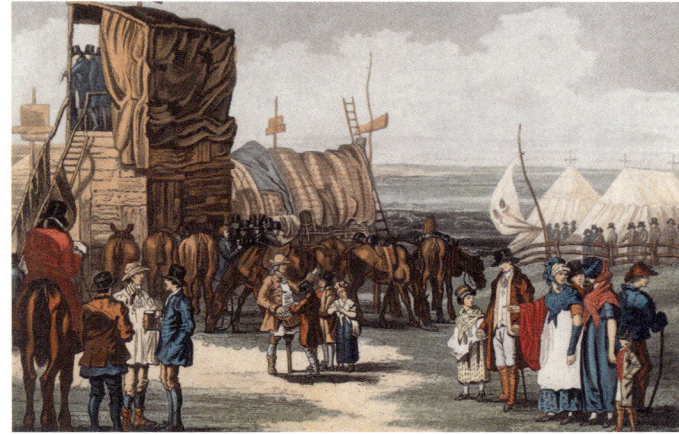

FIG. 34. Jacques Laurent Agasse, *Peasants Coming to the Race,* 1807, cat. no. 3

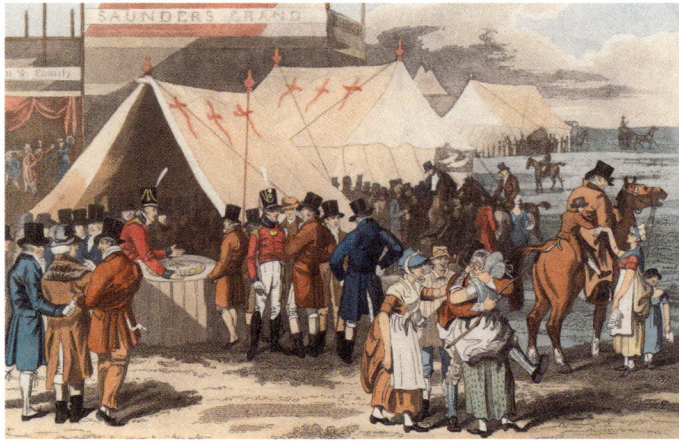

FIG. 33. Isaac Cruikshank, *London Sportsmen Recharging,* ca. 1800, cat. no. 33

FIG. 35. Jacques Laurent Agasse, *Sketch from a Race Ground,* 1807, cat. no. 2

An important development occurred at the turn of the nineteenth century with the movement away from high-art references toward more stereotypical images, which consolidated the image of sporting prints. This transition is readily apparent in the racehorse portrait, which in the first decades of the nineteenth century attained a typological perfection in such works as John Frederick Herring's *Mango* (fig. 36) and Henry Bernard Chalon's *Pavilion* (fig. 37).

Chalon's image, in its measured, not to say parsimonious, approach to presenting information, furnishes an important visual precedent for quintessentially "modern" paintings that derived inspiration from sporting prints at the beginning of the nineteenth century — for example, Theodore Géricault's *A Horse with Jockey Up* (fig. 38). Géricault's image depicts the

banality of everyday life for horse and jockey with an equally dull composition — horse, jockey, and post set in a barren landscape — that directly depends on the visual precedent of Chalon's print. Herring's *Mango,* fully worked up in color and including extensive inscriptions (the Chalon is a proof before lettering), shows the aesthetic culmination of the development in horse portraiture of a more accomplished yet still rudimentary style that nonetheless provides a maximum of precise information, particularly when coupled with legends recounting the genealogies and successes of the horse.

A similar visual change from the complexities of the eighteenth century to a clearer and simpler style occurred especially in depictions of the hunt and the steeplechase. The visual richness of Samuel Howitt's

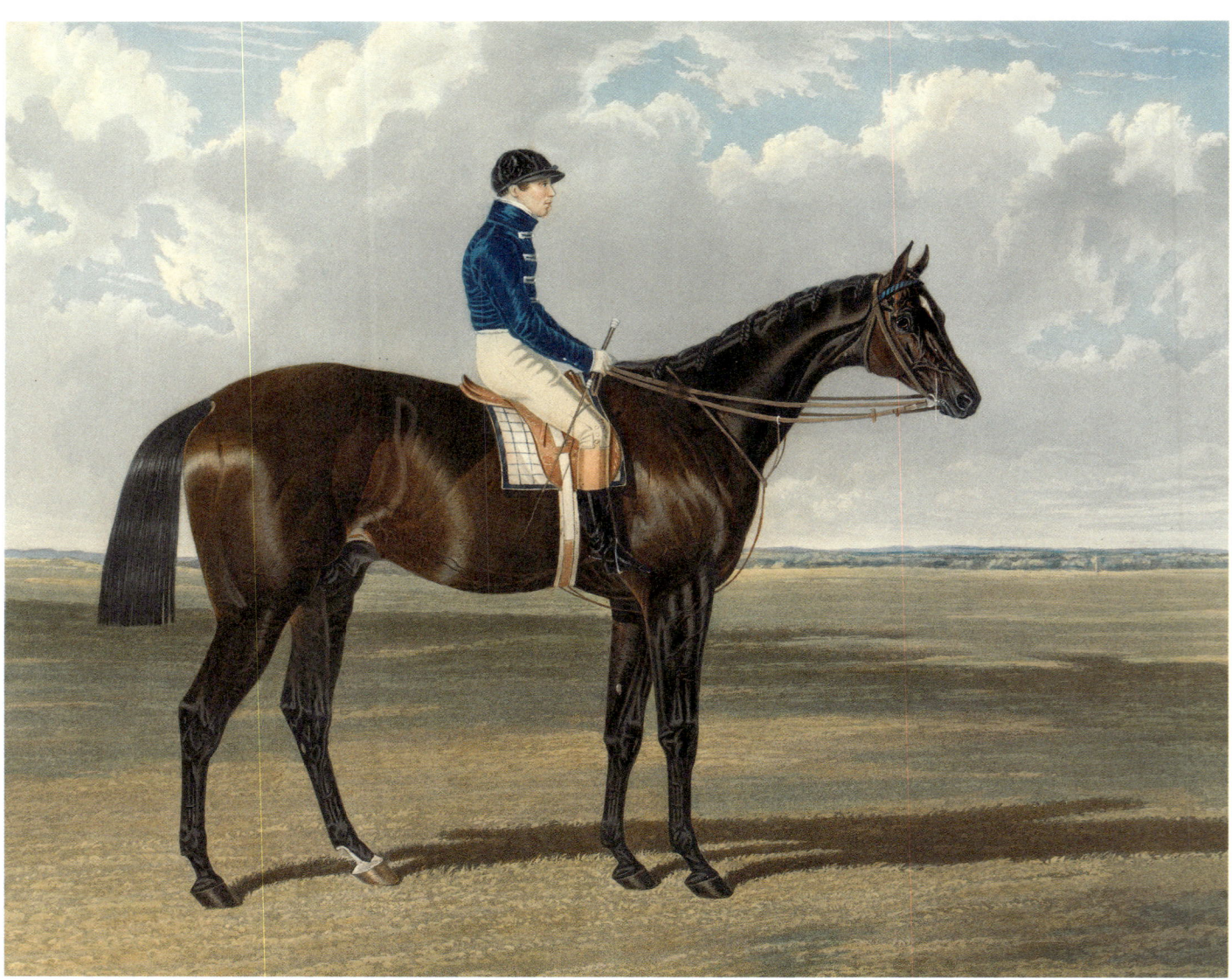

FIG. 36. John Frederick Herring, *Mango,* 1837, cat. no. 45

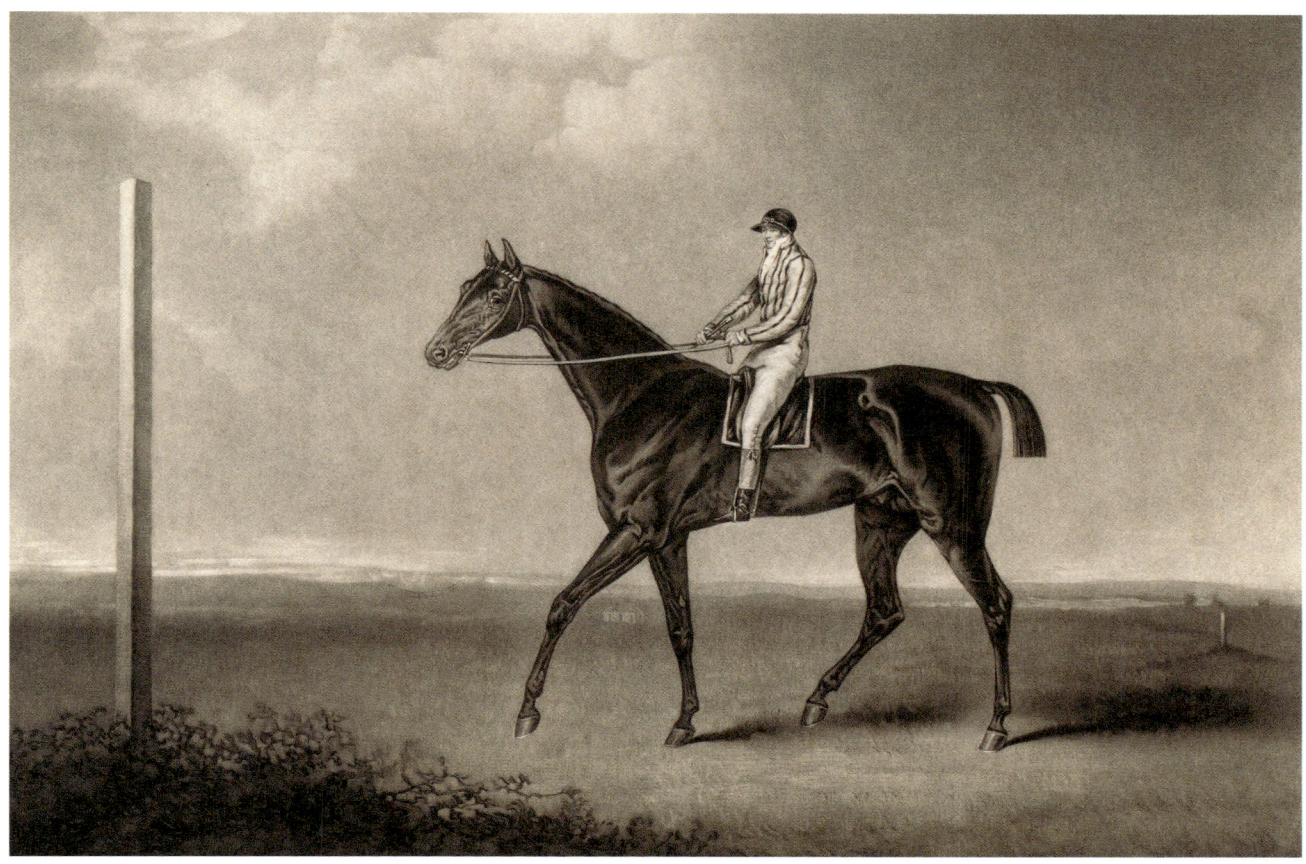

FIG. 37. Henry Bernard Chalon, *Pavilion, Ridden by Chifney,* 1803, cat. no. 32

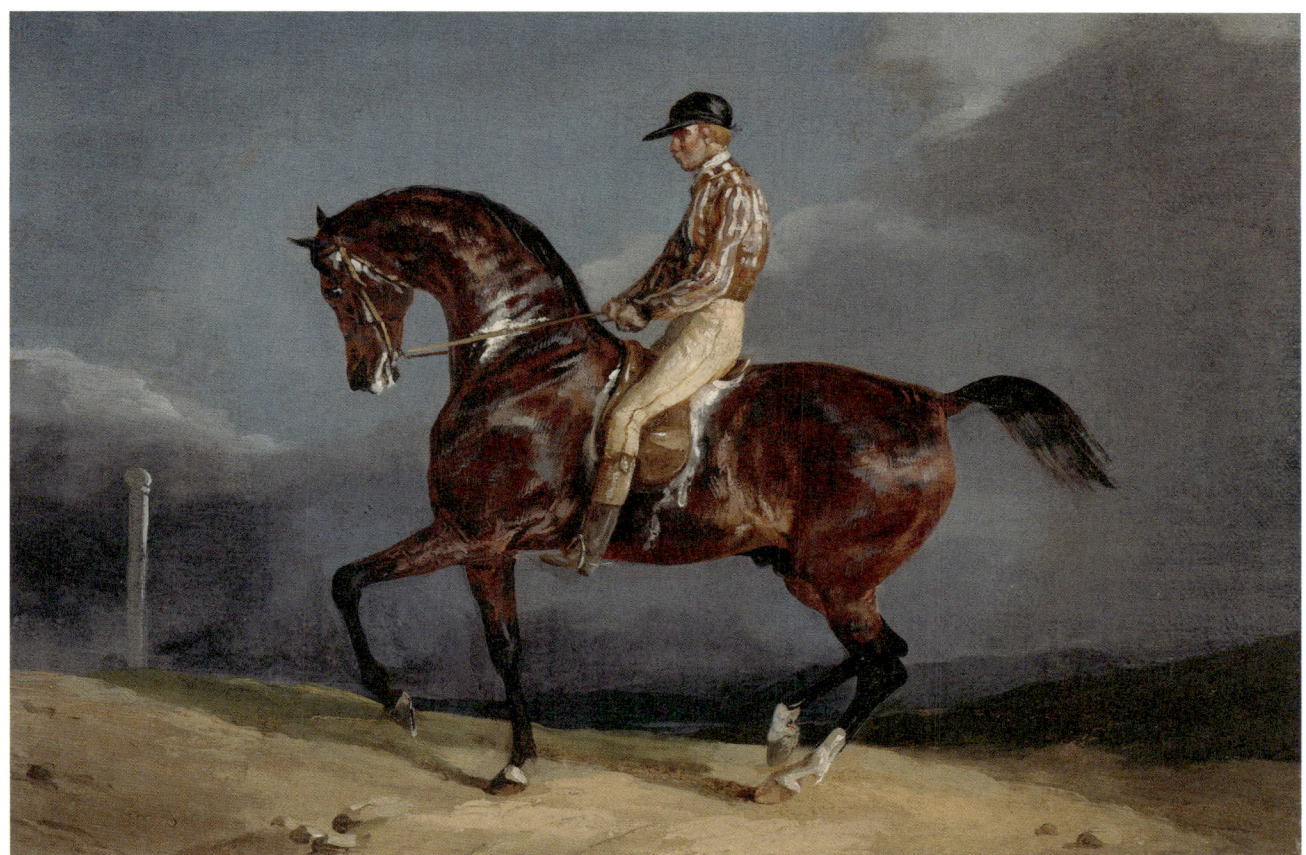

FIG. 38. Théodore Géricault (French, 1791–1824), *A Horse with Jockey Up,* oil on canvas, 1821–22. Virginia Museum of Fine Arts, Paul Mellon Collection

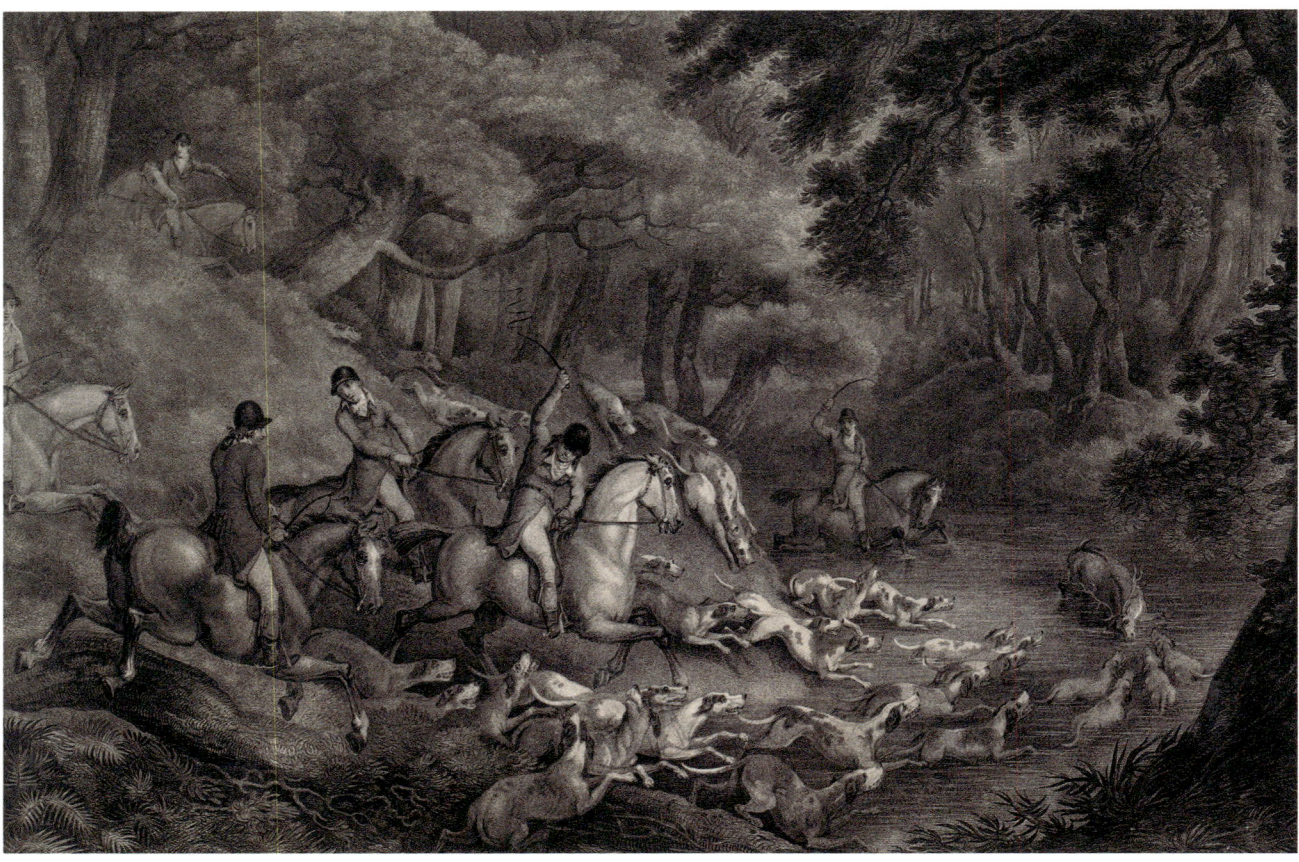

FIG. 39. Samuel Howitt, *The Stag at Bay and Whipping Off the Hounds,* 1802, cat. no. 47

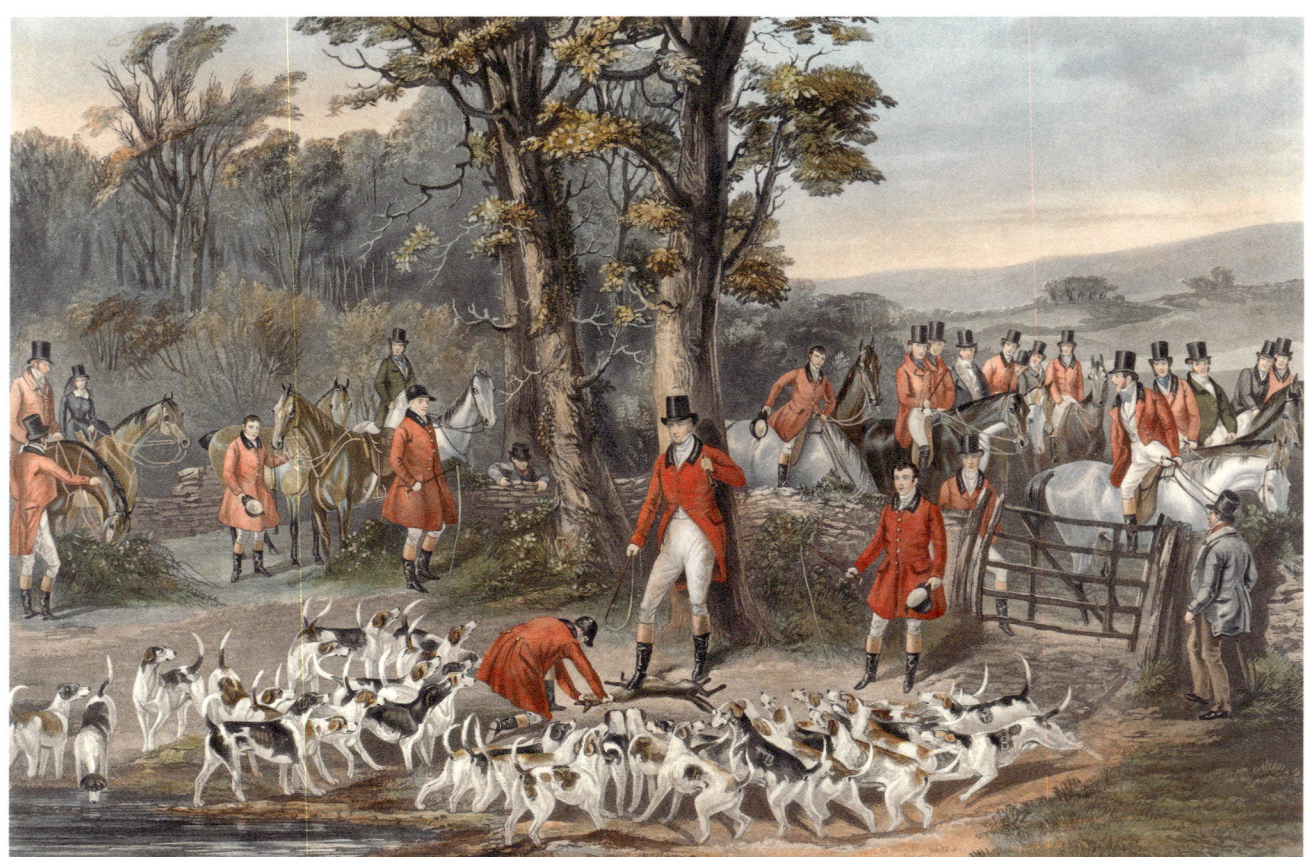

FIG. 40. Francis Calcraft Turner, *The Death,* 1842, cat. no. 77

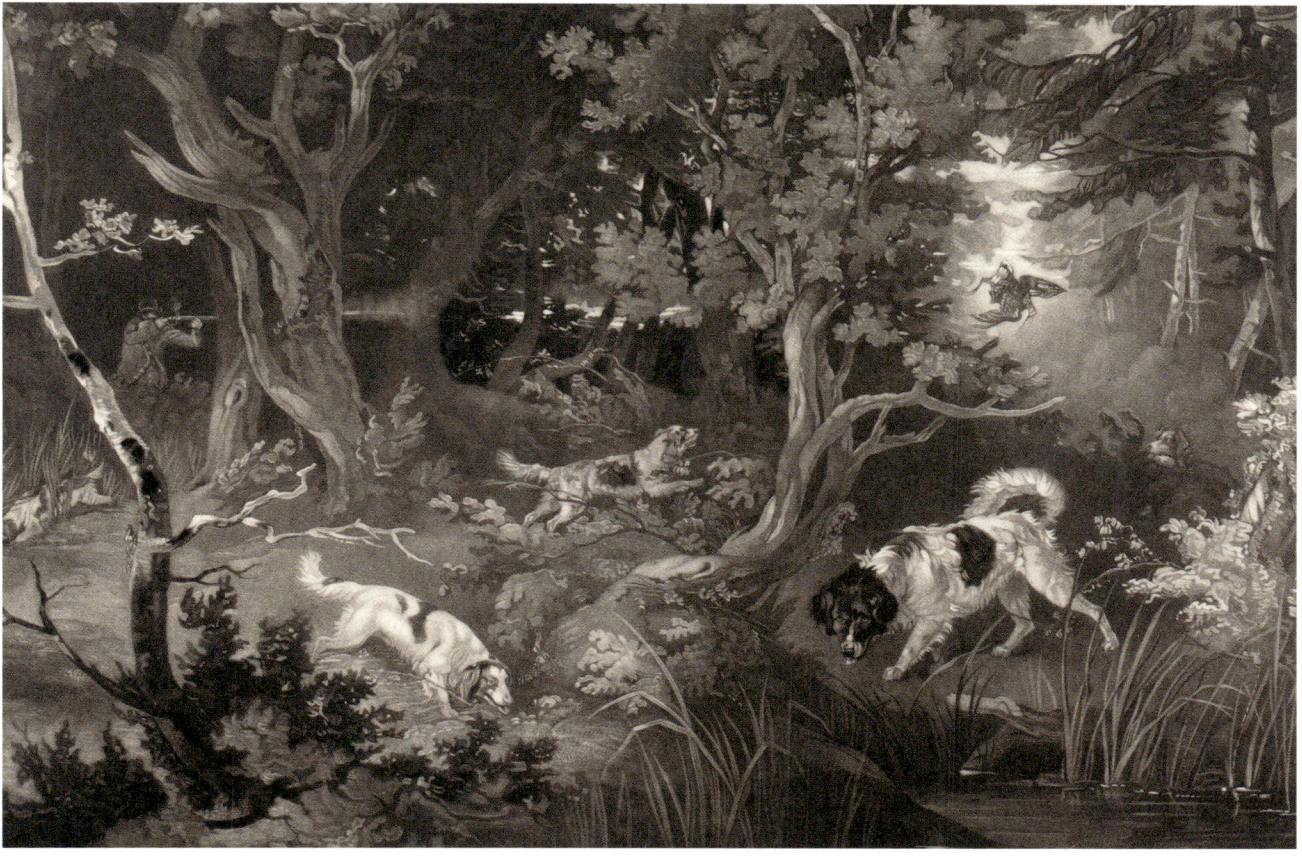

FIG. 41. Philip Reinagle, *Fowling,* 1810, cat. no. 57

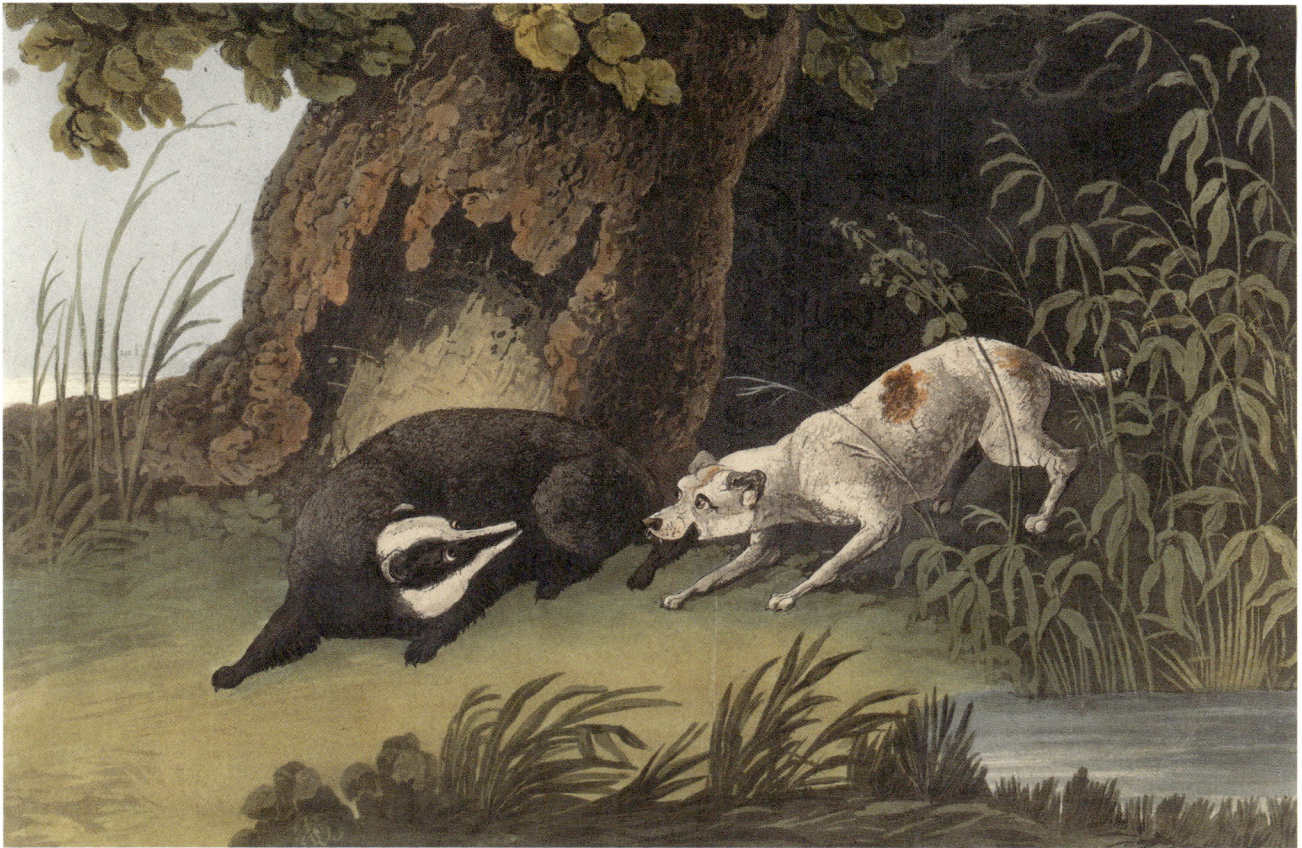

FIG. 42. Dean Wolstenholme, the Elder, *Dog and Badger,* ca. 1820–30, cat. no. 80

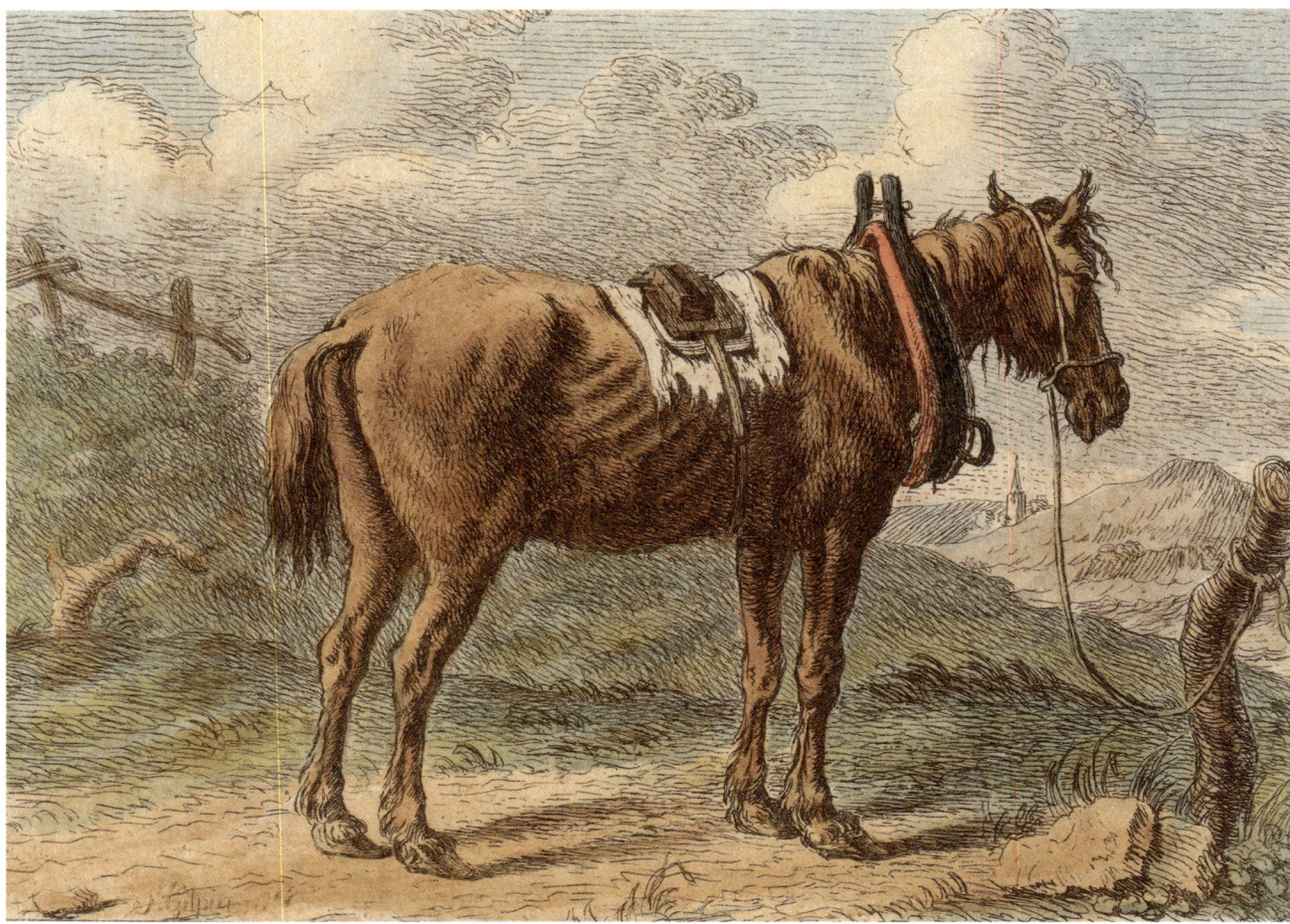

FIG. 43. Sawrey Gilpin, *The Cart Horse,* 1793, cat. no. 43

1802 mezzotint *The Stag at Bay* (fig. 39), which represented a sport long superseded by foxhunting, is replaced in Francis Calcraft Turner's prints of *The Berkeley Hunt* (or *The Death*) by a more direct mode of expression that borders on stereotype (fig. 40). The same development toward a more linear, reductive style is evident in the contrast between Phillip Reinagle's richly detailed mezzotint *Fowling* of 1810 (fig. 41) and the charming straightforwardness of Dean Wolstenholme's 1820s–30s scene of badgering (fig. 42).

This shift toward simplicity nevertheless still allowed self-referential and even witty elements. Sawrey Gilpin was an artist steeped in the culture of sympathy for animals; his well-known painting illustrating an episode from Jonathan Swift's *Gulliver's Travels* features the human protagonist conversing with horses.[17] In his *Characters of Horses* series, Gilpin pictures the various types of horse as they exist under the dominance of men. Though the shaggy

Cart Horse tethered to a tree under a heavy yoke again derives from Dutch examples such as Paulus Potter, the comic model of Henry Bunbury is also detectable (fig. 43). *The Pad* (a horse for easy riding) (fig. 44), with its African servant indicating submissiveness, is reminiscent of the plate illustrating the outskirts of Wellbeck [*sic*] in the Duke of Newcastle's fundamental *Nouvelle methode* manual of equestrian prints. The contortions of *The Managed Horse* (fig. 45) recall the pictorial paradigm of Stubbs's print *Lord Pigot* (fig. 46). While Gilpin does not ignore the visual traditions of high art, he increasingly uses sporting prints themselves rather than other art forms as his chief point of reference.

This concern with finding a pictorial language appropriate to each type of horse (hunter, pad, racer, etc.) is also common to Géricault's lithographs. Géricault spent nearly two years, from 1820 through 1821, working in England, where he was influenced

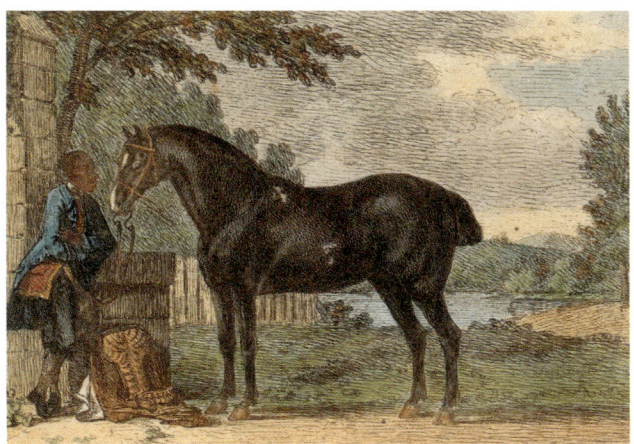

FIG. 44. Sawrey Gilpin, *The Pad,* 1793, cat. no. 42

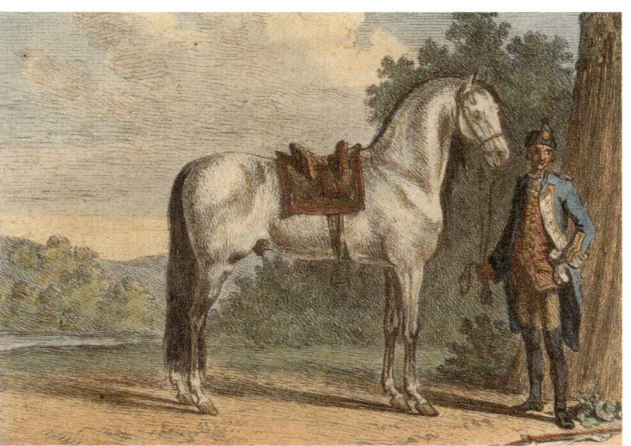

FIG. 45. Sawrey Gilpin, *The Managed Horse,* 1793, cat. no. 41

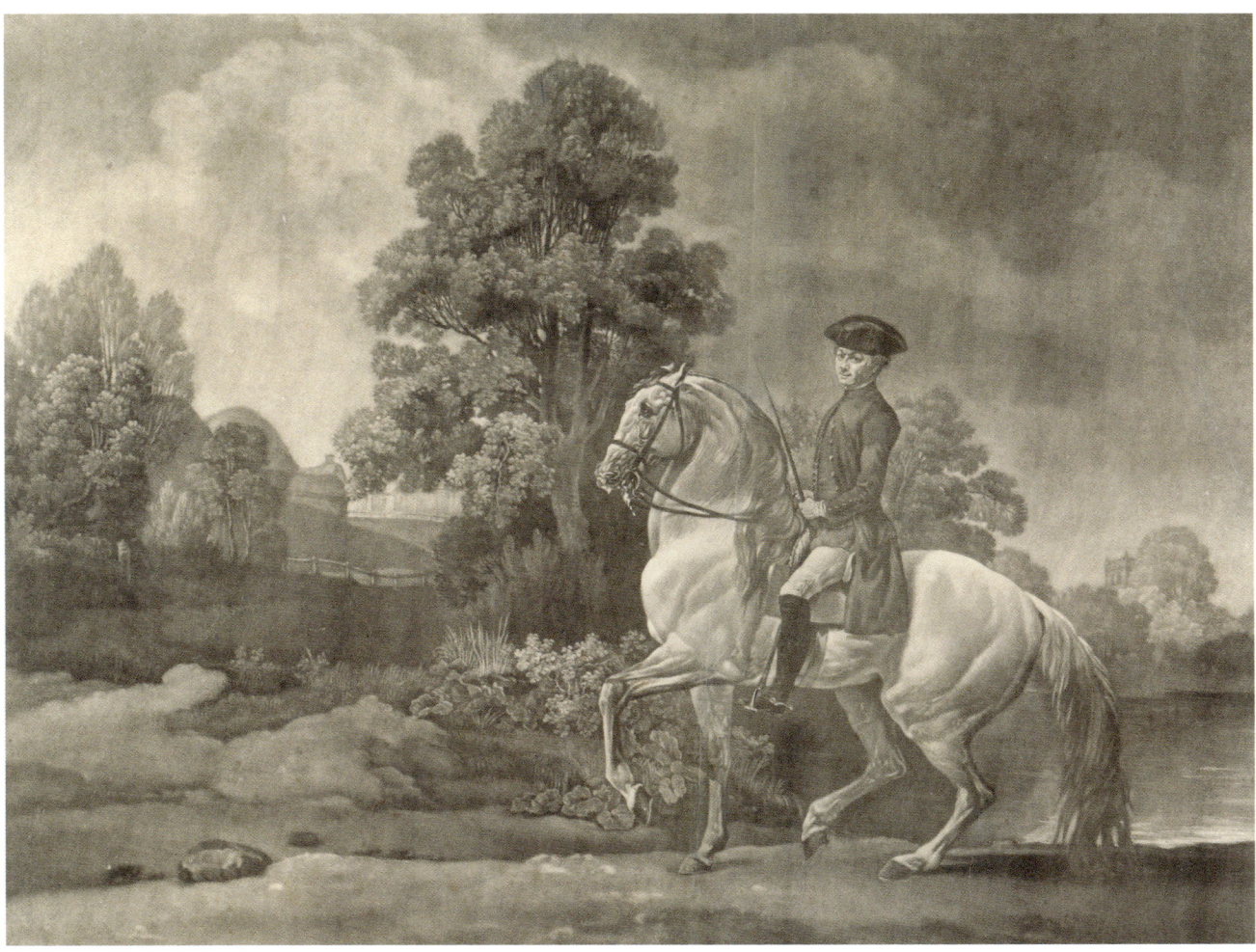

FIG. 46. George Stubbs, *The Right Honorable Lord Pigot Governor of Madras,* mezzotint, 1777. Virginia Museum of Fine Arts, Paul Mellon Collection, 85.1412

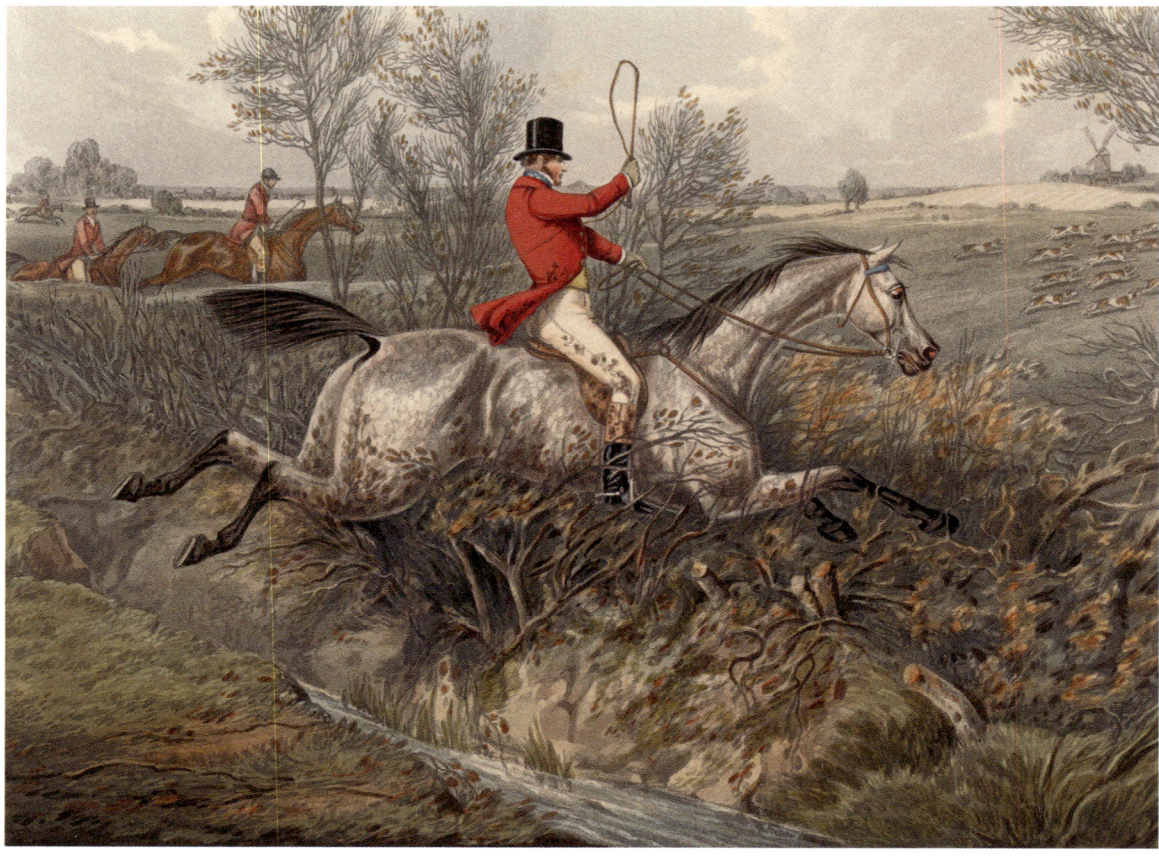

FIG. 47. Henry Thomas Alken, *Swishing a Rasper,* 1850, cat. no. 21

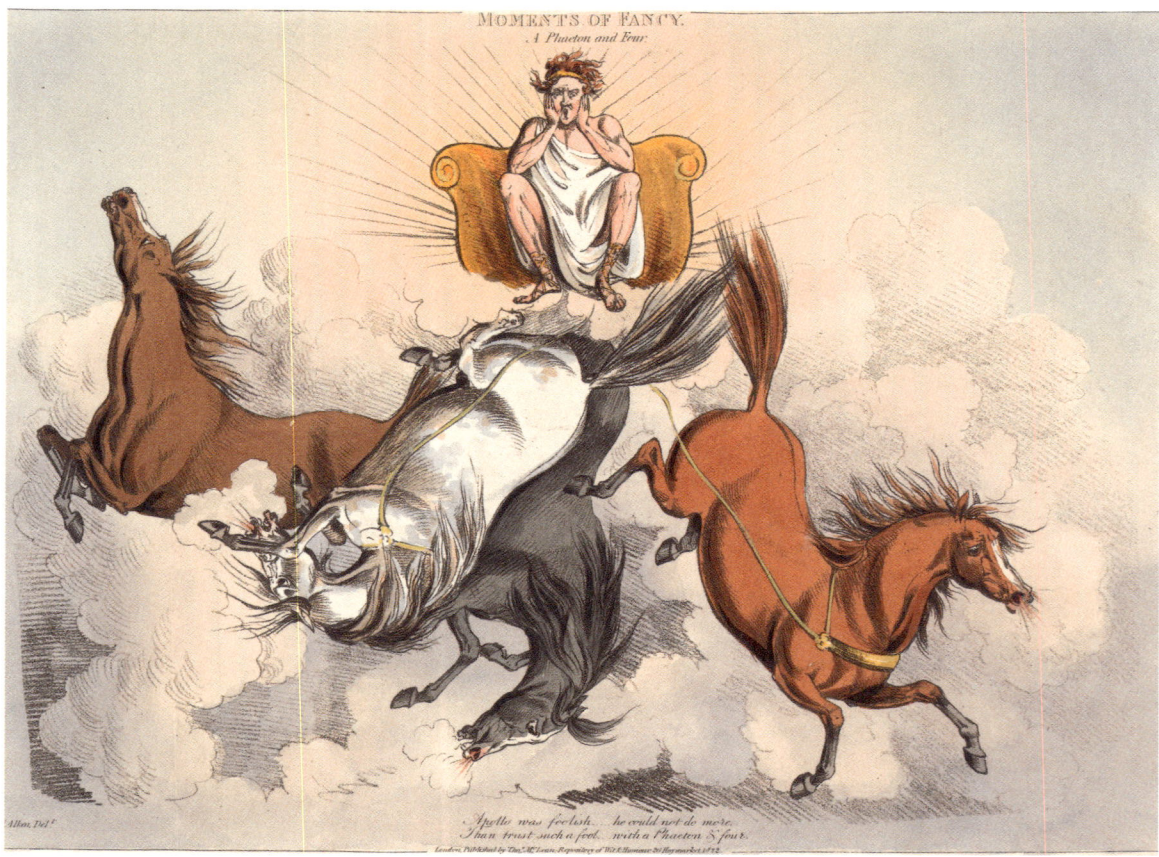

FIG. 48. Henry Thomas Alken, *A Phaeton and Four,* 1822, cat. no. 6

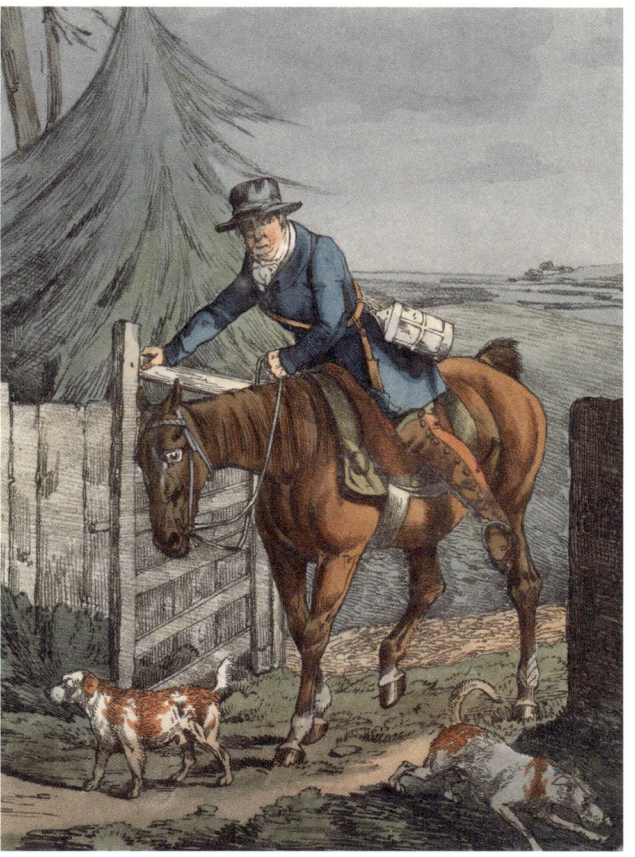

FIG. 49. Henry Thomas Alken, *Earth Stopper,* 1823, cat. no. 9

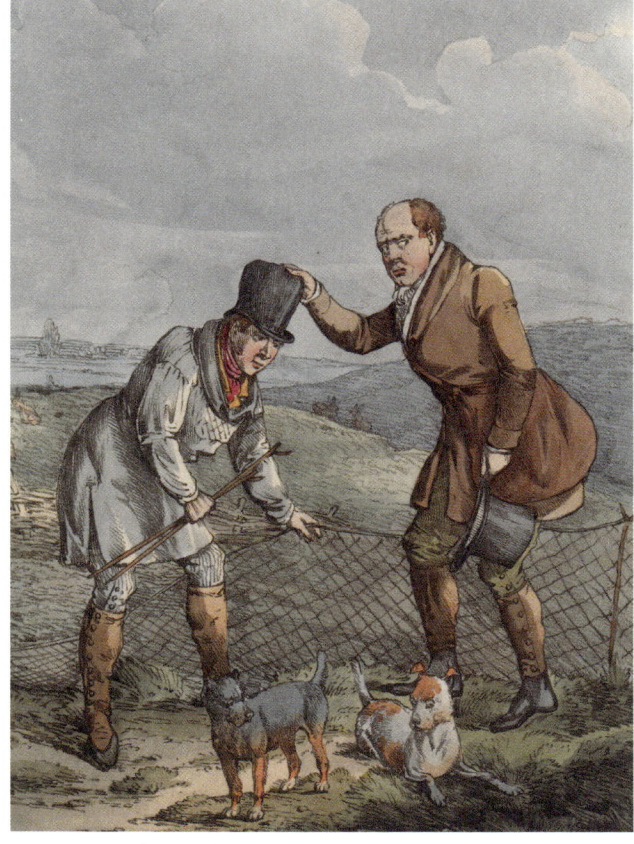

FIG. 50. Henry Thomas Alken, *Poachers,* 1823, cat. no. 10

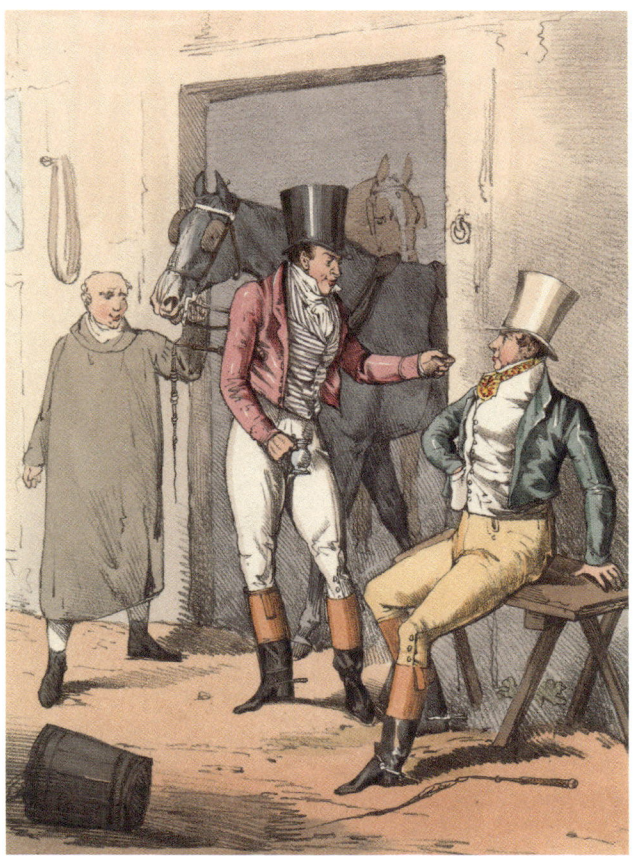

FIG. 51. Henry Thomas Alken, *Post Lads,* 1823, cat. no. 8

by the prolific Henry Alken and the British school generally.[18] Géricault's interest in Alken appears to indicate their common concern not only with sport but also with exploiting different pictorial styles. In addition to providing a complete chronicle of all sports pursued in Britain, Alken's oeuvre encompasses many modes — from the heroic *Swishing a Rasper* to the comic *A Phaeton and Four* (figs. 47 and 48), which anticipates French artist Honoré Daumier's mocking caricatures of the Roman gods. Alken also mastered the genre scene in his pictures of the everyday activities of non-aristocratic characters in sporting prints such as *Earth Stopper, Poachers,* and *Post Lads* (figs. 49, 50, and 51). With equal ability, he managed single-figure compositions such as *Right Sort* and *Wrong Sort* as well as large multi-figured scenes (figs. 52 and 53). The fleeting effects of weather — the great nemesis of the sportsman and coachman — becomes an important pictorial theme in the work of Alken and his contemporaries. Another

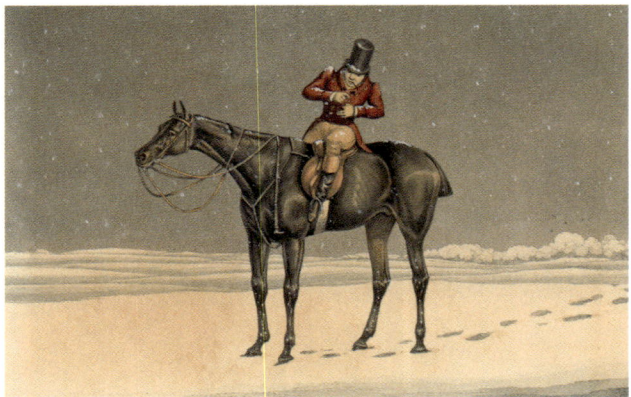

FIG. 52. Henry Thomas Alken, *One of the Right Sort,* ca. 1820, cat. no. 4

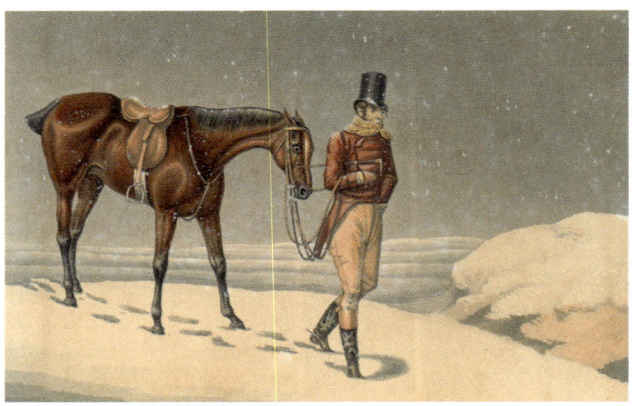

FIG. 53. Henry Thomas Alken, *One of the Wrong Sort,* ca. 1820, cat. no. 5

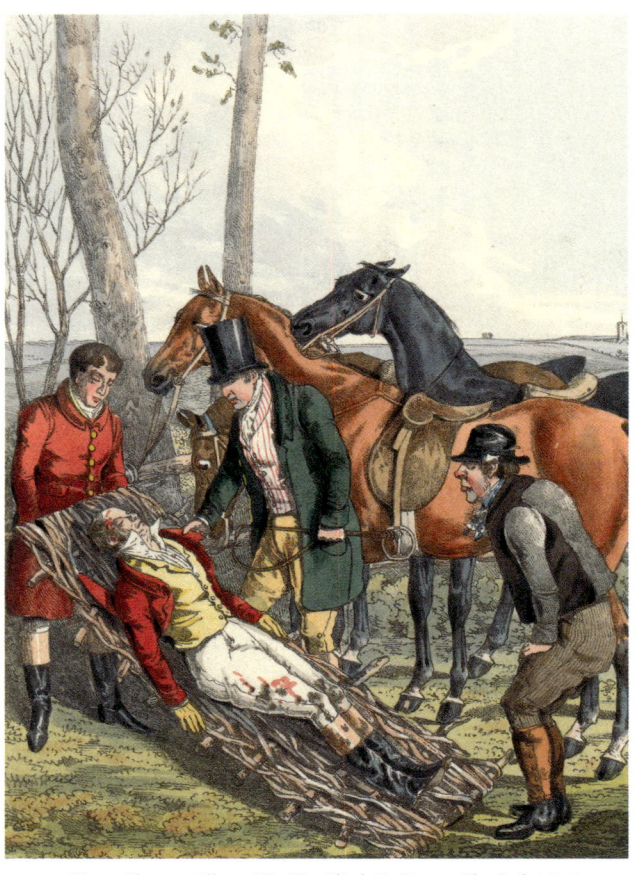

FIG. 54. Henry Thomas Alken, *I Do Not Think He Has an Idea Left,* 1826, cat. no. 12

pitfall of sport was speed, and Alken graphically illustrated its terrible consequences in prints such as those in *A Few Ideas* (fig. 54).

In the coaching prints of Alken, James Pollard, and Charles Cooper Henderson, the speed of the vehicle is implicitly tied to the theme of modernity, the Royal Mail coaches being a then-recent institution.[19] Though the popularity of the coaching print has been explained in terms of its timeliness, the entire genre of the sporting print is itself concerned with the subject: the times of the day, the endlessly repeatable moments of the race or the hunt, the seasons of the year, the life cycle of the horse. The coaching print takes as its theme the progression from the vehicle's novelty to its later obsolescence as the railway network spread across Britain. When new, the coach was celebrated for its fashionable smartness, but nostalgia for the short-lived great days of coaching is already evident in such prints as those in *Fores's Coaching Recollections* (fig. 55). In its purest expression, fear

of the future and of the downside of progress itself is evidenced in *A View in Regent's Park* (fig. 56).

While sporting prints have typically been considered to present a single style that remained unchanged, this account of the sophisticated visual vocabulary suggests instead that artists actually employed a complex and broad array of sources to arrive at distinctive modes of representation of sport and country life. This development has important implications for the understanding of not only sporting art but British visual culture as a whole.

While art history has sought to define strict boundaries between sporting and mainstream art, within the world of the British sporting print, that delineation was not always so clear. The many artists who created sporting prints both drew upon and influenced larger aesthetic currents. The genre functioned as a symbol of the pictorial commitment to representing modern life; hence, Degas's inclusion of Herring's *Steeple Chase Cracks* in his painting

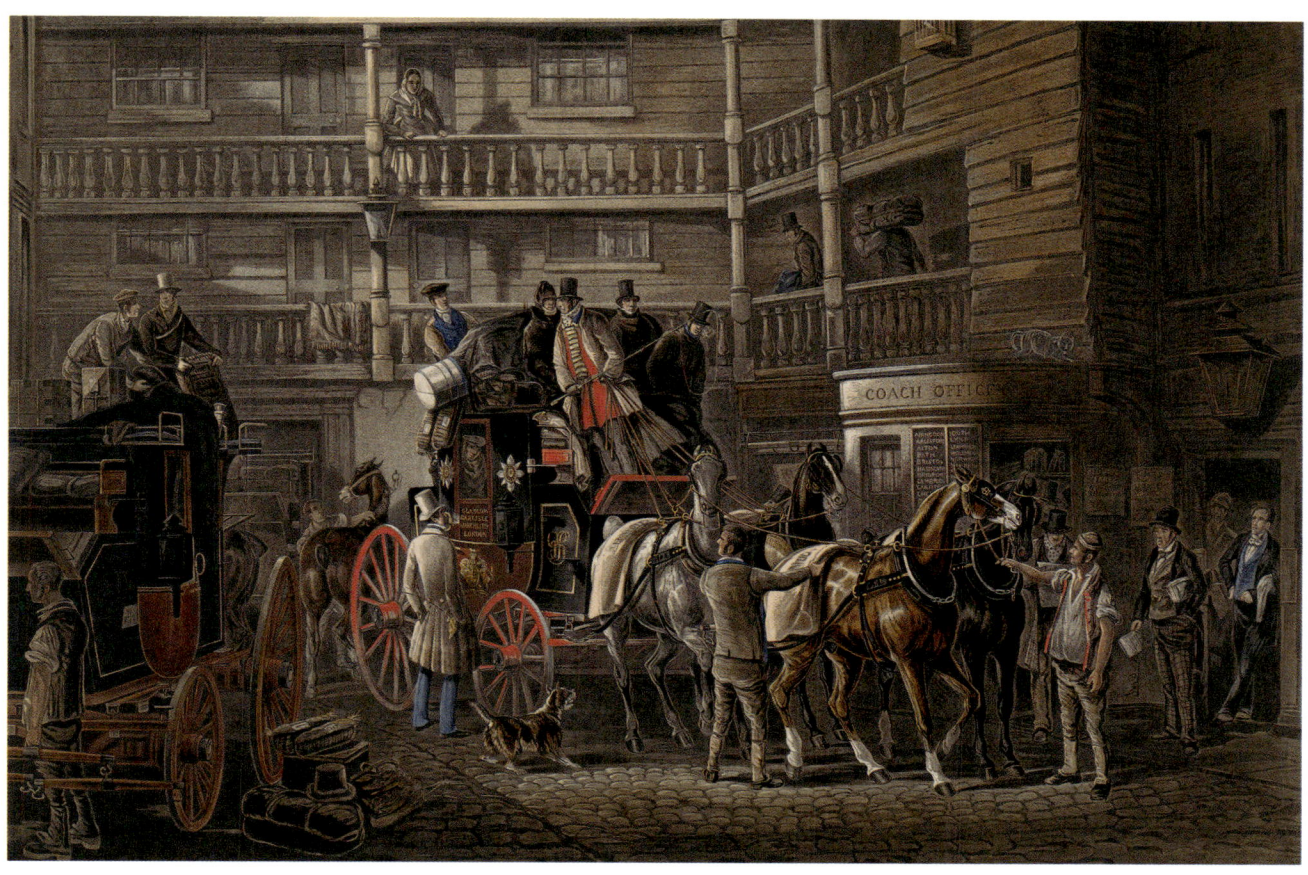

FIG. 55. Charles Cooper Henderson, *The Olden Time,* 1846, cat. no. 44

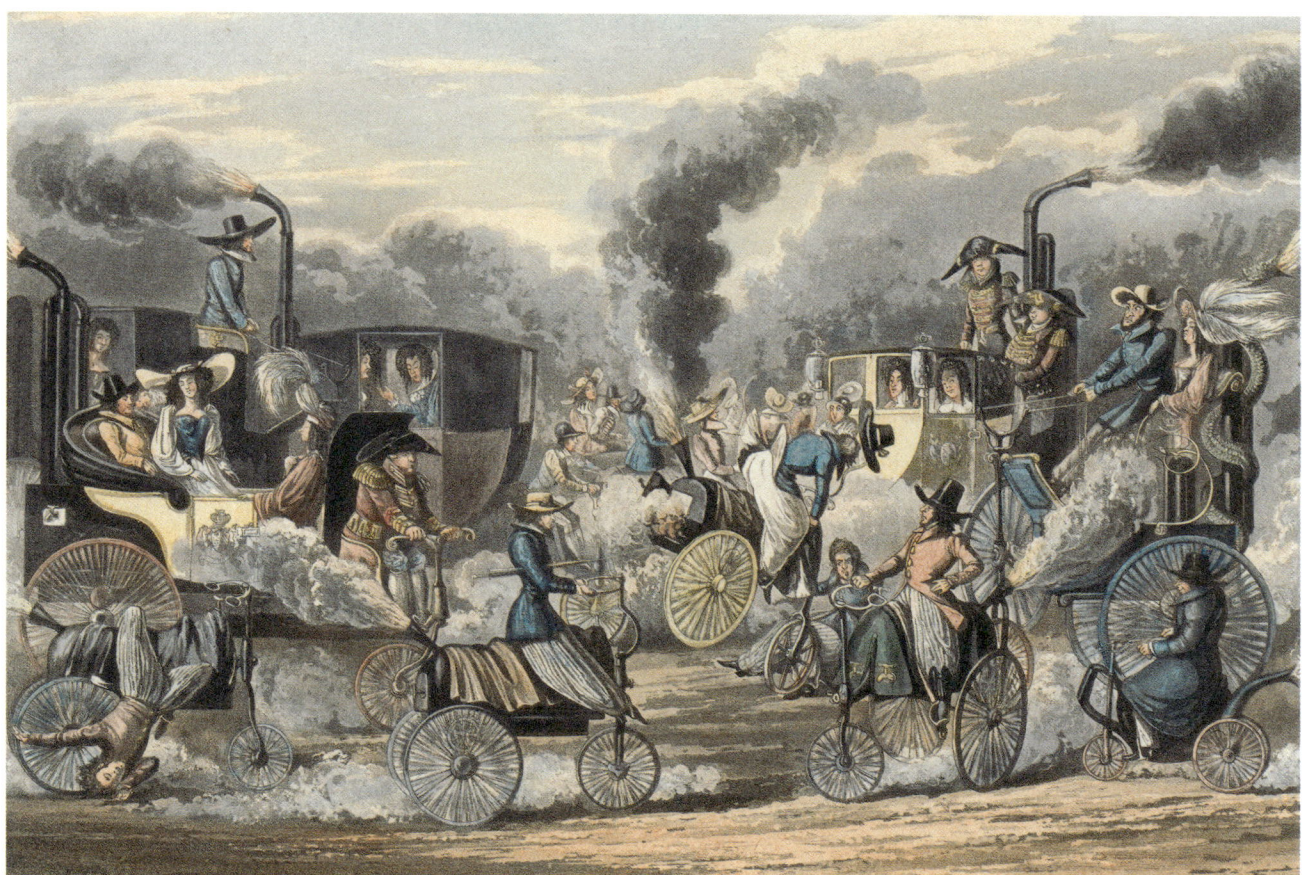

FIG. 56. Henry Thomas Alken, *A View in Regent's Park, 1831,* 1828, cat. no. 19

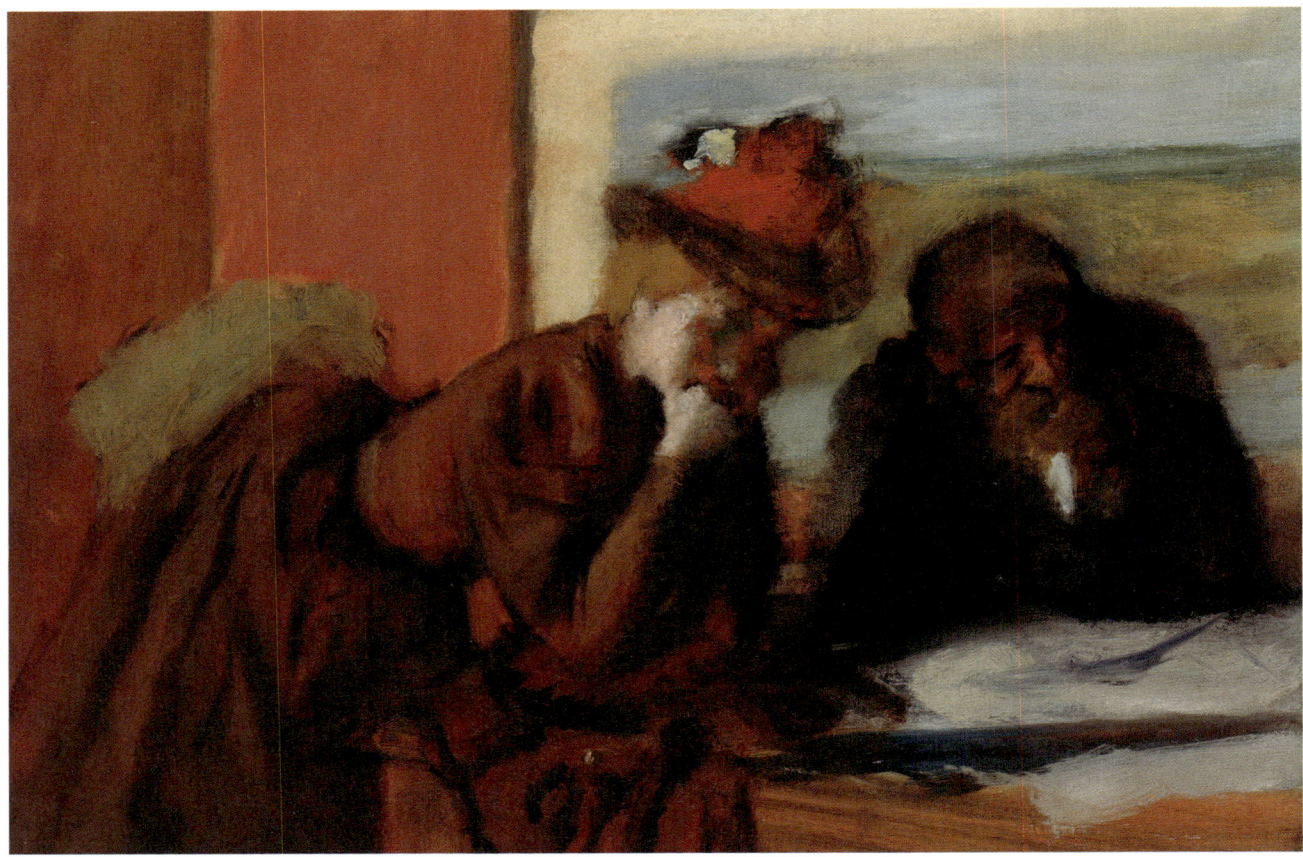

FIG. 57. Edgar Degas (French, 1834-1917), *The Conversation,* oil on canvas, 1885-95. Yale University Art Gallery, Collection of Mr. and Mrs. Paul Mellon, B.A. 1929, L.H.D.H. 1967, 1983.7.7

Sulking. As sporting printmakers shifted away from traditional models drawn from classical and Continental sources in depicting sport, their art became more sophisticated and had greater contemporary relevance. It was this very currency, not only as representations of modern life, but also as representations in a modern style, that brought the sporting print to the notice of nonsporting Continental artists who sought inspiration in the genre.

Though field sports continue today to be a popular pursuit both in Britain and America (despite new restrictions and regulations), the sporting print as a genre became exhausted within a short space of time, whether because artists and public turned to a new preoccupation with urban life and industrial change or maybe because the expressive possibilities of the genre had reached their limit around the middle of the nineteenth century.

This perception that over time sporting prints lost relevance as signifiers of contemporary life might best be confirmed by returning to Degas, and to Theodore Reff's insightful essay. As Reff also noticed in his groundbreaking study, Degas later reprised the composition of *Sulking* in a painting called *The Conversation* (late 1880s — early 1890s, fig. 57). There, the artist elided the specific reference to the sporting print by picturing it as a mere blur, perhaps therefore foreshadowing the future low esteem in which some audiences and historians would hold the genre. However, I would argue that Degas quite possibly omitted the Herring not only because his later art became more abstract and less reliant on precise pictorial points of reference,[25] but also because, for Degas, what was once seen as a paradigm of pictorial modernity had by his time become a symbol of tradition itself.

NOTES

1. Republished in Reff 1976, 116–19.

2. For the purposes of this essay, the artist is considered the person who was substantially responsible for the overall conception of the image and was therefore the person ultimately responsible for the style and visual language of the print. While this essay will draw upon a wide variety of art historical sources, the focus remains upon the development and significance of sporting prints as an independent genre.

3. Snelgrove 1981, Deuchar 1982, Deuchar 1988, and Donald 2007.

4. For Barlow the best account remains Deuchar 1988, 12–14. On Hollar see Pennington 1982, Godfrey 1994, and Podeschi 1981, 37–39.

5. The reference is to Henry Alken's series of the same name. The idea that the sports of Great Britain were their own subject was immensely fecund for later artists such as Alken, who in the early nineteenth century produced his own compendium of this subject. Alken 1825.

6. Kendall 1932–33, Meyer 1984.

7. Reproduced in Meyer 1984, 77–78.

8. For the earlier example from the British Museum see Meyer 1984, 78.

9. On Wootton's classicizing landscapes see Meyer 1984, 61–69. For Seymour's style see Deuchar 1988, 74–75.

10. Lennox-Boyd et al. 1989.

11. See Deuchar 1988 for a discussion of the specialized audience for whom sporting art was produced.

12. Warner and Blake 2004, 106.

13. See Barrell 1980, 25–33. For this painting and *Lord Torrington's Hunt Servants* see also Egerton 2007, 275–76. For the print see Lennox Boyd et al. 1989, 210.

14. Barrell 1980, 89–131.

15. Despite considerable differences between the two artists, there is a direct link between Morland and Rowlandson, documented by Rowlandson's aquatints after Morland — cf. Snelgrove 1981, 122.

16. For the moralistic condemnation of sportsmen, see Deuchar 1982, 93–105.

17. See Donald 2007, 203–4, for Gilpin and more generally pp. 199–232.

18. Lodge 1965, 616–27.

19. For coaching, see Bovill 1959, 127–69.

20. See Kendall 1966.

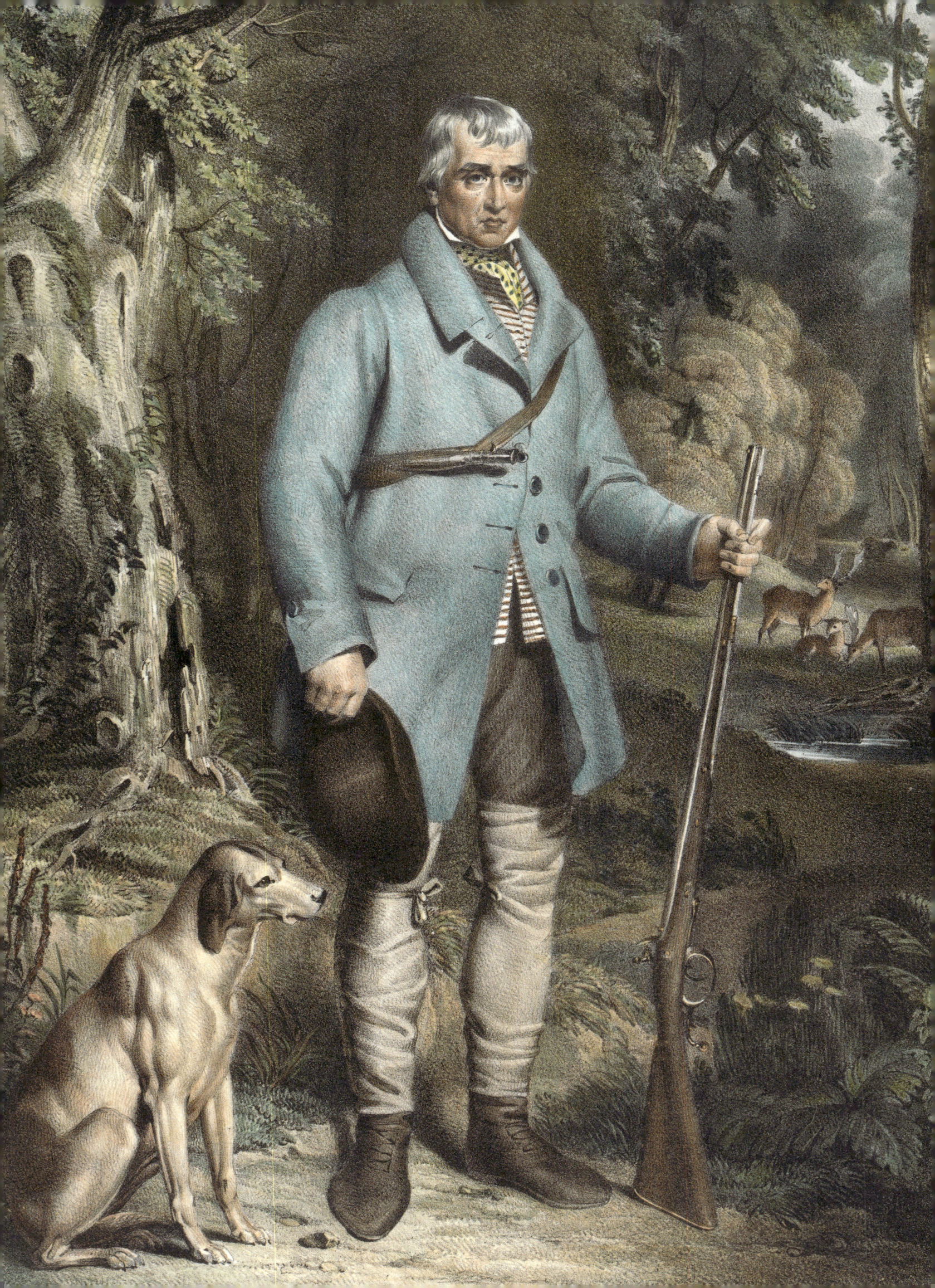

The Social World of the British Sporting Print

COREY PIPER

*Man is the same now that he was in the days
of Solomon; he must, and will be amused if
he can . . . rational amusements and innocent
recreations have ever been considered essential
to his very existence, and of these, the master
of fox-hounds or the owner of race-horses contributes his share, if not a good deal more.*[1]

NIMROD

On his many excursions into the field, sporting
correspondent Nimrod chronicled dozens of people
engaged in all the various professions and pursuits
associated with field sports and country life. Nimrod
was the pseudonym of Charles James Apperley, a
gentleman by birth, who was perhaps the most sought-
after sporting author of the early nineteenth century.
More inclined to the diversions of the field than the
commerce and activity of London, Apperley found
his calling writing detailed and grandiose accounts
of sporting happenings throughout Britain for the
newly minted *Sporting Magazine,* which paid him a
handsome retainer and furnished all of his stabling
and traveling expenses.[2] Nimrod's appeal derived
from his thorough insider knowledge — acquired as
both participant and observer — of the wide array of
people and customs associated with hunting, shooting, coaching, racing, and other field sports. While

Nimrod's perspective was that of the gentleman
sportsman — like the "master of fox-hounds or owner
of race-horses" — sporting periodicals enjoyed a much
broader readership, and in his anecdotal tours through
the countryside, he often saw fit to include the names
of those huntsmen, grooms, and servants who distinguished themselves in the performance of their duties.

The frequency and specificity with which Nimrod
refers to this broad cast of characters indicates their
importance to those from all levels who engaged in
country pursuits.[3] While the sporting press developed
rather late in the eighteenth century, many readers
were already familiar with the types and personalities
that appeared on the pages of sporting magazines
through the growing popularity of sporting art, and
in particular sporting prints. During the second half
of the century the market for sporting prints both in
London and all of England grew considerably, with
numerous sellers advertising a wide variety of subjects
throughout the country. In addition, the prints were
available at a range of prices, suggesting a strong interest from many levels of society. Indeed, contemporary
accounts show that prints decorated settings both public and private, from large estates to modest homes,
taverns, inns, and even stables.[4] At the same time, the
traditions of grand sporting art — such as aristocratic
and equine portraiture — became increasingly insular,

with paintings being removed from halls and public spaces of country homes and themes more focused on the exclusive concerns of the upper classes.[5]

Because of their broad appeal, sporting prints offer a distinctive insight into the nature of the sporting economy and society of the period. As sophisticated and significant works of art, sporting prints that depicted various characters engaged in field sports and country life were employed to negotiate the increasingly complex social relationships that developed around agrarian and sporting societies. Such images — far from benign reflections of a neutral sporting culture — often carried deep social and ideological implications ranging from the proper conduct of gentlemen and servants to the inalienability of rights bestowed upon property owners.

The height of the sporting print genre is generally considered to be from 1750 to 1850. During the same period Britain's countryside experienced great social, geographic, and economic change that has traditionally been termed the agricultural revolution.[6] Spurred by key advances in farming and legal developments in property ownership, a new system of enclosure put an end to the traditional practice of farming or grazing open fields communally. Instead, such land was fenced and entitled to one or more individual owners. In turn, larger and more productive farms were created, the number of once-prominent yeoman farmers and small landowners decreased, and wage employment rose.

The transformation of the countryside also had important implications for sport. For decades, overhunting of deer had decimated the population, leading hunting enthusiasts to pursue smaller game such as foxes and hares, which were previously considered only vermin. The Game Act of 1671 — one of many laws concerning the hunting of game enacted by Parliament over the course of several centuries — raised the value of property required for taking game from a mere 40 shillings to £100. While this act reduced the number of qualified persons allowed to shoot and take game, it also extended formerly royal rights to them, permitting hunting on any and all land unless specifically forbidden by a landowner.[7] Sanctioned to roam over many miles, lawful hunters actually expanded their range, venturing wherever the pursuit might lead. The progress of enclosure in the eighteenth century further improved

circumstances for foxhunting as access to larger tracts of land offered better chances for hounds to catch the scent, more space for pursuit, and fences and hedges for riders to jump — increasingly one of the principal attractions for participants. Indeed the commencement of the celebrated Grafton and Pytchley hunts around midcentury followed closely on the heels of enclosure.[8] Enclosure also changed the nature of coursing, a sport in which sight hounds chase a hare across an open field. Confining the landscape left few avenues for escape and the outcome of the contest much more certain. Eventually the focus of the sport turned toward gambling on matches that became staged affairs in which captive hares were released before large audiences. Concurrently, the development of gun technology changed the nature of shooting sports from simple rambles through the countryside in pursuit of game to major endeavors in which large parties followed beaters, taking scores, even hundreds, of birds in a single outing.[9]

The rise in popularity and transformation of sport also had important social implications for those who lived and worked in the countryside as well as for those who participated in the sport. A complex and highly organized sporting economy developed, requiring the employment of a range of people, from jockeys, grooms, huntsmen, loaders, and gamekeepers to service providers, namely innkeepers, farriers, and coachmen. At the same time that wage employment was becoming more prevalent in rural areas, the sporting economy provided an alternative to traditional agricultural labor.

For the small landowner or tenant farmer, field sports could cause tensions. Such residents were prohibited from killing foxes or hares (which were seen as a great nuisance), while larger landowning neighbors might be free to maintain covers, or safe havens for animals to live and reproduce, or even pursue game across tenants' fields. Not only were social relations affected, but interactions with the landscape itself changed as the rise of railroads in the early nineteenth century led many urban dwellers to travel to the countryside as a destination for leisure.

As works of art, sporting prints reveal a great deal of information about the complex layers of social exchange that developed around field sports in the eighteenth and nineteenth centuries. Artists employed different strategies in their portrayals of human sporting subjects in order to navigate the social world of the countryside for a broad public.[10] A close examination of several different figures featured in the sporting print — the gamekeeper and poacher, the sportsmen and servants engaged in the hunt, and the residents and workers of the countryside — demonstrates how these images go beyond simply illustrating rural types to convey broader ideologies about the rules of propriety operating within rural Britain's intricate social fabric.

The figure of the gamekeeper appears frequently in sporting prints, though the individual portrait of John Giffin by Henry Bone (fig. 58), presents a curious subject for a picture meant to have a broad appeal. Certainly those connected to Waltham Forest or to John Giffin would have admired this image, but Bone and Sir Thomas E. Tomlins, a steward of the forest courts (the body charged with enforcing laws of the forest) who commissioned the original painted portrait, must have foreseen a larger audience. While Bone may have intended to represent the gamekeeper as an archetype, of interest to all who valued the work of such men, for Tomlins the print served as a powerful symbol of legal and social control over the countryside. The gamekeeper was a contentious figure who often stood literally and figuratively at the intersection between property owners asserting their rights and the greater population striving for common access to land and resources.

In his portrait, John Giffin appears powerfully in command of his dominion, asserting the sole right of the landowner to take game within the forest. He is an imposing figure with gun in hand and a sure menace to would-be poachers, while remaining devoted and humble (with hat in hand), guarding the landowner's deer in the distance. Though the portrayal of Giffin is unequivocally positive, gamekeepers actually occupied an ambivalent position within the countryside. Often feared or even reviled by the lower classes (from whose ranks keepers themselves were drawn), keepers were given a great deal of trust and responsibility by landowners who sought to preserve the sanctity of their property. Such autonomy was not lightly extended, and the propriety of gamekeepers remained a great concern for some landowners who were weary of granting too much authority to servants. Therefore great attention was paid to the

selection of a gamekeeper. The popular periodical *Annals of Sporting* detailed the ideal qualities that should be considered:

> If he avoid too much tippling, and keep himself within reasonable bounds, he is rarely discharged; and as he is generally fond of his employment, we cannot imagine a more agreeable or happy life. . . . A game-keeper should have received a good, if not a classical education; should have some knowledge of natural history, and properly understand the breeding of dogs; and should at the same time, possess a superior address and be civil and obliging in his manners.[11]

Sobriety was a significant worry for employers of gamekeepers, who were largely left to their own devices throughout the day. Samuel Egbert Jones's *Gamekeepers Refreshing* print presents an ideal picture of temperance and good work habits (fig. 59). Although shown in the midst of "tippling," the two keepers are neatly dressed, and the game lying on the ground beside them indicates that they have earned their respite after a hard day's work.

Gamekeepers had a reputation for being rough characters, freely exhibiting the ruggedness and quick temper that were considered by some as important traits for their profession. However, these very behaviors could sometimes be viewed as indicators of a moral shortcoming. The *Annals of Sporting* warns readers against relying too heavily on those coarser attributes:

> When we consider that a desperate or incorrigible poacher is but too often raised from infamy to respectability, and placed in the responsible and important position of Game-Keeper, we shall not be surprised at the bad effects which have been produced by engaging men to fill this office, whose best recommendations have usually been those of cunning and culpable dexterity. The game-keeper is no sooner invested with the ensigns of authority than he fancies himself a privileged or superior being, and, with an air of self-importance, endeavours to impress the same notion on the rustics who regard him with jealousy.[12]

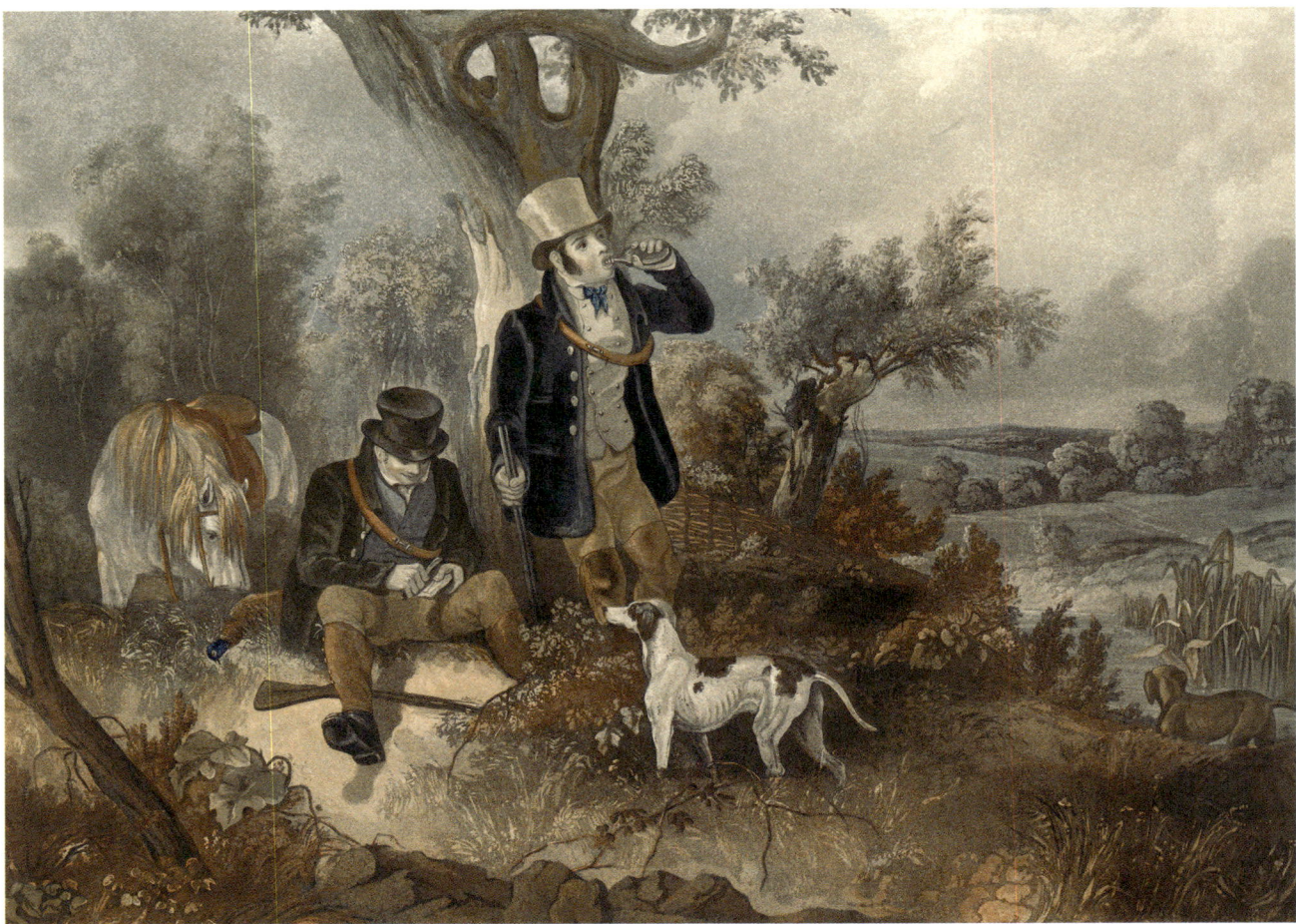

FIG. 59. Samuel John Egbert Jones, *And 'neath Some Aged Oak's Umbrageous Shade,* 1829, cat. no. 48

While in Bone's portrait Giffin appears very much the upstanding figure that the steward of the forest courts thought him to be, he nevertheless became embroiled in a long-running conflict over the rights and responsibilities of landowners. During the 1820s a contentious debate broke out over whether to enclose Waltham Forest, where Giffin served as keeper. In a pamphlet arguing in favor of the enclosure (thereby limiting the authority of the keeper to roam throughout the common land), John Elsee, a landowner whose holdings abutted the forest, recounted a litany of incidents in which he claimed Giffin had abused his power on behalf of the Crown and the steward.[13] One incident involved two servants whom Elsee had dispatched to retrieve a gun, which required them to pass through Waltham Forest. Giffin and his assistant fired at the servants, taking them to be poachers. Despite Elsee's efforts to have Giffin arrested, he was quickly freed by the magistrate, who argued that it could not be proven that the servants

were not in fact poachers. A second incident occurred five years later when Elsee observed Giffin firing his gun and then fleeing into the forest. He later found that Giffin had shot and killed his greyhound. The final charge Elsee leveled against Giffin was that he falsely accused a man in Elsee's employ of taking a fallow deer and, with a gang of fellow keepers, abducting the man without warrant or charge and confining him for a night. During the illegal arrest, Giffin was reported to have declared, "We are superior to constables, we are King's men," a claim that surely suggested a vastly inflated sense of authority.[14]

Elsee's pamphlet was not simply an indictment of a particular gamekeeper, but rather an argument for the system of enclosure, which he saw as a more rational way to regulate land than assigning authority over vast common areas to a few designated individuals deemed unworthy of such distinction. However, for many other landowners, the gamekeeper represented the front line of defense against the serious threat of poaching and other affronts to the game laws. The severity of the game laws did diminish during the era with the reduction of property qualifications in 1831. However, changes did not come about easily and at times resulted in great social conflict and even violence, as well as a corresponding vehemence in the press and Parliament in defense of the established order.[15] In the midst of such conflict, the gamekeeper served as an instrument in maintaining physical control over the land on behalf of the landowner or the Crown. For landowners who subscribed to such a view, the positive and steadfast depiction of a particular gamekeeper like John Giffin would certainly serve both to assert and validate their claims for authority over the land.

While Elsee focused his ire on the role of the gamekeeper, many landowners saw poachers as a much more serious and readily identifiable threat. Sporting magazines were filled with accounts of the nefarious deeds of unqualified persons who were caught taking game. Henry Alken's depiction of two poachers stealing into a rabbit warren, for example, neatly matches an account in the *Sporting Magazine:* "W. Peverett has been committed to Bury Gaol, charged with having, on Sunday night, the 16th ult. Entered into an inclosed warren used for the breeding and keeping of rabbits in Santan Downham and having then and there killed and taken there from two rabbits"[16] (fig. 60). Poaching carried serious consequences, from fines and imprisonment with hard labor to public whippings and deportation. Alken's poachers, shown raiding the warren in the darkness, would have been the most serious type of offenders, as night poaching carried additional penalties. Despite the almost universal opposition among landowners to poaching and systematic attempts to legislate against it, the activity remained a regular, if not common, occurrence throughout the eighteenth and nineteenth centuries. In addition to taking game for their own consumption and to control pests, unqualified persons (those owning property worth less than £100) were also motivated by the increasingly lucrative black market for game, fueled by demand among well-to-do urban dwellers for whom it was a much-loved part of their diet.

The game laws ostensibly existed to control the animal population, but they also asserted a certain type of social control over the human inhabitants of

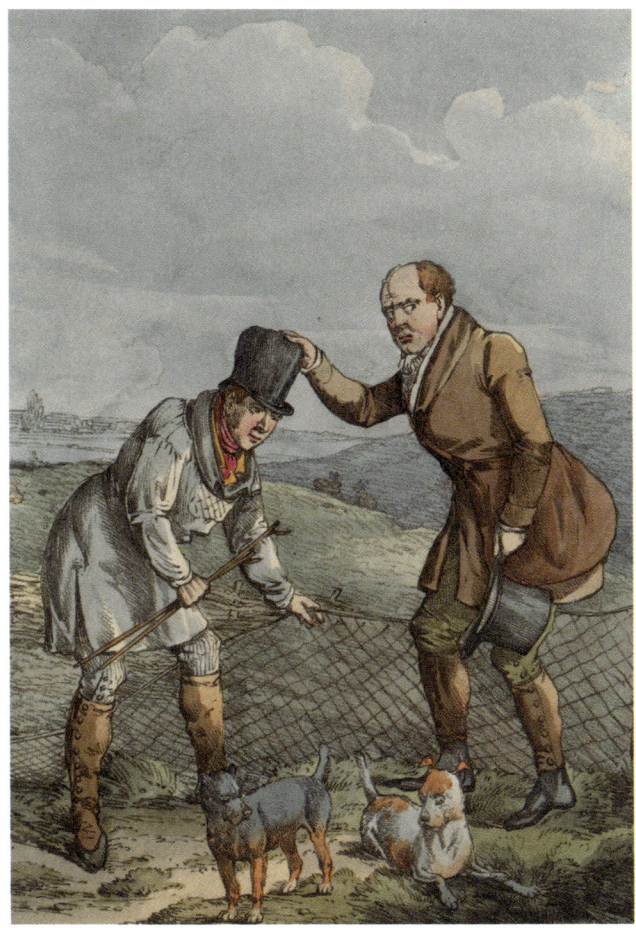

FIG. 60. Henry Thomas Alken, *Poachers,* 1823, cat. no. 10

the countryside. Many ardent defenders of these laws held them up as a guard against vices to which they believed the lower classes would inevitably succumb. The reasoning of Henry Zouch, a justice of the peace who ruled in many cases involving the game laws, epitomized such a view:

> It is not for the preservation of the Game alone (tho' this with the qualified sportsmen of England is held to be a matter of general and national concern) that we ought to be so much solicitous; it is not to secure the right of this Game to those whom the law hath given it, which we ought to principally regard, but it is to keep those of our fellow subjects within the bounds of their duty, who are now become a burthen or even a terror to the places where they live.[17]

According to Zouch, poaching represented just one aspect of the lawlessness that would arise if the

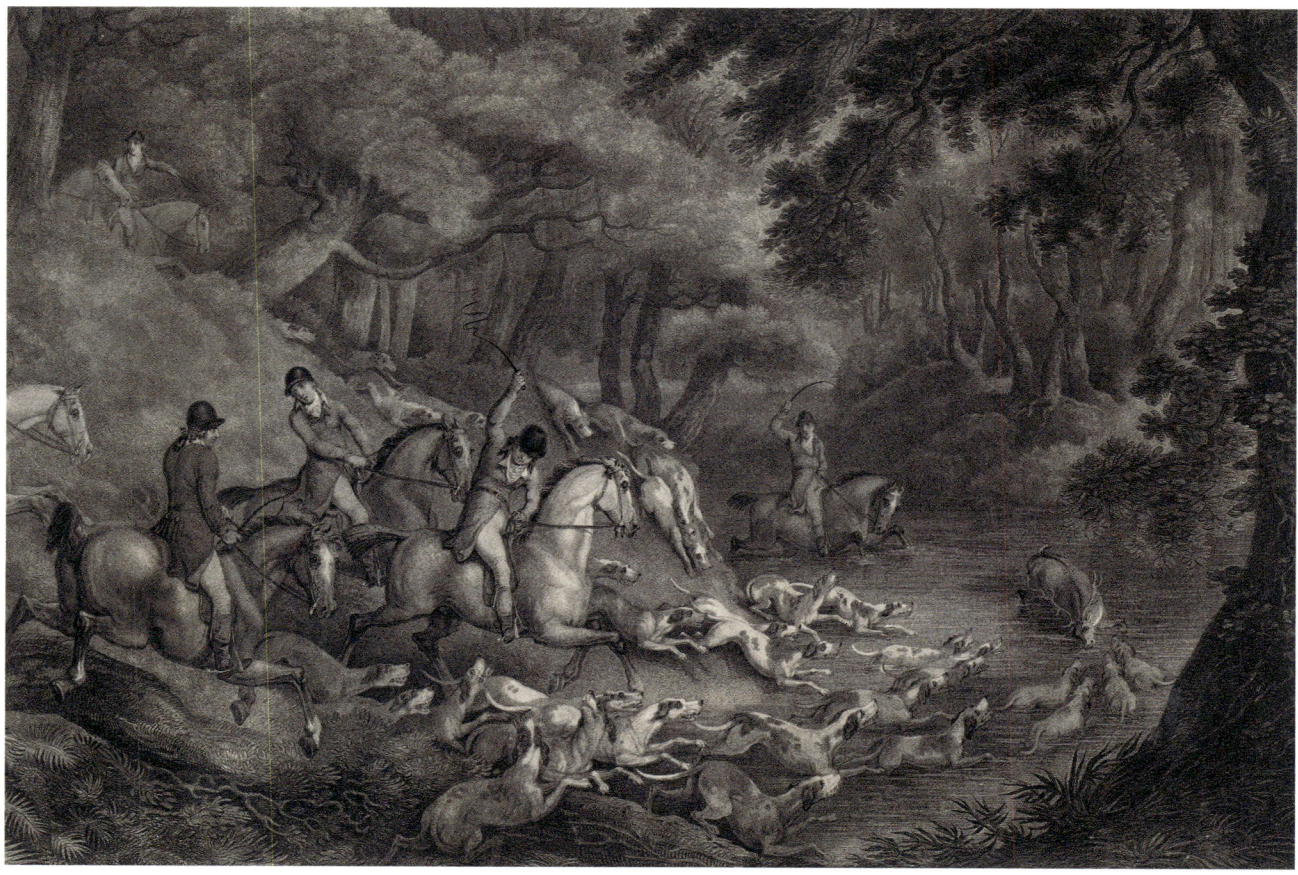

FIG. 61. Samuel Howitt, *The Stag at Bay and Whipping of the Hounds,* 1802, cat. no. 47

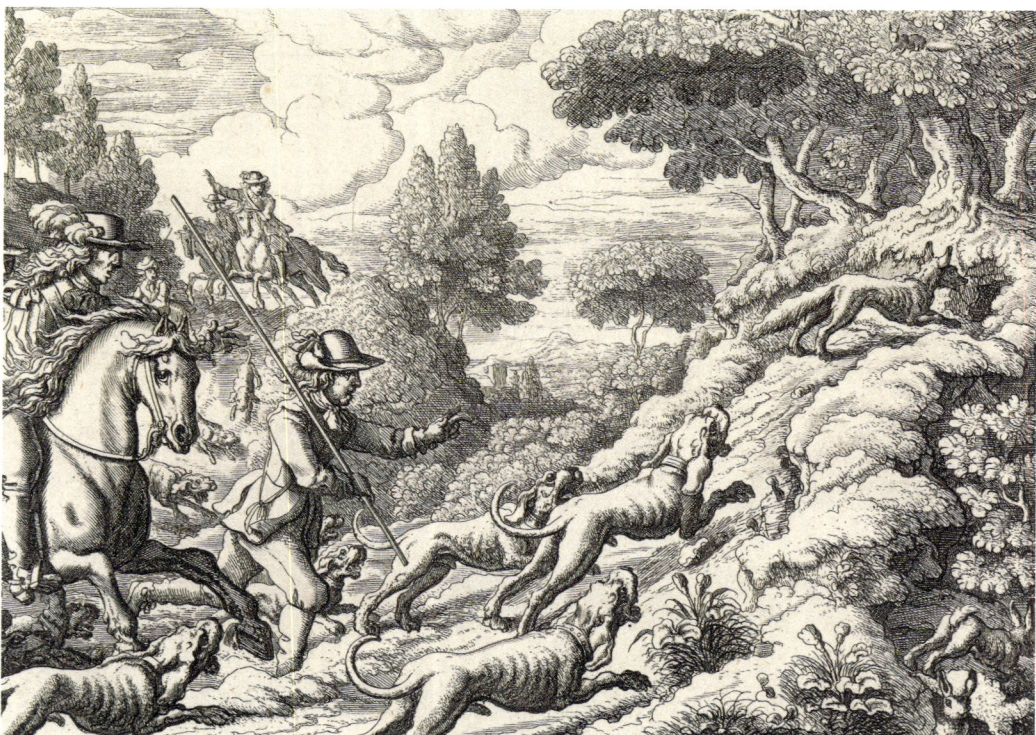

FIG. 62. Francis Barlow, *Fox Hunting,* ca. 1671, cat. no. 27

lands were not well regulated and the rural lower classes were given over to idleness. In his pamphlet decrying the practice of night poaching, he goes on to describe how alehouses served as breeding grounds for criminality, of which poaching was only one example. Writing fifty years later in a pamphlet arguing in support of the game laws, Grantley Berkeley, a member of Parliament and an avid sportsman, claimed, "In almost all cases of poaching by night, the inclination to murder arises from that curse upon the morals of the lower orders, *the beer shop*."[18] For these authors the game laws exerted a moral order upon the countryside for the benefit of all its inhabitants; enforcing property rights and the rights to take game served as a check against the tendency of the lower classes toward idleness and vice.

The prints by Jones, Bone, and Alken depicting honorable gamekeepers and the sinister deeds of poachers illustrated the kind of social and moral order espoused by the authors above. While debates over the justness of the game laws broiled for decades, often spilling over into physical conflict between poachers, keepers, and landowners, these sporting prints offered a simple visual argument for the establishment and enforcement of the game laws — both for those who were qualified (through property ownership) to profit from them and those who were not.

While the game laws restricted certain sports like shooting and coursing to a select minority, foxhunting presented fewer barriers to inclusion and an arguably more egalitarian nature. Participation in most hunts required only an annual subscription, and there was no legal requirement of property ownership to join in the pursuit. Foxhunting rose from humble beginnings as a lowly regarded alternative to stag hunting (fig. 61). Traditionally, deer were considered noble prey and the fox a mere vermin. However, by the sixteenth century, deer populations had diminished considerably, prompting many to turn to foxhunting as an alternative. Selective breeding of hounds in the eighteenth century also led to faster packs, giving rise to the modern form of the sport in which riders follow the hounds at great speed over considerable distances. While such changes led to a great surge in popularity for the sport, hunts were transformed during the second half of

the eighteenth century and the early nineteenth into highly organized, elaborate, and increasingly socially stratified affairs. Early foxhunts might have consisted of a handful of riders (fig. 62), but by the nineteenth century they could number in the hundreds.[19] These large-scale events relied on a corps of servants and other workers who were engaged in a variety of related activities.

Grand painted portraits of hunts such as Francis Grant's *The Melton Hunt Going to Draw the Ram's Head Cover* (fig. 63) were largely concerned with the depiction of the fashionable members (the whipper-ins, or whips, who were assistants to the huntsmen, are shown with their backs to the viewer). Sporting prints, however, often featured a wider range of participants from varying ranks. Prints were affordable and thus available to many classes, and they were frequently displayed in public places throughout the countryside where classes intermingled, such as taverns, inns, and stables. All involved — from sportsmen to spectators to employees — could see something of themselves in these scenes. Depictions of the hunt itself and the world surrounding it served to reinforce ideologies of proper conduct and sportsmanship. As such they functioned as valuable tools in negotiating the complex relationships among sportsmen, servants, and rural dwellers that grew out of the sporting economy.

As hunts grew in size, the role of the staff became highly important and increasingly specialized. The earth stopper's responsibility was to traverse the field the night before a hunt, filling up holes while the fox was out chasing its own prey and thus foiling its easy escape underground next day. The job was a solitary one, often essential to the event's success, but it cast doubts on the "sporting" nature of the contest. Alken's depiction of an earth stopper presents a commanding but somewhat shadowy figure, carrying out his duty in the dark of night (fig. 64). An earth stopper's pay typically depended on the effectiveness of his efforts; he might lose a whole night's wages if the fox proved able to escape underground.[20] Charles Loraine Smith's *A Leicestershire Burst* acknowledges the earth stopper's important contribution, placing him at the forefront of the composition proudly gesturing toward the action unfolding in the field beyond.

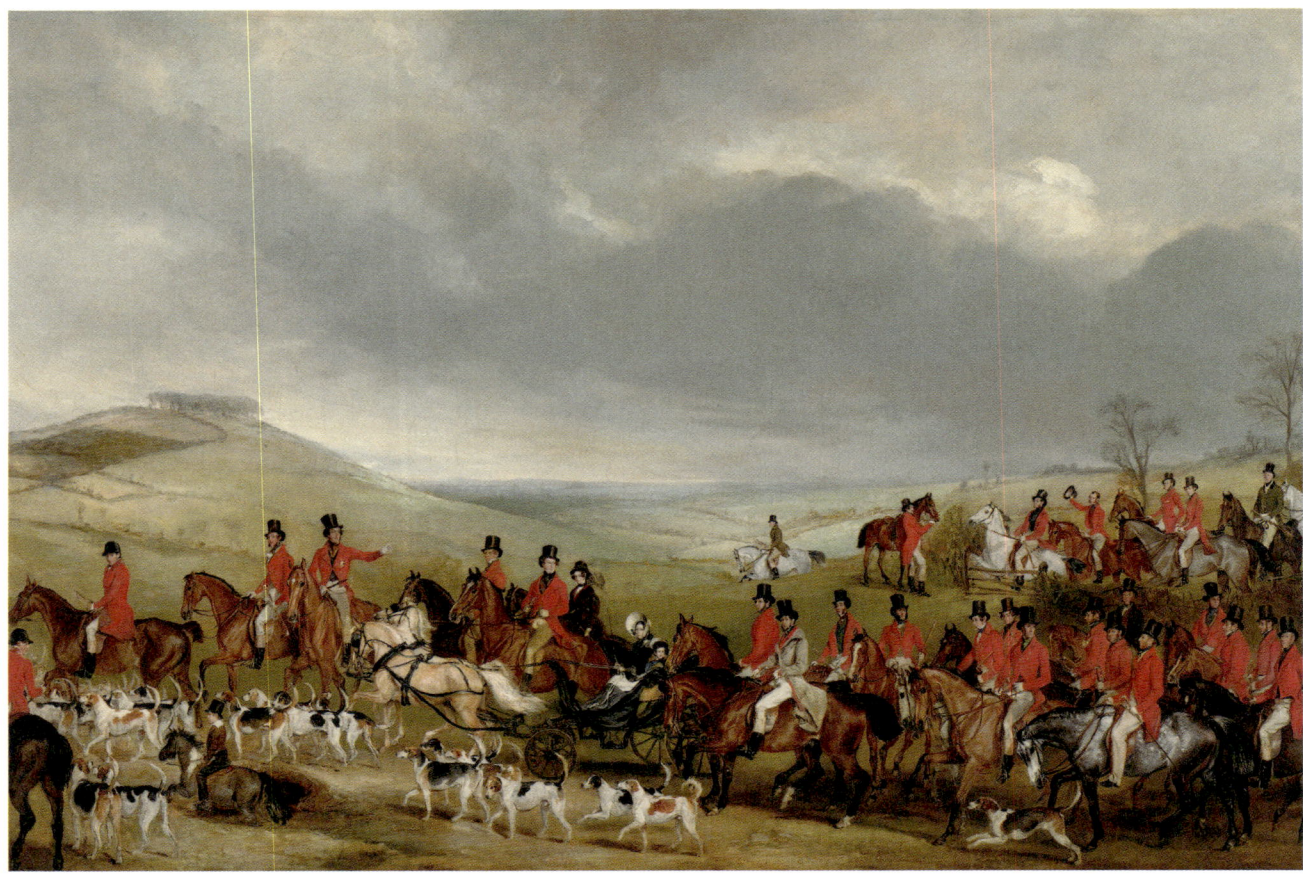

FIG. 63. Sir Francis Grant (Scottish, 1803-1878), *The Melton Hunt Going to Draw the Ram's Head Cover,* oil on canvas, 19th century, Virginia Museum of Fine Arts, Paul Mellon Collection, 85.494.1

Among those engaged in the hunt, the huntsman had the most profound influence on the progress of the chase. As the leader of the pursuit, he was responsible for directing the hounds, alerting the field when the pack had taken up the fox's scent, and generally maintaining order over the proceedings. Befitting such a central figure, the huntsman had to live up to high expectations, in terms of his performance as well as character. In 1781 Peter Beckford, renowned sportsman and employer of such servants, described a model huntsman:

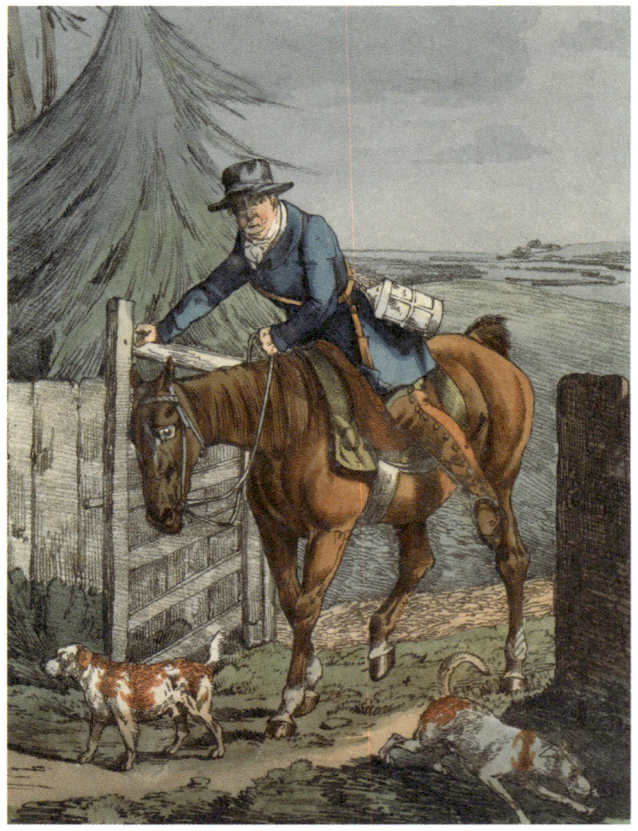

> He should be young, strong, and active, bold and enterprising; fond of the diversion, and indefatigable in the pursuit of it; he should be sensible and good tempered; he ought also to be sober; he should be exact, civil and cleanly; he should be a good horseman, and a good groom; his voice should be strong and clear, and he should have an eye so quick as to perceive which of his hounds carries the scent, when all are running; and should have so excellent an ear, as always to

FIG. 64. Henry Thomas Alken, *Earth Stopper,* 1823, cat. no. 9

distinguish the foremost hounds, when he does not see them.[21]

These lofty qualifications were not often spelled out so plainly. In sporting prints, however, these ideals were frequently expressed in the depiction of hunt servants.

The huntsman (as well as his whipper-in) appears prominently in a number of sporting prints, embodying many of the qualities that Beckford describes. In James Seymour's *Making a Cast at a Fault,* the prowess of the huntsman in managing the hounds is the central theme. He is shown communicating with the pack as they search for the fox's scent, which has been lost in the thick underbrush. In contrast to the huntsman, the followers of the hunt mill about idly all the while. In Francis Calcraft Turner's print showing the death of the fox, the huntsman assumes a commanding position, central to the climactic action of the day's events. He maintains control over not only the hounds but also his assistants and the entire field, who stand back as he sees to the death of the fox. While the character of the huntsman is perhaps the most difficult to capture in a print, Dean Wolstenholme succeeds notably in *Returning.* By moonlight, after what was surely an exhausting day of sport, the huntsman ably leads the pack (with several of the hounds looking up to him for instruction) and participants safely back home. Wolstenholme's huntsman is not only a reliable worker but also a capable leader.

Besides servants, sportsmen, naturally, figured prominently in the iconography of the sporting print genre.[22] Images of the sportsman engaged in the chase or at leisure before or after the hunt also prescribed proper forms of behavior, in many cases even more forthrightly than corresponding depictions of servants. In Henry Alken's pair of prints *One of the Right Sort, Who Hunts Because He Likes It* and *One of the Wrong Sort, Who Goes Out with the Hunters Because It Is the Fashion* (figs. 65 and 66), the artist has plainly juxtaposed the figure of the ideal sportsman and his counterpart, who has no real interest in sport other than to maintain the appearance of a gentleman. The former is a stalwart type, seemingly undeterred by the harsh conditions. Indeed his only complaint, as indicated by the inscription, is that the

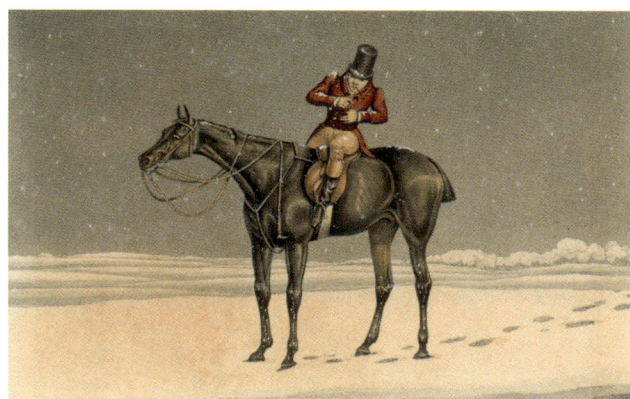

FIG. 65. Henry Thomas Alken, *One of the Right Sort,* ca. 1820, cat. no. 4

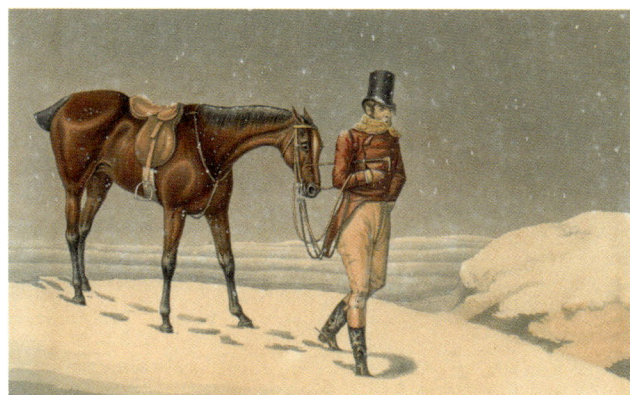

FIG. 66. Henry Thomas Alken, *One of the Wrong Sort,* ca. 1820, cat. no. 5

snow will postpone the next day's hunt. The "Wrong Sort" by contrast is dismounted, unable to endure the weather or rigor of the chase, and is concerned only with his own comfort. Those sportsmen who conducted themselves admirably in the field while also embodying the proper expectations of sportsmanship could be described colloquially as "doing the thing well," while those who fell short of the sporting ideal were merely "doing the thing."

Prints portraying both types of sportsmen served a valuable purpose in enforcing proper conduct in the field. Robert Frankland-Russell's *Taking a Lead* pokes fun at a common sporting mishap but also issues a serious warning to the overeager sportsman who rides too far ahead of the group, putting the chase off course. The consequences of unruly behavior could be much more dire; Alken's *I Do Not Think He Has an Idea Left* depicts a sportsman who has died of injuries sustained during the hunt. Conversely, the rider in Alken's *Swishing a Rasper* expertly navigates the jump, endangering neither himself nor the outcome of the chase. Foxhunting was governed by a complex set of principles, rituals, and procedures, and while the sporting press and instructional manuals outlined proper etiquette, no universal code of conduct existed. In the absence of codified rules or procedures, such images helped by demonstrating the essentials of a successful hunt and the consequences (often humorous) of improper behavior and incompetence.

Images of sportsmen also upheld the benefits of sport for its proponents and society at large.[23] While the merits of hunting were frequently contested in the public sphere, among sporting enthusiasts there was an almost universal belief in the righteousness of country pursuits and their positive contributions for humankind. Typical of this certitude is Delabere Blaine's claim in *An Encyclopaedia of Rural Sports*: "As the pursuit of animals is a divine command and the love of the chase is instinctively implanted in our breast, we cannot be injuriously or unworthily employed when we cherish the one and engage in the other."[24] The author goes on to chronicle the positive influence of sport on health, long life, social character, and even preparation for war.

The Old Free Method of Rouzing a Brother Sportsman (by an unknown artist) presents a striking contrast to the ideal of the virtuous sportsman. A nearly contemporary account in the *Sporting Magazine* of an actual event involving an amorous encounter could easily have been describing the outcome of the scene in this print: "A singular trial occurred at Bradford General Quarter Sessions last week. James Mackmanus was indicted for entering a house at midnight with intent to seduce the wife of the owner. The case was made out to the satisfaction of the Court, and the gallant was sentenced to be confined for the term of one year in York Gaol."[25] Images like this one and Francis Wheatley's *The Amorous Sportsman* no doubt compared unfavorably to portrayals of more upstanding pursuits, such as George Morland's *Morning, or the Benevolent Sportsman* and John Raphael Smith's *Sportsman's Repast* (fig. 67).[26] In Wheatley's image, a sportsman returning from a day's shooting comes across a peasant family in the road and proceeds to make unwanted advances toward the young woman. Her humiliated children turn away from the impropriety. The dead rabbit on the ground seems to suggest that the hunter's quest for game has

transformed into lust, the unwitting woman his latest prey. While the moral implication is unambiguous, Wheatley's critique becomes even more pointed when contrasted with Morland's print, in which a sportsman encountering a similar peasant family offers only charity. Moreover, the sportsman pictured drinking at a tavern in Smith's scene stands as a model for the respectable interaction between men and women of differing classes.

Overindulgence was another shortcoming represented in the sporting print in opposition to the ideal conduct of sportsmen. Thomas Rowlandson's *The Breakfast* shows a slovenly hunt party readying themselves for the day's action. While some of the group are still dressing, others have already begun imbibing heavily and gorging themselves on the meal. The satirical depiction of gluttony in William Hogarth's *The Rake's Progress* has here been transported from the late night to early morning. The respectable sportsman's morally superior habit of early rising is particularly mocked in this discordant image.[27] Overindulgence was typically considered a symptom of urban vice. An article in the *Sporting Magazine* describing an anonymous "Bon Vivant" chronicled the enormous amount of alcohol he consumed as well as his idleness and general lack of vigor. The author concluded by asking, "Of how many in the metropolis is this Journal the epitome? Oh that men, possessing the attributes of reason and intellect should clothe themselves in the sensual habits of brutes."[28] To likeminded inhabitants, such plagues of urban living stood in stark contrast to the ideals of sport and country life.

The increased involvement of urban dwellers in rural sports was of great concern to those who guarded traditional sporting values from perceived urban vices such as licentiousness and overindulgence. Apprehension over the intrusion found visual expression in prints depicting the foibles of the Cockney sportsman — a neophyte transplanted from the city with absolutely no skill at sport or spirit for outdoor pursuits. In a print attributed to Charles Ansell, three Cockney sportsmen bring menace to the countryside, shooting wildly at anything that moves — in this case an owl and bat setting out at dusk. In their ineptitude, however, they have managed to hit only the poor laborer fixing a roof, their own hound, and one of

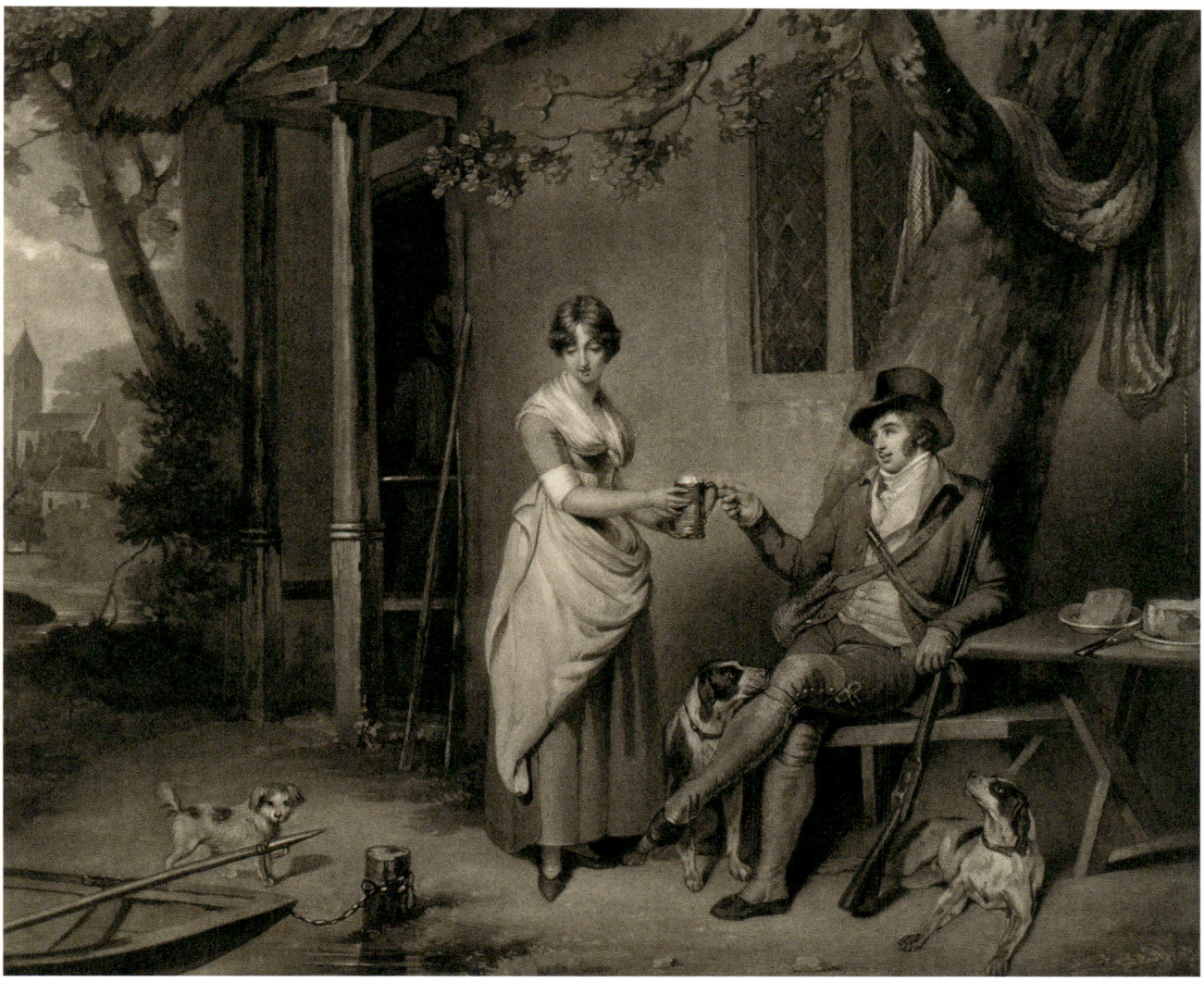

FIG. 67. John Raphael Smith, *Sportsman's Repast,* 1801, cat. no. 69

their own party. The full basket of the sportsman at center indicates that they have terrorized not only the human inhabitants but also the game population. The clear message is that certain men may meet the property qualifications to shoot game, but they are not "qualified" in regard to their sense of sportsmanship and respect for the countryside.

Those who saw themselves as guardians of a traditional sporting order often phrased their objections in terms of protecting the property of the small landowner and tenant farmer. As one former huntsman wrote:

It is fair to suppose that those who have not resided in the country cannot be so much aware at times of the mischief they are doing in riding as those who are constantly resident there,

and who have more opportunities of getting acquainted with the crops. If these men would only consider this, they would not be surprised at seeing a farmer extremely irate with them for riding on a field of tares for instance (which they had mistaken for weeds).[29]

Such apprehension was not just speculation, as the sporting press often carried reports of transgressions by unruly sportsmen.[30] Indeed, in sporting prints it was frequently the small farmer who appeared most affected by the carelessness of unfit types. Alken's *Down Charge* depicts two urban sportsmen who, whether by incompetence or drunkenness (a previous print in the series shows them enjoying a hearty meal with plenty of drink), have killed a farmer's pig. The

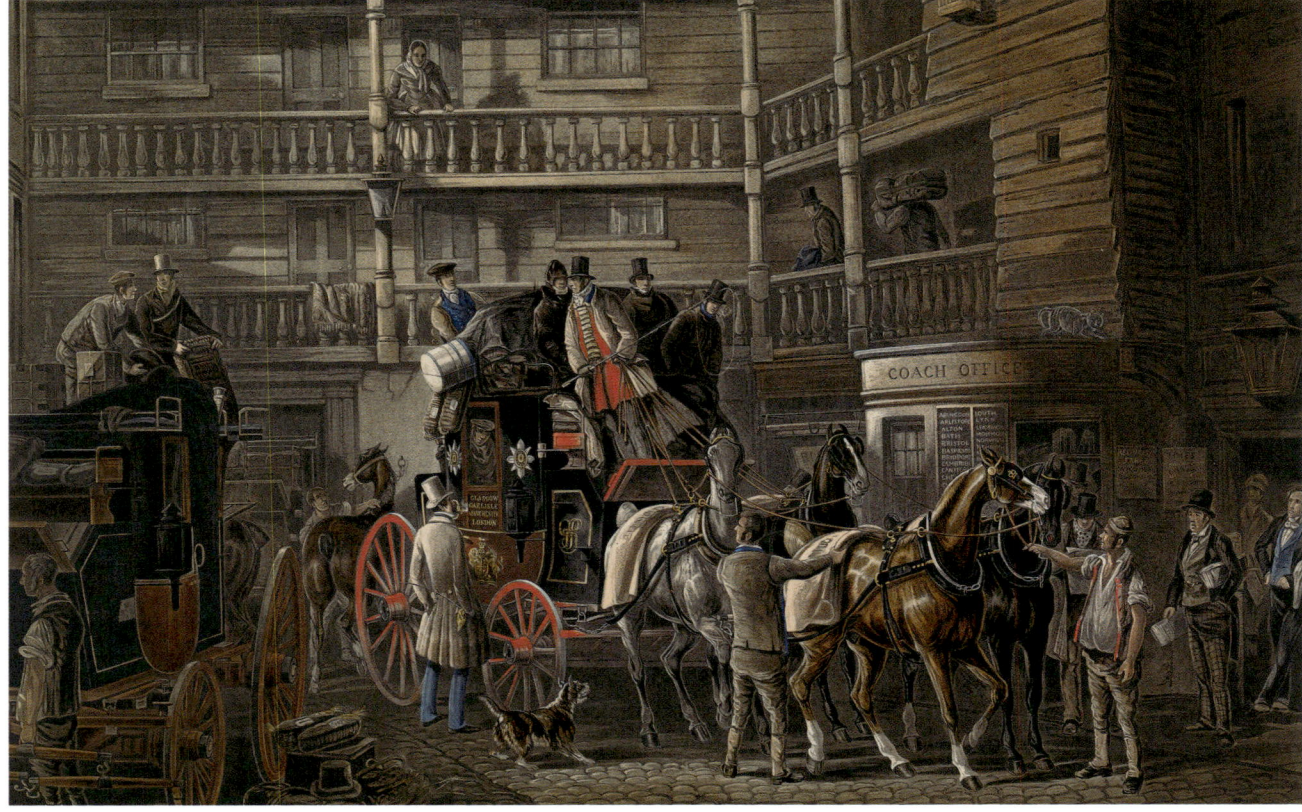

FIG. 68. Charles Cooper Henderson, *The Olden Time,* 1846, cat. no. 44

farmer's angry response to the sportsmen's sheepish offer of compensation reflects the hardship that the loss of a single pig could cause.

Despite the infusion of so many city participants, prints and hunting literature perpetuated social customs that favored insider status and resisted idleness, intemperance, and vice — commonly perceived as "urban." While prints expressed anxiety over an urban invasion, the popularity of field sports as a fashionable pursuit for the urban upper classes grew during the nineteenth century, leading to ever more city residents taking to the country to shoot and hunt. With the advent of the railroad, including special cars to carry horses, gentleman could easily travel from London to any number of hunts in just a few hours. Prints and sporting literature continued to stress the importance of strong ties to the countryside, bolstering the traditional views against any new customs introduced by the increasingly urban participants. Such a viewpoint stands in opposition to the common myth put forth during that period that foxhunting was an egalitarian pursuit in which

the only prerequisites for success were skill at riding and love of the open air.[31]

A preference for the old order of sport and countryside among artists and purchasers of sporting prints is evident in the proliferation of coaching prints that arose around the time of the development of the steam engine and railroad. Henry Alken's *A View in Regent's Park* presents an absurdist vision of the future (in a distinctly urban setting) in which steam travel has replaced the horse and clogs the air with dense smoke. Created around fifteen years later, Charles Cooper Henderson's print from the series *Fores's Coaching Recollections* (fig. 68) presents coach travel as a nostalgic relic of the past. The booming growth of railways in the 1830s and 1840s signaled the inevitable end of coaching, considered essential to the way of life of the countryside for nearly a century. Henderson's image captures the transformative nature of coach travel as passengers are transported from a dense urban scene to the open air of the countryside. While rail travel offered the opportunity to shrink the country by drastically reducing travel times, it also brought the city closer to the rural world and weakened a conceptual barrier that had existed between the two for a significant period of Britain's history.

By the second half of the nineteenth century the countryside had undergone tremendous change, spurred by numerous economic and social factors. The growth in popularity and organization of field sports was an important component of that transformation. Sporting art and field sports have traditionally been thought to concern only a small stratum of society. However, the issues that defined the agricultural revolution, such as the changing nature of property ownership and employment in the countryside, were inextricably tied to the progress and development of sport. While a relatively small number of people actually participated regularly in field sports, the cultural significance of sport loomed much larger as it came to signify the established social order of the country and define itself against urban values and way of life.

Sporting prints served as a crucial tool in understanding the complex modes of social interaction that derived from the increased demand placed on the countryside by those seeking to engage in leisure pursuits. Prints were not neutral documents reflecting an impartial representation of those who participated in field sports — as employees, enthusiasts, and bystanders. Instead, artists actively shaped perceptions of the people they depicted in service to a variety of different interests. While field sports enjoyed great popularity during the second half of the nineteenth century, the countryside continued to undergo demographic and economic change well into the twentieth. After the 1850s, though, sporting prints diminished in popularity and significance. Changing networks of communication and technological advances led to innovations such as illustrated newspapers, which brought images of events and people to even larger national audiences. Sporting prints, however, remain significant as works of art that not only reflect the intense social change of the period but participated in the larger ideological and cultural currents surrounding the countryside, sport, and class interaction.

NOTES

1. Nimrod 1843, 85.

2. Lawley 1892, 13.

3. Apperley was a regular contributor to the *Sporting Magazine* from 1822 to 1829, submitting reports from the field. As a typical example of the range of people he profiled, in "Nimrod's Tour," from the August 1825 issue, over nine pages the author introduces his readers to aristocratic landowners, horse owners, jockeys, a training groom, a horse dealer, cock fighting enthusiasts, a "pad-boy" (or hunt assistant), among others. Nimrod 1825, 274–82.

4. Clayton 1997, 141–45.

5. Deuchar 1988, 91.

6. There are many sources on the agricultural history of the period approaching the topic from multiple perspectives. The following are not meant to be exhaustive but to provide an starting point: Beckett 1990, Chambers and Mingay 1968, Overton 1996, Williamson 2002.

7. Griffin 2007, 110–11.

8. Williamson 2002, 45–46.

9. Griffin 2007, 117–19.

10. While relationships with the sporting world have been firmly established for some artists, such as Alken and Stubbs, for others whose biographies are less well known in present scholarship, these connections remain comparatively murky. For the purposes of this essay, the prints themselves serve as the primary markers of the points of contact between artist and subject. Previous authors such as Clayton 1997 have documented the urban marketplace for sporting prints. The source of the sociological and historical factors that drove the intense interest in sporting prints among urban clientele has not been fully resolved and remains a question perhaps to be taken up by future scholars.

11. *Annals of Sporting* 1822, 143.

12. Ibid., 142.

13. Elsee 1818.

14. Ibid., 16–27.

15. For an overview of the history of the Game Laws and the conflict that surrounded them in Britain see Munsche 1981 and Hopkins 1985.

16. *Sporting Magazine* 1811, 191.

17. Zouch 1793, 9.

18. Berkeley 1845, 7 (author's own italics).

19. *Sporting Magazine* 1835, 108. The author counted about 400 participants in a day's hunt.

20. Thomas Smith 1841, 201.

21. Beckford 1781, 123.

22. The eighteenth century saw the steady decrease of women engaged in field sports. While women still did participate and do appear in sporting prints, prints from this period overwhelmingly feature male participants, so the term "sportsman" has been used throughout. See Griffin 2007, 133–35.

23. See Deuchar 1988, 41–44.

24. Blaine 1841, 152.

25. *Sporting Magazine* 1797, 220.

26. Deuchar 1988, 43.

27. Ibid., 41.

28. *Sporting Magazine* 1800, 67–68.

29. Smith 1841, 102.

30. To cite one example: "On Monday, the 14th of January, 1811, a pack of hounds, said to belong to a gentleman of Bath, with a set of vagabonds on foot, and an idle unthinking set on horseback, made four or five rings not less than six miles in circumference and leveled gates, stiles and fences in such a manner that was never before seen.; not less than twenty of those idle unthinking jockies (not one of them qualified for pursuing game) entered the field, some on horses more fit to feed the hounds than follow them." *Sporting Magazine* 1811, 227–28.

31. Griffin 2007, 132.

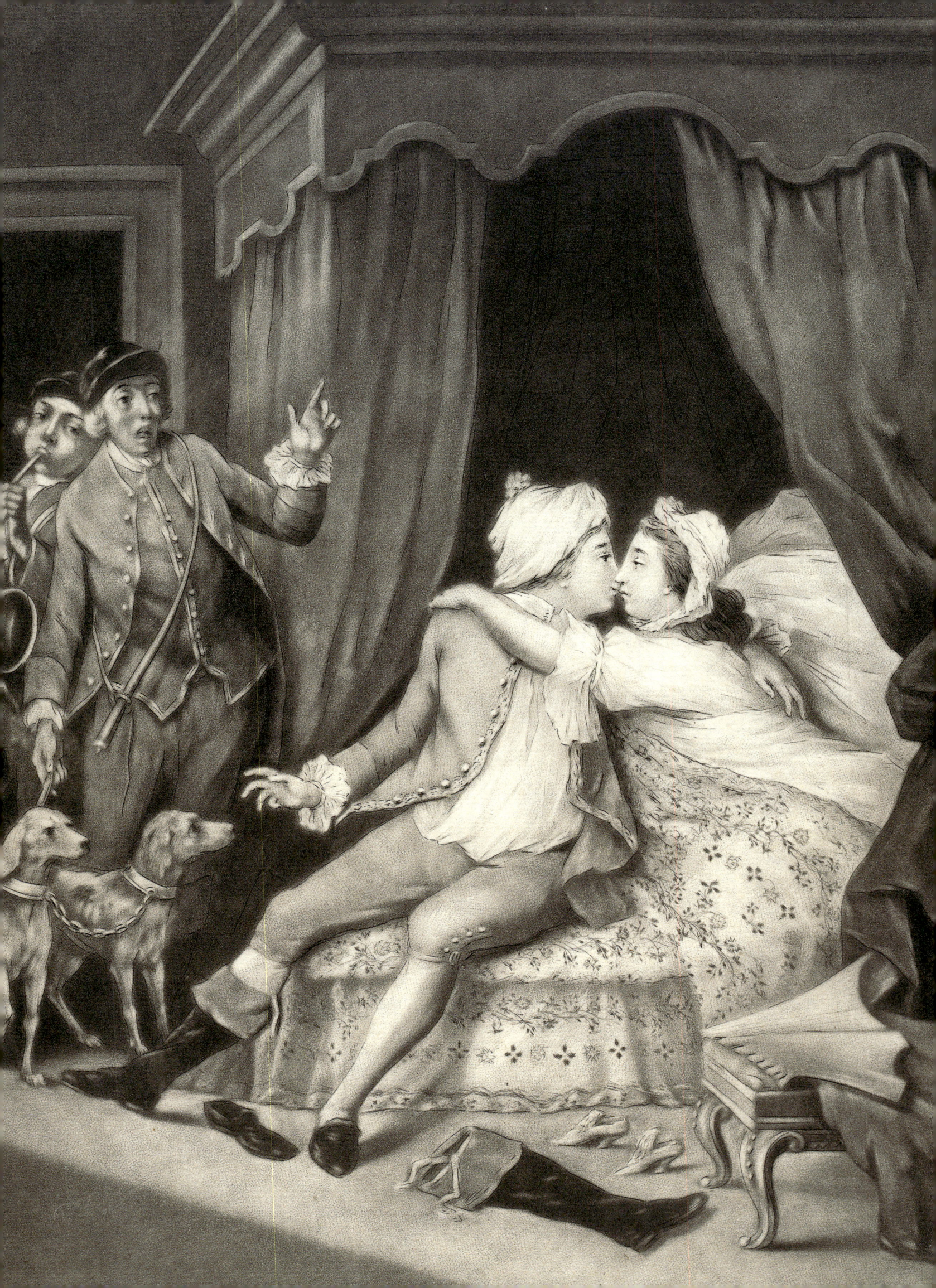

Catching Sight Catalogue

NOTE TO THE READER

The entire Mellon collection of sporting prints was meticulously catalogued by Dudley Snelgrove in *British Sporting and Animal Prints, 1658–1874,* published by the Tate Gallery for the Yale Center for British Art in 1981. The present catalogue takes that volume as the primary source for much of the information contained within this checklist, except where new information has come to light or as it pertains to those works that are not part of the Mellon collection. Prints are categorized according to the primary painter or draftsman with engravers and publishers included when known. Inscriptions that appear on the print are shown in italics with additional information in brackets.

Technical descriptions were verified by Rosemary Smith, Mellon Project, 2005–6. Titles are not repeated in inscription line unless they appear with significant variation on the print itself. Dimensions given are of image size (including inscriptions). All dimensions are height x width.

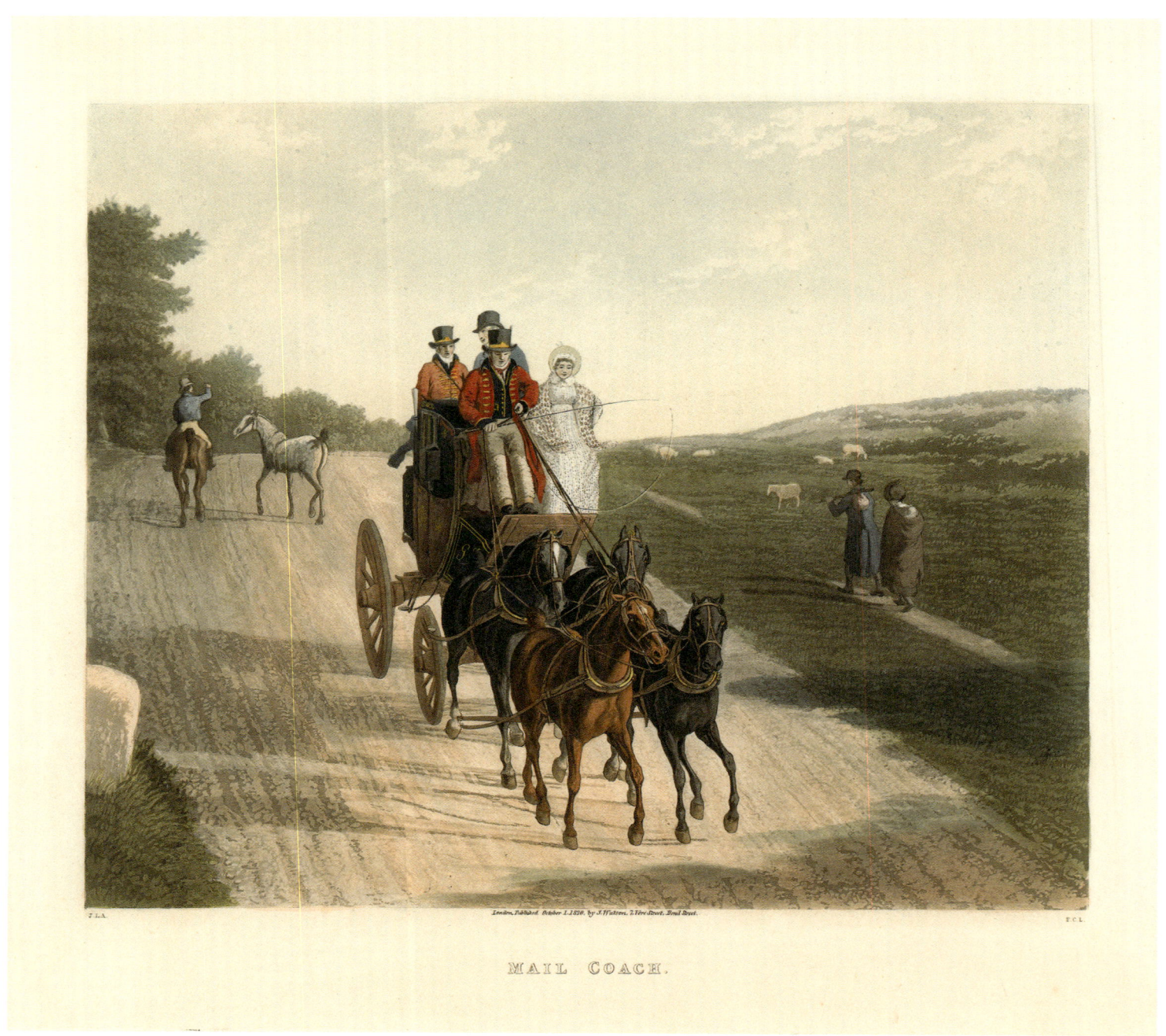

MAIL COACH.

1

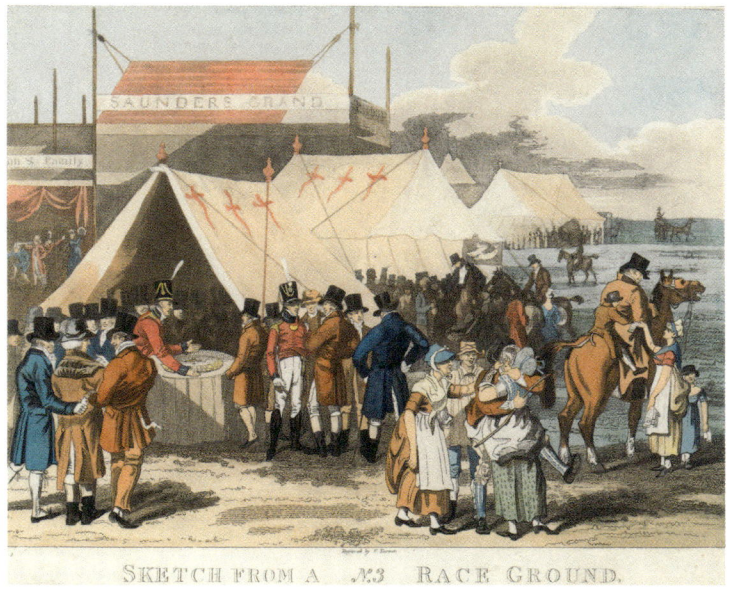

2

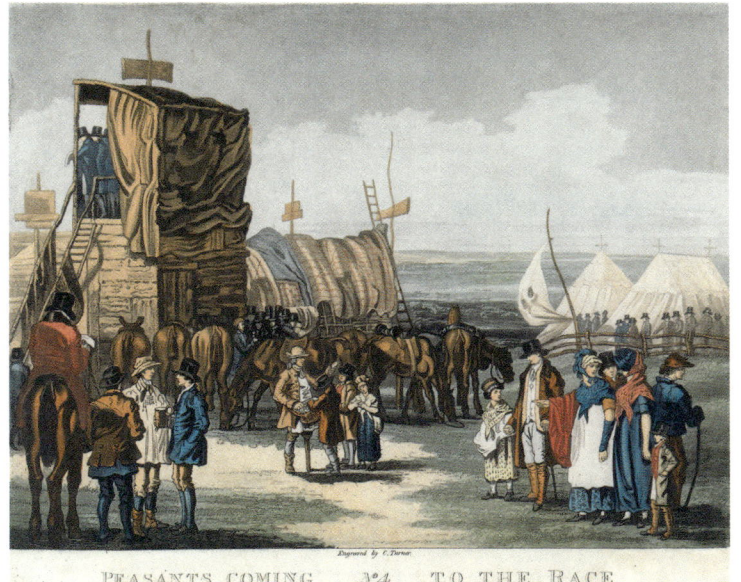

3

1. JACQUES LAURENT AGASSE (after)
Swiss, 1767–1849
Mail Coach, 1820
Color-printed and hand-colored etching and aquatint,
11 ⁷⁄₁₆ x 14 ¹³⁄₁₆ in.
Paul Mellon Collection, 85.1372

J.L.A. F.C.L. [F.C. Lewis]. *London, Published October
1. 1820, by J. Watson, 7. Vere Street, Bond Street.*

2. JACQUES LAURENT AGASSE (after)
Swiss, 1767–1849
Sketch from a Race Ground, No. 3
[from a set of six], 1807
Hand-colored etching with aquatint,
8 ⁹⁄₁₆ x 11 ½ in.
Paul Mellon Collection, 85.1298.3

Engraved by C. Turner.

3. JACQUES LAURENT AGASSE (after)
Swiss, 1767–1849
Peasants Coming to the Race, No. 4
[from a set of six], 1807
Hand-colored etching with aquatint,
8 ⁹⁄₁₆ x 11 ½ in.
Paul Mellon Collection, 85.1298.4

Engraved by C. Turner.

4. HENRY THOMAS ALKEN (after)
British, 1785–1851
*One of the Right Sort, Who Hunts Because
He Likes It* [from a pair], ca. 1820
Hand-colored aquatint with touches of etching,
9 ³⁄₁₆ x 11 ⁵⁄₈ in.
Paul Mellon Collection, 85.1263.1

*One of the Right Sort, / Who hunts because he likes
it. / "Confound this Snow I shall never get a light; but the
worst of it is, it will put a stop to hunting / for a few days
at least."*

[Engraved by E. Duncan; Published by S. & J. Fuller]

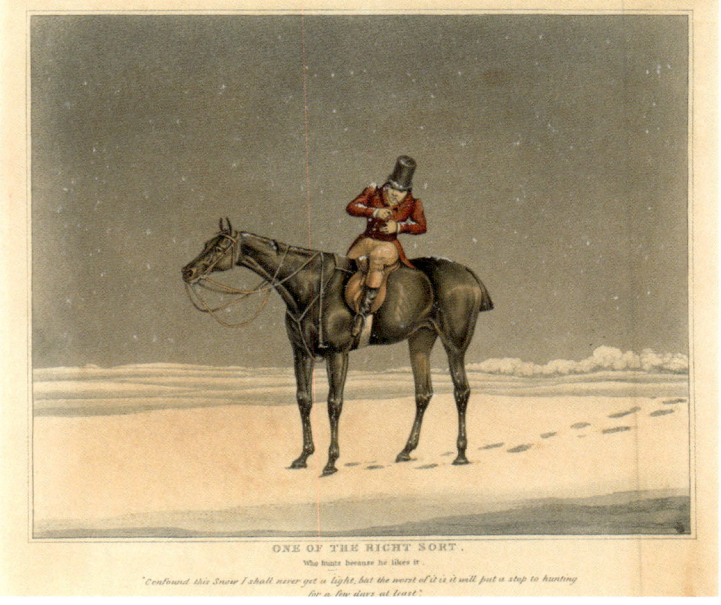

4

5. HENRY THOMAS ALKEN (after)
British, 1785–1851
*One of the Wrong Sort, Who Goes Out with the Hunters
Because It Is the Fashion* [from a pair], ca. 1820
Hand-colored aquatint with touches of etching,
9 ³⁄₁₆ x 11 ⁵⁄₈ in.
Paul Mellon Collection, 85.1263.2

*One of the Wrong Sort. / Who goes out with the
hunters because it is the fashion. / "Confound the
Snow is not hunting bad enough without this; but
there's one comfort we shall not be / able to go out
again for some time."*

[Engraved by E. Duncan; Published by S. & J. Fuller]

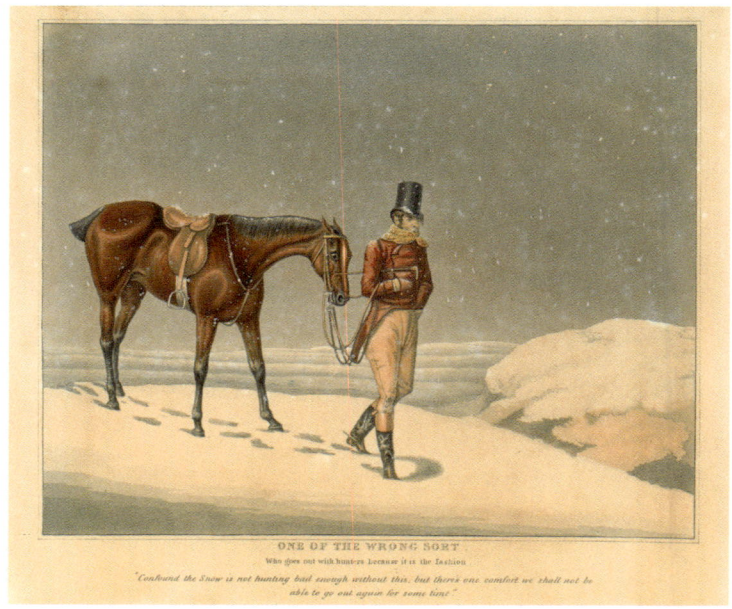

5

6. HENRY THOMAS ALKEN
British, 1785–1851
A Phaeton and Four [from *Moments of Fancy*], 1822
Hand-colored soft-ground etching, 9 ⁹⁄₁₆ x 13 ½ in.
Paul Mellon Collection, 85.1266.1

*A Phaeton and Four. / Apollo was foolish . . . . .
he could do no more, / Than trust such a fool
. . . with a Phaeton & four.*

*Hy. Alken, Delt. London, Published by Thos. McLean;
Repository of Wit & Humour, 26 Haymarket, 1822.*

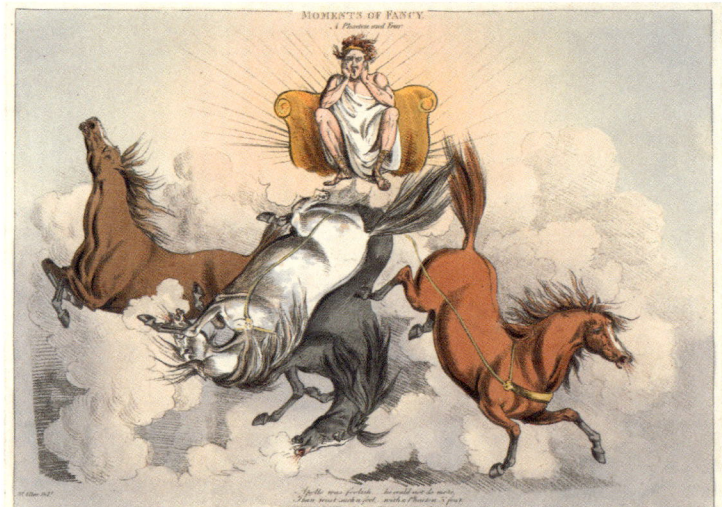

6

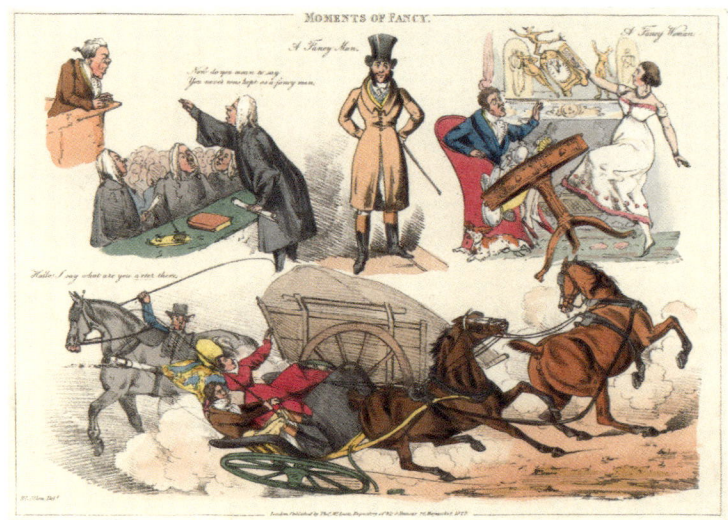

7

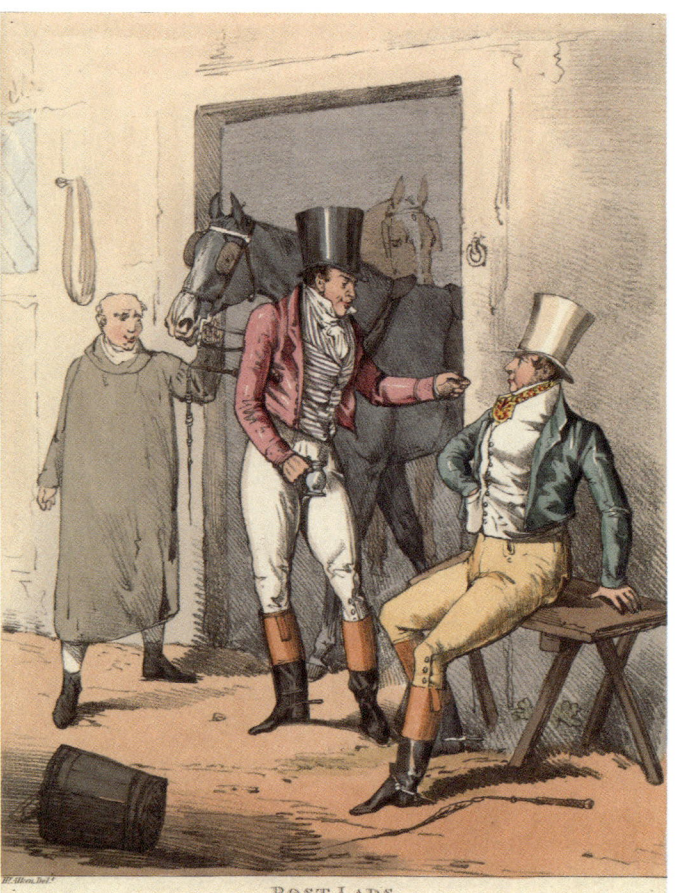

8

7. HENRY THOMAS ALKEN
British, 1785–1851
A Fancy Man [from *Moments of Fancy*], 1822
Hand-colored soft-ground etching, 9 ⁹⁄₁₆ x 13 ½ in.
Paul Mellon Collection, 85.1266.6

*A Fancy Man. / A Fancy Woman. / Now do mean to
say / You never was kept as a fancy man. / Hallo! I say
what are you <u>arter</u> there.*

*Hy. Alken, Delt. London, Published by Thos. McLean;
Repository of Wit & Humour, 26, Haymarket, 1822.*

8. HENRY THOMAS ALKEN
British, 1785–1851
Post Lads [from a set of six], 1823
Hand-colored soft-ground etching, 9 ⅜ x 7 ⁵⁄₁₆ in.
Paul Mellon Collection, 85.1261.2

Hy. Alken, Delt. [Published by Thomas McLean, 26
Haymarket, London]

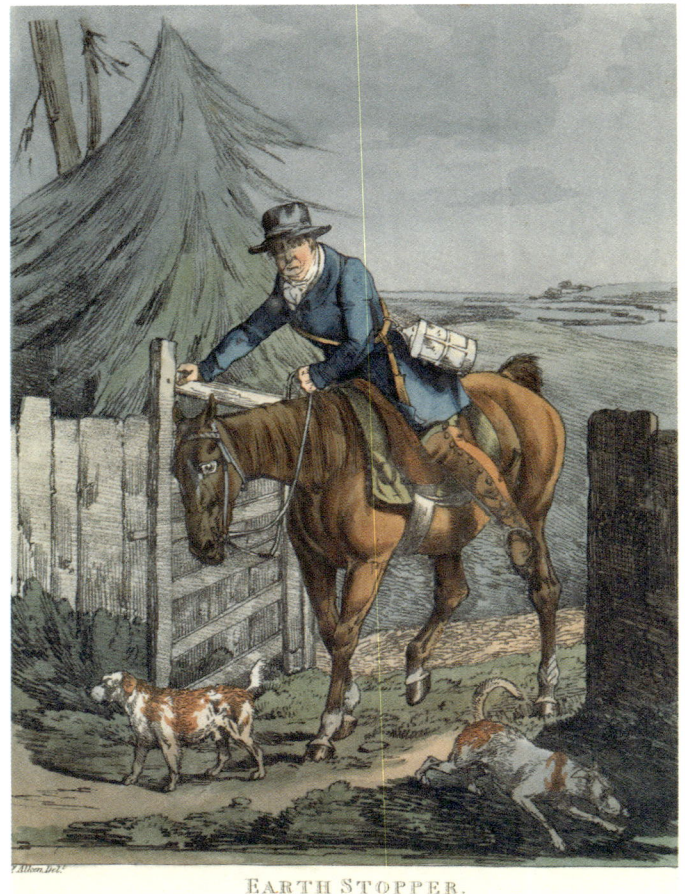

EARTH STOPPER.

9

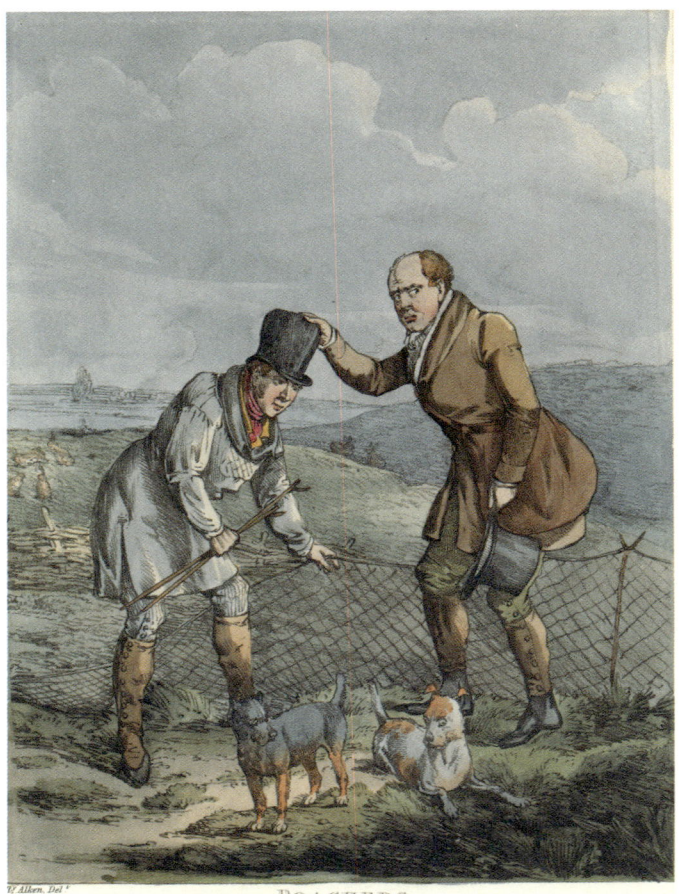

POACHERS.

10

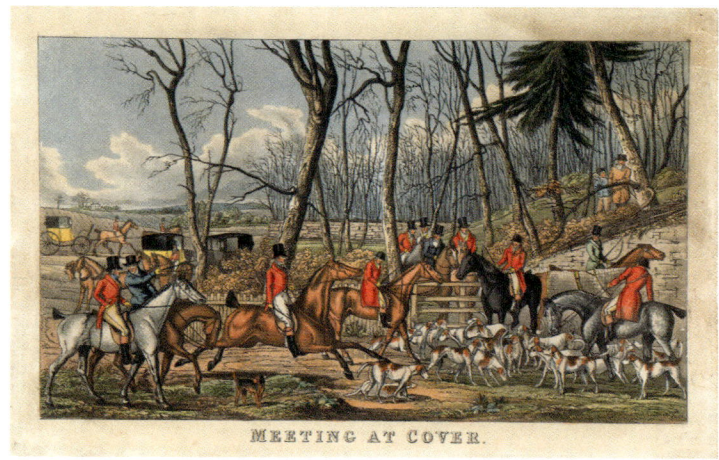

11

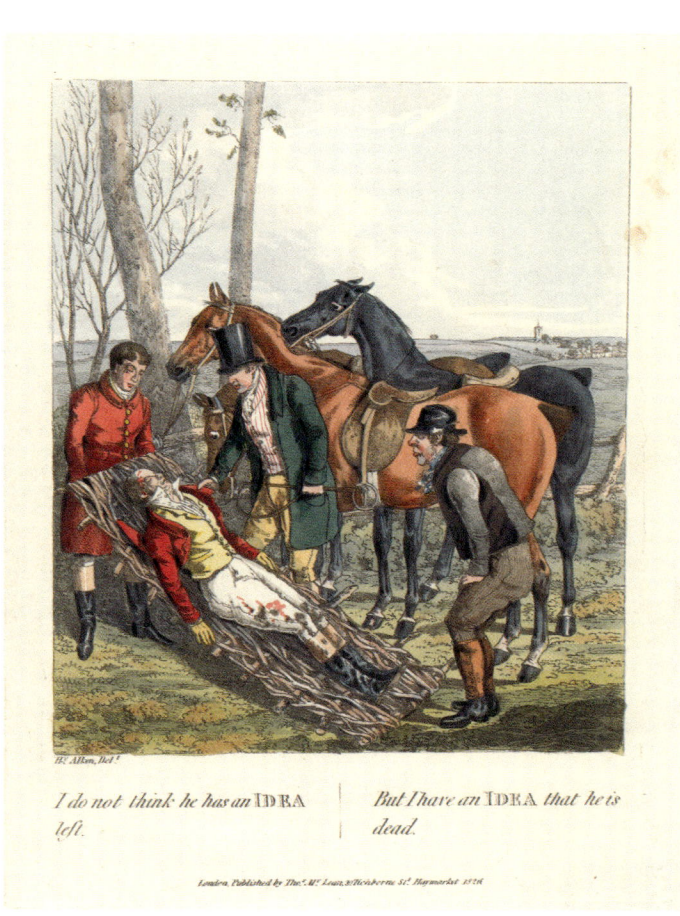

12

9. HENRY THOMAS ALKEN
British, 1785–1851
Earth Stopper [from a set of six], 1823
Hand-colored soft-ground etching, 9 ⅜ x 7 ⁵⁄₁₆ in.
Paul Mellon Collection, 85.1261.6

Hy. Alken, Delt. [Published by Thomas McLean, 26 Haymarket, London]

10. HENRY THOMAS ALKEN
British, 1785–1851
Poachers [from a set of six], 1823
Hand-colored soft-ground etching, 9 ⅜ x 7 ⁹⁄₁₆ in.
Paul Mellon Collection, 85.1261.5

Hy. Alken, Delt. [Published by Thomas McLean, 26 Haymarket, London]

11. HENRY THOMAS ALKEN
British, 1785–1851
Meeting at Cover [from a set of four], 1824
Hand-colored etching with aquatint, 7 ⁹⁄₁₆ x 12 ¹⁵⁄₁₆ in.
Paul Mellon Collection, 85.1262.1

[Etched by Henry Alken; Aquatinted by T. Sutherland; Published by Thomas McLean, 26 Haymarket, London]

12. HENRY THOMAS ALKEN
British, 1785–1851
I Do Not Think He Has an Idea Left [from *A Few Ideas: Being Hints to All Would-Be Meltonians*], 1826
Hand-colored soft-ground etching, 8 ⅜ x 7 ¹⁄₁₆ in.
Paul Mellon Collection, 85.1306.12

I do not think he has an Idea / left. / But I have an Idea that he is / dead.

Hy. Alken, Delt. London, Published by Thos. McLean, 20, Tichborne Stt. 1826.

13. HENRY THOMAS ALKEN
British, 1785–1851
As a Foal You First See Him, PL. 1
[from *The High Mettled Racer*], 1828
Hand-colored soft-ground etching, 3 ⅜ x 4 ¹³⁄₁₆ in.
Paul Mellon Collection, 85.1315.1

*As a Foal you first see him ev'n then highly
match'd, / With tenderness rear'd lest the prize should
be snatch'd; / From the grasp of his owner, whose
principle fort, / Is in "play or pay bubbles", and
things of that sort. / He now is all nature his limbs
finely formed, / His mouth never bitted, his whole
form unadorned; / By rich colour'd silks, platted
mane, and such stuff, / For a thorough bred Foal is
quite handsome enough.*

*Hy. Alken, Delt. London, Published by Thos.
McLean. 26. Haymarket. 1828.*

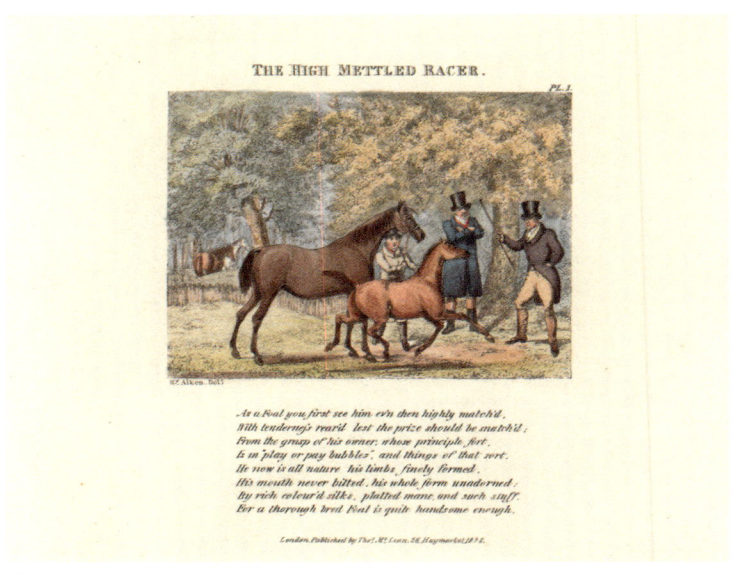

13

14. HENRY THOMAS ALKEN
British, 1785–1851
*He Is Now Put in Trammels of
Bit, Rein, and Girth*, PL. 2
[from *The High Mettled Racer*], 1828
Hand-colored soft-ground etching, 3 ⁵⁄₁₆ x 4 ¹¹⁄₁₆ in.
Paul Mellon Collection, 85.1315.2

*He is now put in trammels of Bit, Rein & Girth, / But
is treated with kindness, on account of his birth. / He
is charmingly cloath'd, and most daintily fed. / His
lodgings quite warm with a soft & dry bed. / But if he
is restive, kick, fidget, or plunge, / He is punish'd by
having more work in the [word omitted] / Improv'd
in his form, his tail still remaining, / You here see the
thorough bred Colt in his training.*

*Hy. Alken, Delt. London, Published by Thos.
McLean. 26. Haymarket. 1828.*

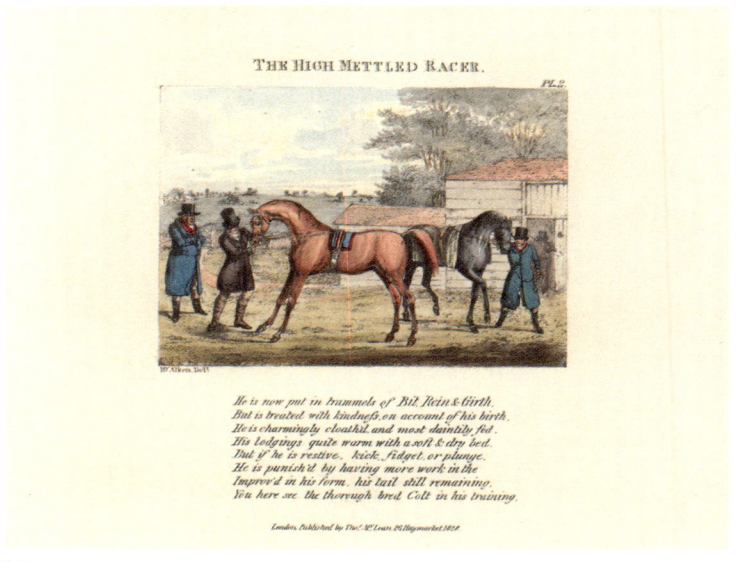

14

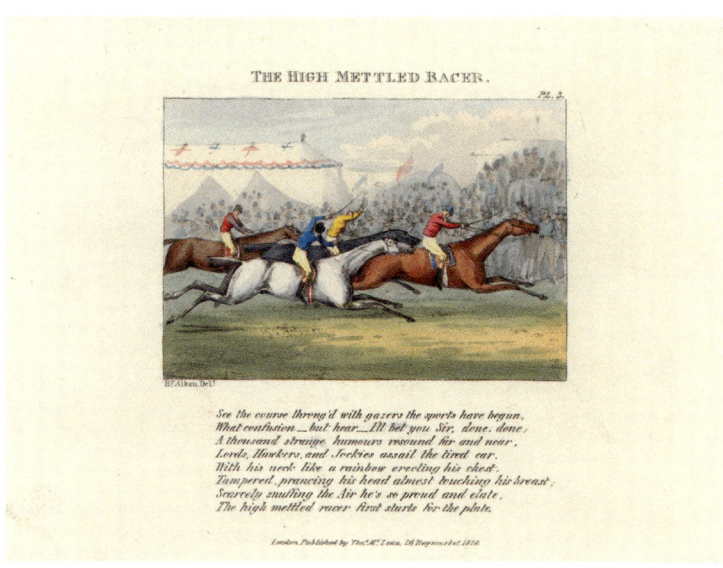

15

15. HENRY THOMAS ALKEN
British, 1785–1851
See the Course Throng'd with Gazers, PL. 3
[from *The High Mettled Racer*], 1828
Hand-colored soft-ground etching, 3 5/16 x 4 3/4 in.
Paul Mellon Collection, 85.1315.3

See the course throng'd with gazers the sports have begun, / What confusion — but hear — I'll bet you Sir, done, done; / A thousand strange humours resound far and near, / Lords, Hawkers, and Jockies assail the tired ear, / With his neck like a rainbow erecting his chest, / Tampered, prancing his head almost touching his breast; / Scarcely snuffing the Air he's so proud and elate, / The high mettled racer first starts for the plate.

Hy. Alken, Delt. London, Published by Thos. McLean. 26. Haymarket. 1828.

16

16. HENRY THOMAS ALKEN
British, 1785–1851
Now Renard Turn'd Out, PL. 4
[from *The High Mettled Racer*], 1828
Hand-colored soft-ground etching, 3 5/16 x 4 7/8 in.
Paul Mellon Collection, 85.1315.4

Now Renard turn'd out, and o'er hedge and ditch rush, / Men, Horses and Dogs, who are hard at his brush; / Oe'r heath and hill moorland led by the sly prey, / By scent and by view create a long tedious way. / When alike born for joys of the field and the course, / Always sure to come through a staunch and fleet horse; / And when fairly run down the fox yields his breath, / The high Mettled racer is in at the death.

Hy. Alken, Delt. London, Published by Thos. McLean. 26. Haymarket. 1828.

17. HENRY THOMAS ALKEN
British, 1785–1851
Grown Aged Used Up and Turned Out of the Stud, PL. 5
[from *The High Mettled Racer*], 1828
Hand-colored soft-ground etching, 3 ⅜ x 4 ⅞ in.
Paul Mellon Collection, 85.1315.5

Grown aged used up and turned out of the stud, / Lame spavin and wind gall'd but yet of some blood, / Whilst knowing postilions his pedigree trace, / And his dam won that sweepstake, his sire gain'd that race; / And what money he made the ostlers count o'er, / As they loiter their time at some hedge Ale house door, / While the harness sore galls and the spurs his side goad, / The high mettled racer's a hack on the Road.

Hy. Alken, Delt. London, Published by Thos. McLean. 26. Haymarket. 1828.

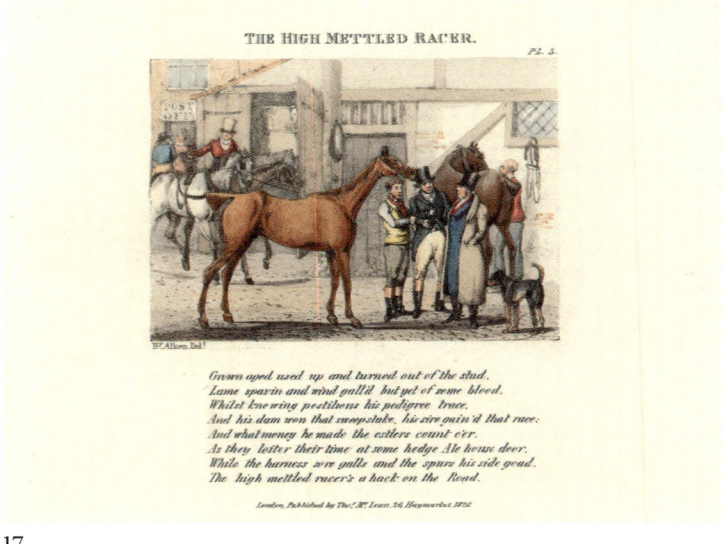

17

18. HENRY THOMAS ALKEN
British, 1785–1851
At Length Old and Feeble, PL. 6
[from *The High Mettled Racer*], 1828
Hand-colored soft-ground etching, 3 ⁵⁄₁₆ x 4 ⅞ in.
Paul Mellon Collection, 85.1315.6

At length old and feeble, trudging early and late, / Bow'd down by degrees he bows down to his fate; / From morning till evening he tugs in a mill, / Or draw sand, till the sand of his hour glass stands still. / And when lifeless & cold he's exposed to the view, / In the very same cart which he yesterday drew; / Whilst a pitying crowd his sad relics surrounds, / The high mettled racer is sold for the hounds.

Hy. Alken, Delt. London, Published by Thos. McLean. 26. Haymarket. 1828.

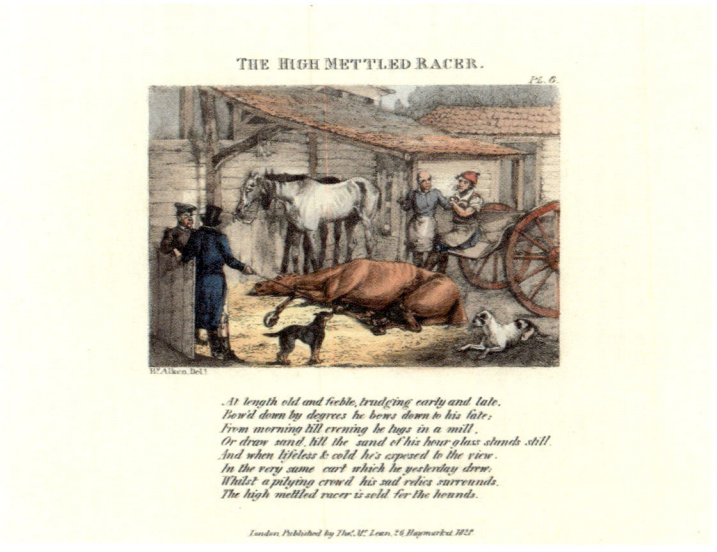

18

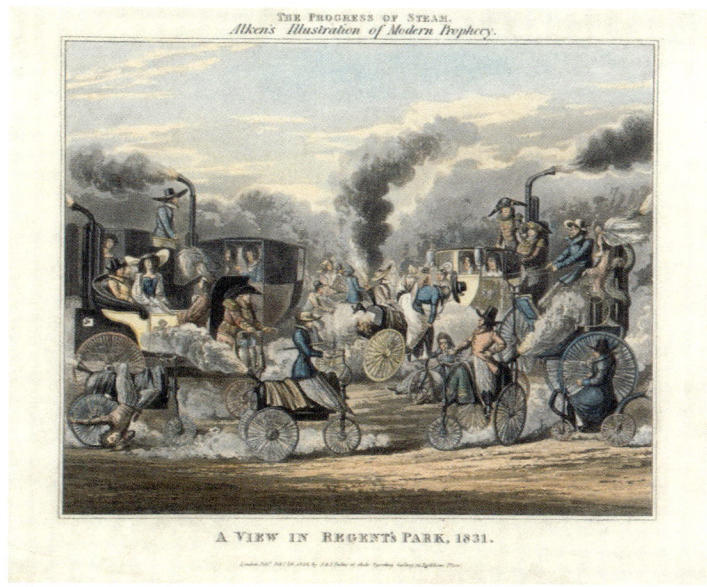

19

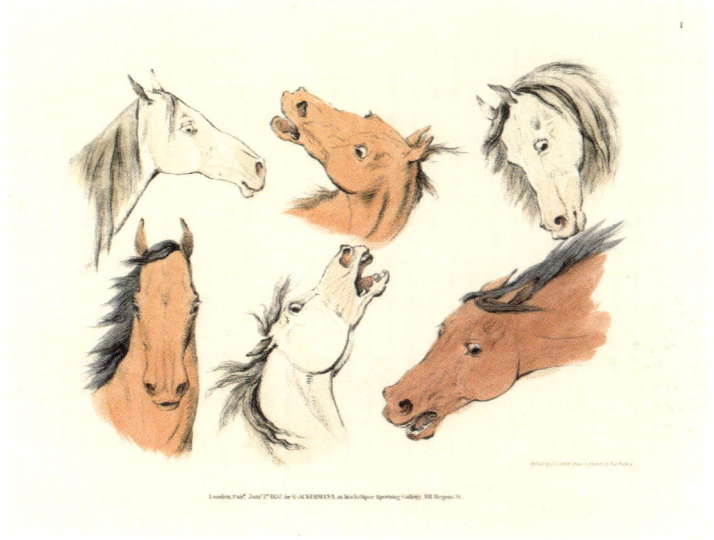

20

19. HENRY THOMAS ALKEN
British, 1785–1851
A View in Regent's Park, 1831 [from *The Progress of Steam: Alken's Illustration of Modern Prophecy*], 1828
Hand-colored etching and aquatint, 8 ⁷⁄₁₆ x 10 ⁵⁄₈ in.
Paul Mellon Collection, 85.1319

London, Pubd. Feby. 20, 1828, by S & J. Fuller. at their Sporting Gallery. 34 Rathbone Place.

20. HENRY THOMAS ALKEN (after)
British, 1785–1851
Six Heads of Horses Showing Expressions, PL. 1
[from *Rudiments for Drawing the Horse*], 1837
Hand-colored etching, 9 ¼ x 12 in.
Paul Mellon Collection, 85.1310.1

Etched by J. C. Zeitter, from a Sketch by his Father. London, Pubd. Jany. 1st. 1837 by R. Ackermann, at his Eclipse Sporting Gallery, 191 Regent St.

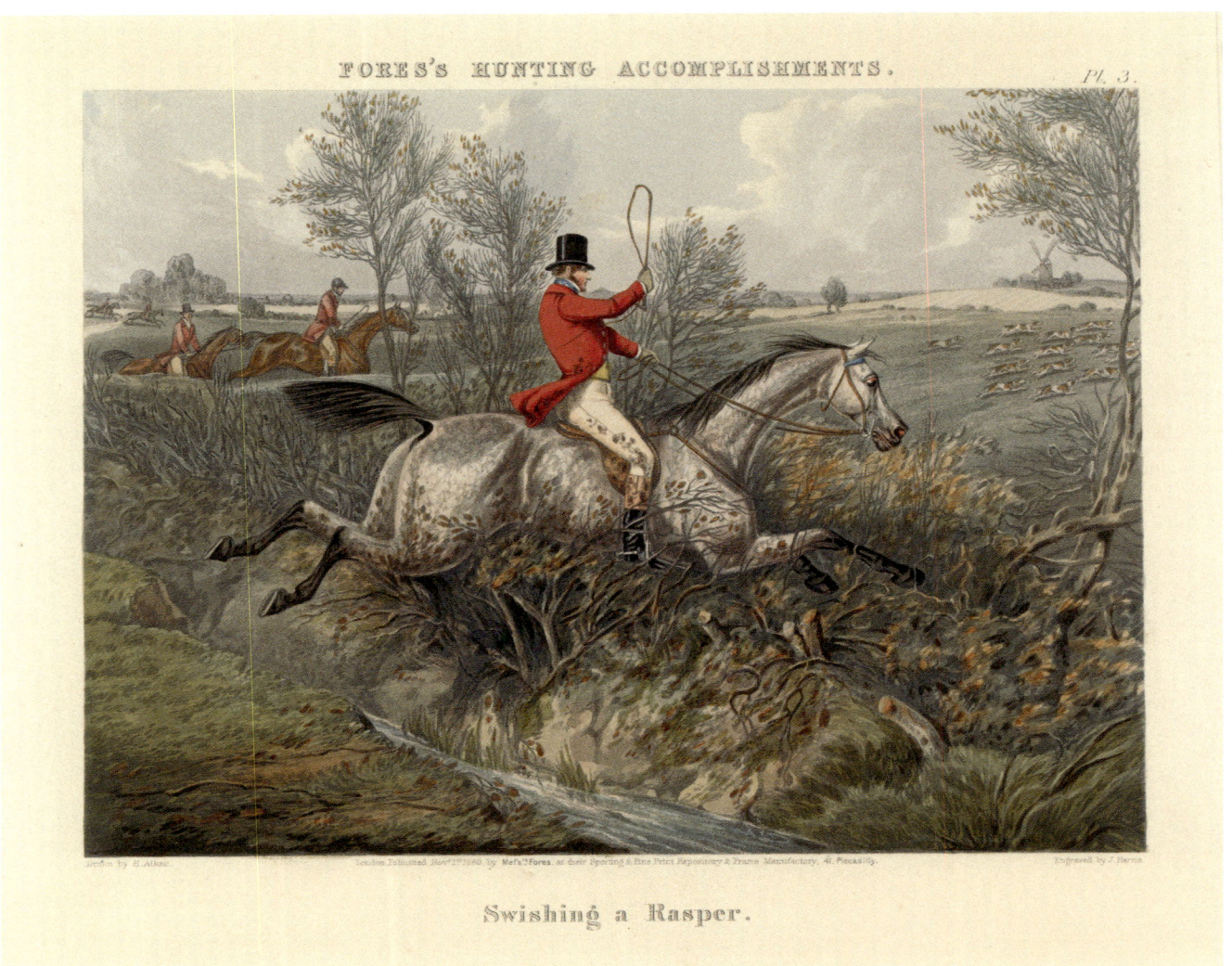

21

21. HENRY THOMAS ALKEN (after)
British, 1785–1851
Swishing a Rasper, PL. 3 [from *Fores's Hunting Accomplishments*], 1850
Hand-colored aquatint with traces of etching, 8 3/16 x 11 3/8 in.
Paul Mellon Collection, 85.1320.3

Drawn by H. Alken. Engraved by J. Harris. London, Published Novr. 1st. 1850, by Messrs. Fores, at their Sporting & Fine Print Repository & Frame Manufactory, 41, Piccadilly.

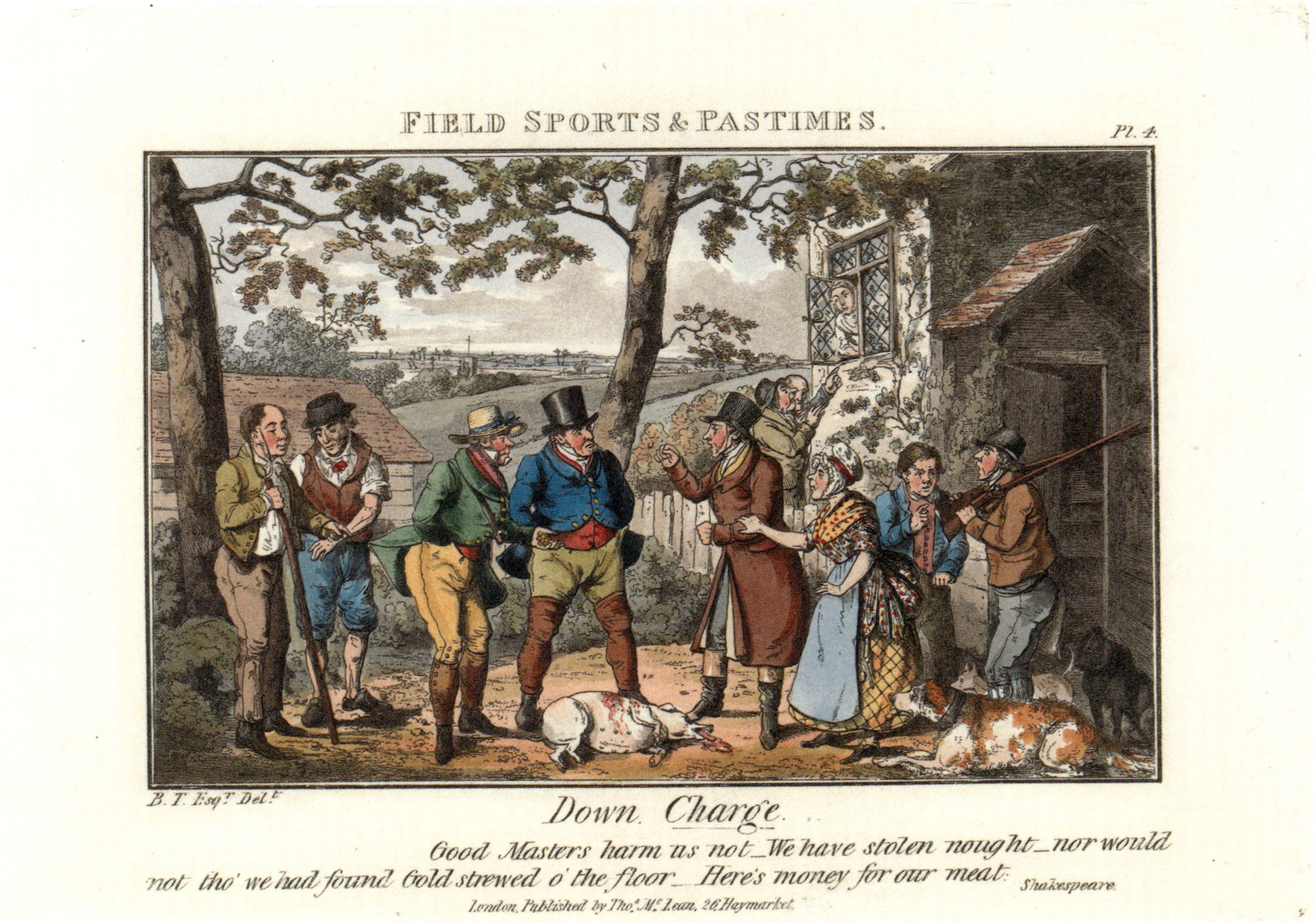

FIELD SPORTS & PASTIMES.

Pl. 4.

B. T. Esqr. Delt.

Down. Charge.

*Good Masters harm us not— We have stolen nought— nor would
not tho' we had found Gold strewed o' the floor— Here's money for our meat.* Shakespeare.

London. Published by Thos. McLean. 26. Haymarket.

22

22. HENRY THOMAS ALKEN (after)
British, 1785–1851
Down Charge, PL. 4 [from *Field Sports & Pastimes*], 1850
Hand-colored etching and aquatint, 4 9/16 x 7 5/16 in.
Paul Mellon Collection, 85.1260.4

*Good Masters harm us not—We have stolen nought—
nor would / not tho' we had found Gold strewed o' the
floor—Here's money for our meat: / Shakespeare.*

B. T. Esqr. Delt. [Ben Tally-Ho] *London, Published by
Thos. McLean. 26. Haymarket.*

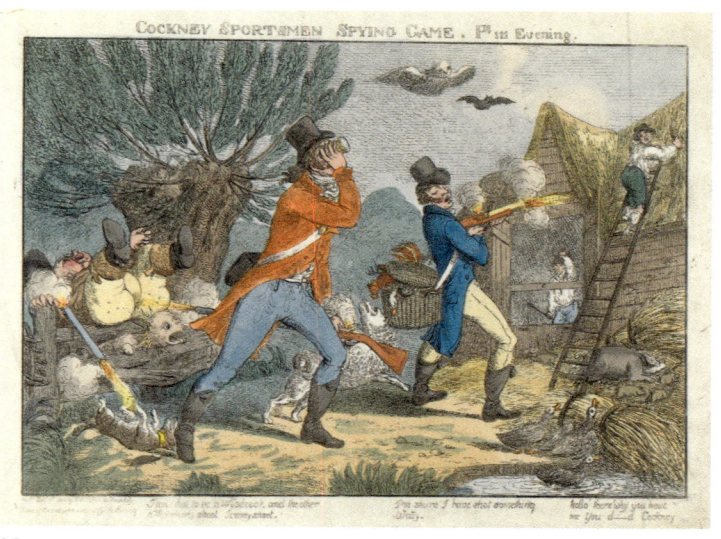

23

23. CHARLES ANSELL (attributed to)
British, active 1780–1800
Cockney Sportsmen Spying Game. Pl III Evening
[from a series of four], ca. 1805
Hand-colored etching, 8 ½ x 12 ½ in.
Paul Mellon Collection   85.1281.3

I take that to be a Woodcock and the other / a
Moorhen, shoot Jemmy shoot. / I'm shure I have shot
something / Walty. / hollo' there' why you have / me You
d___d Cockney

Pubd Decr 8th 1800. by S W Fores 50 Piccadilly Folios
of Caricatures lent out for the Evening

24. GEORGE ARNALD
British, 1763–1841
Spaniels, 1803
Mezzotint, 16 ¼ x 20 ¾ in.
Paul Mellon Collection, 85.1400

Spaniels Belonging to Richard Nowell of Stanstead,
Suffolk

State before all letters, inscribed: *G. Arnold* [sic]
pinxit Robt. Laurie Sculpt. [Published by Laurie
 and Whittle, 1803]

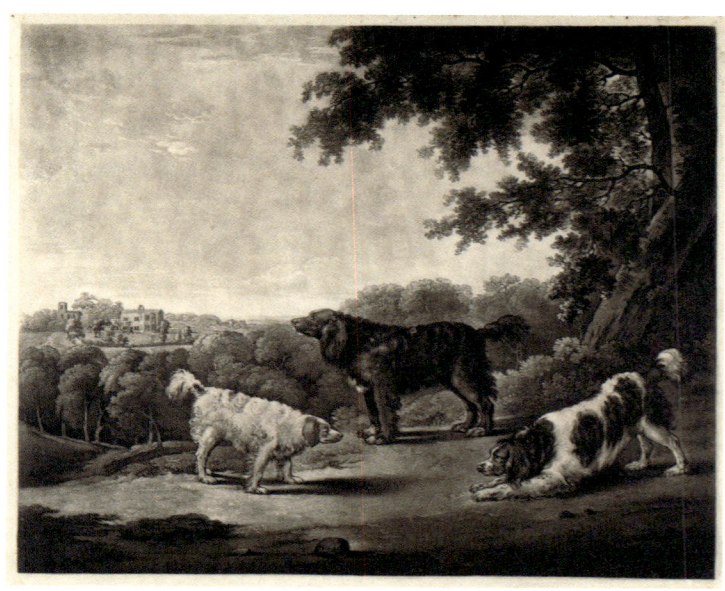

24

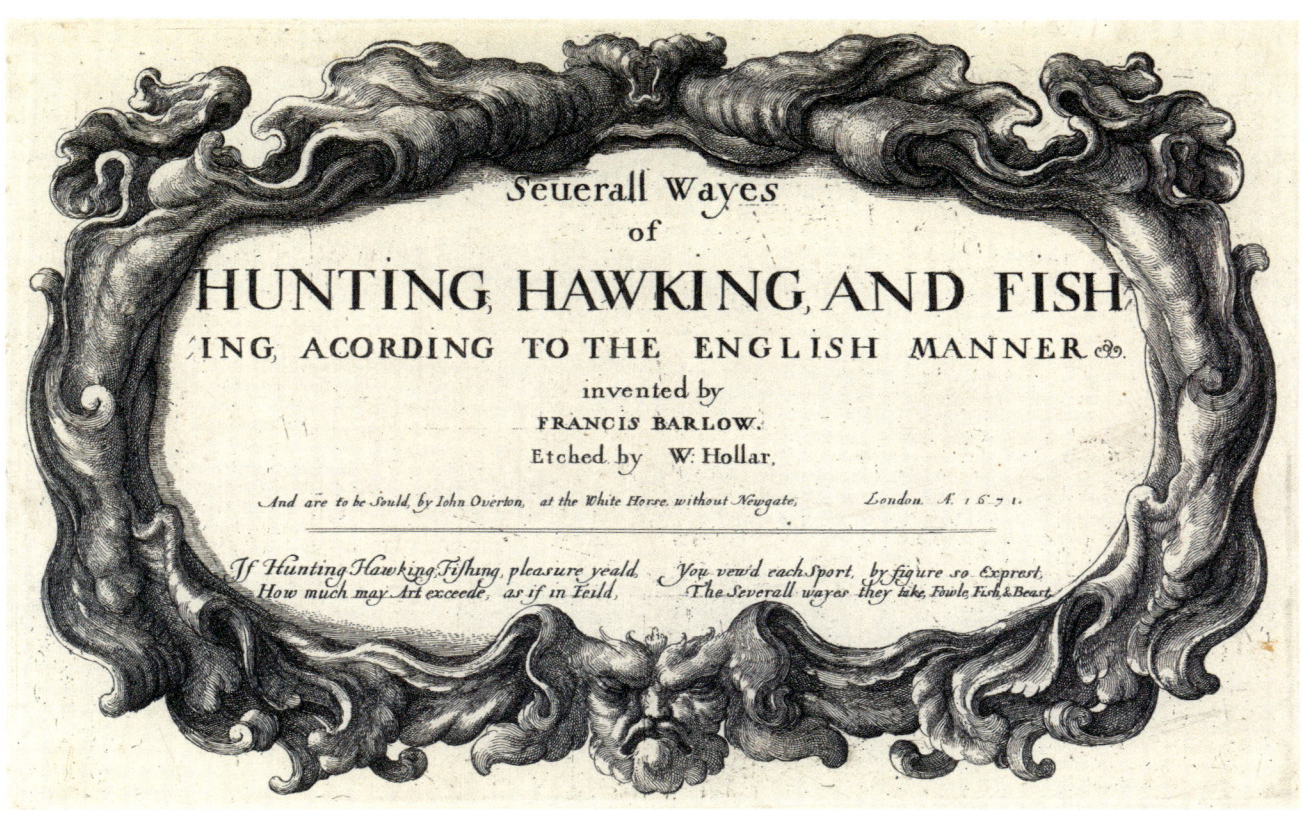

25

25. FRANCIS BARLOW (after)

English, ca. 1626–1704

Frontispiece [from *Severall Wayes of Hunting, Hawking, and Fishing, According to the English Manner*], 1671

Etching, 7 x 11 ½ in.

Promised Gift of Frank Raysor   FR.4977.01

Severall Wayes / of / Hunting, Hawking, and Fish / ing, According to the English Manner / invented by Francis Barlow.

Etched by W: Hollar, / And are to be Sould by John Overton, at the White Horse, without Newgate, London, At. 1671. / If Hunting, Hawking, Fishing, pleasure yeald, / How much may Art exceede, as if in Feild, / You vew'd each Sport, by figure so Exprest, / The Severall wayes they take, Fowle, Fish, & Beast.

26. FRANCIS BARLOW (after)

English, ca. 1626–1704

Hare Hunting [from *Severall Wayes of Hunting,
Hawking, and Fishing, According to the English
Manner*], ca. 1671

Etching, 6 ¾ x 8 ¹⁵⁄₁₆ in.

Promised Gift of Frank Raysor, FR.4977.02

*The timorous Hare, when started from her seat, / by
bloody hounds to save her life soe Sweet, / With
Severall Shifts, much terrour and great payne, / Yet
dyes She by their mouths, all proves but vayne,*

F. Barlow, inv: W Hollar Sculp:

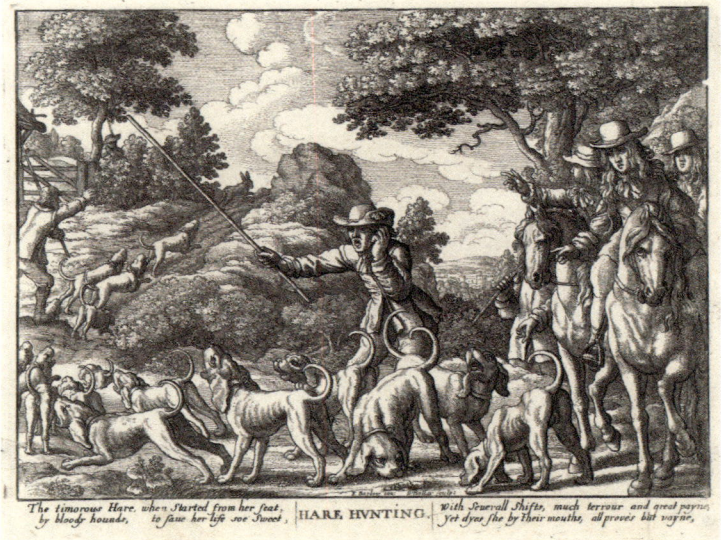

26

27. FRANCIS BARLOW

English, ca. 1626–1704

Fox Hunting [from *Severall Wayes of Hunting,
Hawking, and Fishing, According to the English
Manner*], ca. 1671

Etching, 6 ⁵⁄₈ x 9 in.

Promised Gift of Frank Raysor, L.36.2012

*With Eger Hounds, the Fox is hard pursu'd, / Till him
they Earth, whose Subtile shifts renew'd / Theire noble
chase, and shew'd them Princely Sport / Whose Death
the Cuntrey pleases as the Court.*

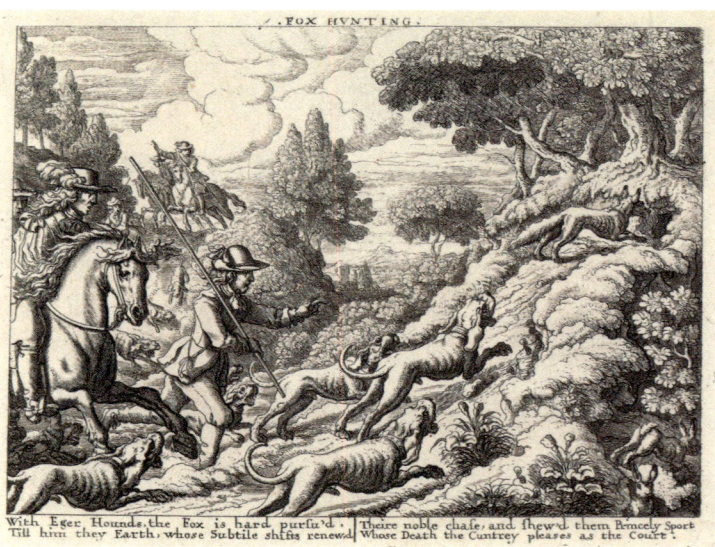

27

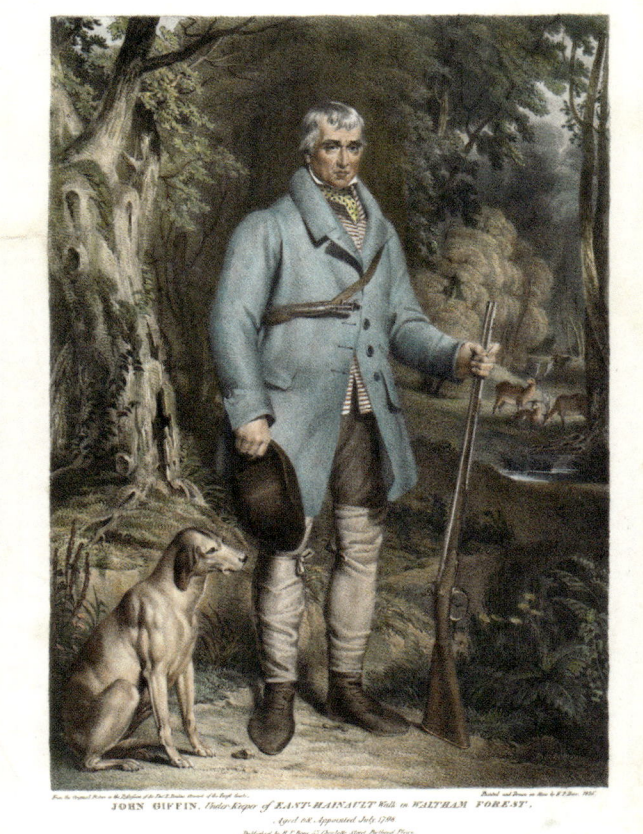

28

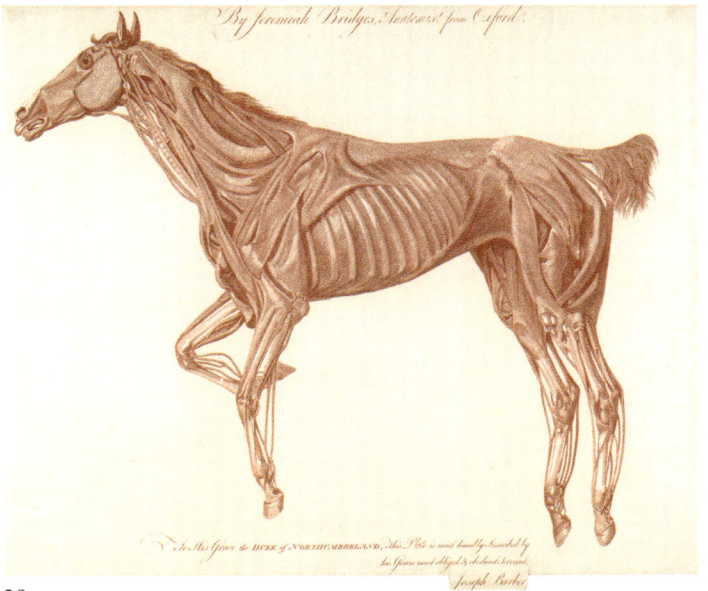

29

28. HENRY PIERCE BONE
British, 1779–1855
John Giffin, Under-Keeper of East-Hainault Walk in Waltham Forest, 1825
Hand-colored lithograph, 17 5/16 x 12 11/16 in.
Paul Mellon Collection, 85.1350

John Giffin, Under-Keeper of East-Hainault Walk in Waltham Forest, / Aged 68, Appointed July, 1798. / From the Original Picture in the Possession of Sir Thos. E. Tomlins, Steward of the Forest Courts.

Painted and Drawn on Stone by H. P. Bone, 1825. Published by H. P. Bone, 47 Charlotte Street, Portland Place.

29. JEREMIAH BRIDGES (after)
British, active 1751
Anatomical Study of a Horse, 1772
Engraving in red ink, 18 5/8 x 23 in.
Paul Mellon Collection, 85.1418

By Jeremiah Bridges, Anatomist from Oxford. / To His Grace the Duke of Northumberland, This Plate is most humbly Inscribed by / his Graces most obliged & obedient Servant, / Joseph Barber.

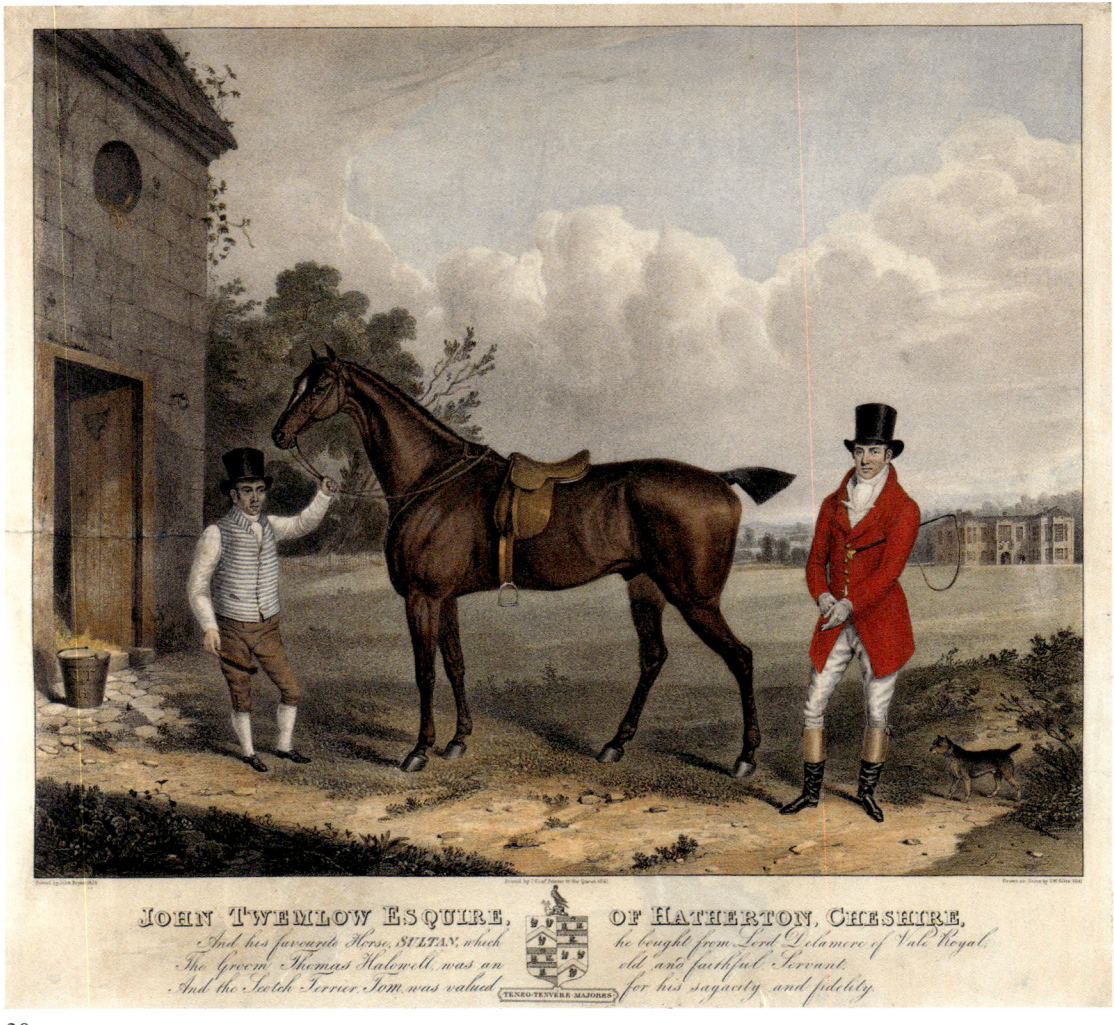

30

30. **JOHN BRYAN** (after)
British, active 1826
John Twemlow Esquire of Hatherton, Cheshire, 1841
Hand-colored lithograph, 16 ⅞ x 21 in.
Paul Mellon Collection, 85.1419

*John Twemlow Esquire, of Hatherton, Cheshire, /
And his favourite Horse, Sultan, which he bought
from Lord Delamere of Vale Royal, / The Groom
Thomas Halowell, was an old and faithful Servant, /
And the Scotch Terrier, Tom, was valued for his
sagacity and fidelity.*

*Painted by John Bryan 1826. Drawn on Stone by
J. W. Giles 1841. Printed by J. Graf Printer to the
Queen 1841.*

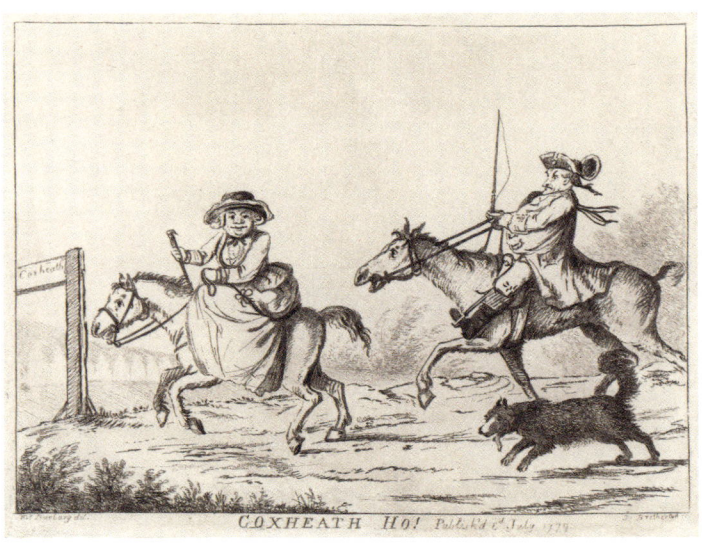

31

31. HENRY WILLIAM BUNBURY
British, 1750–1811
Coxheath Ho!, 1779
Etching, 8 ½ x 11 ¾ in.
Paul Mellon Collection, 85.1322

*Publish'd 3d. July 1779. Mr. Bunbury del. F6.
Bretherton f.*

32. HENRY BERNARD CHALON
British, 1770–1849
Pavilion, Ridden by Chifney, 1803
Mezzotint, proof before letters, 18 ½ x 23 in.
Paul Mellon Collection, 85.1403

[Published March 1, 1803 by Boydell and
Company, 90 Cheapside]

Signed: *Chalon*

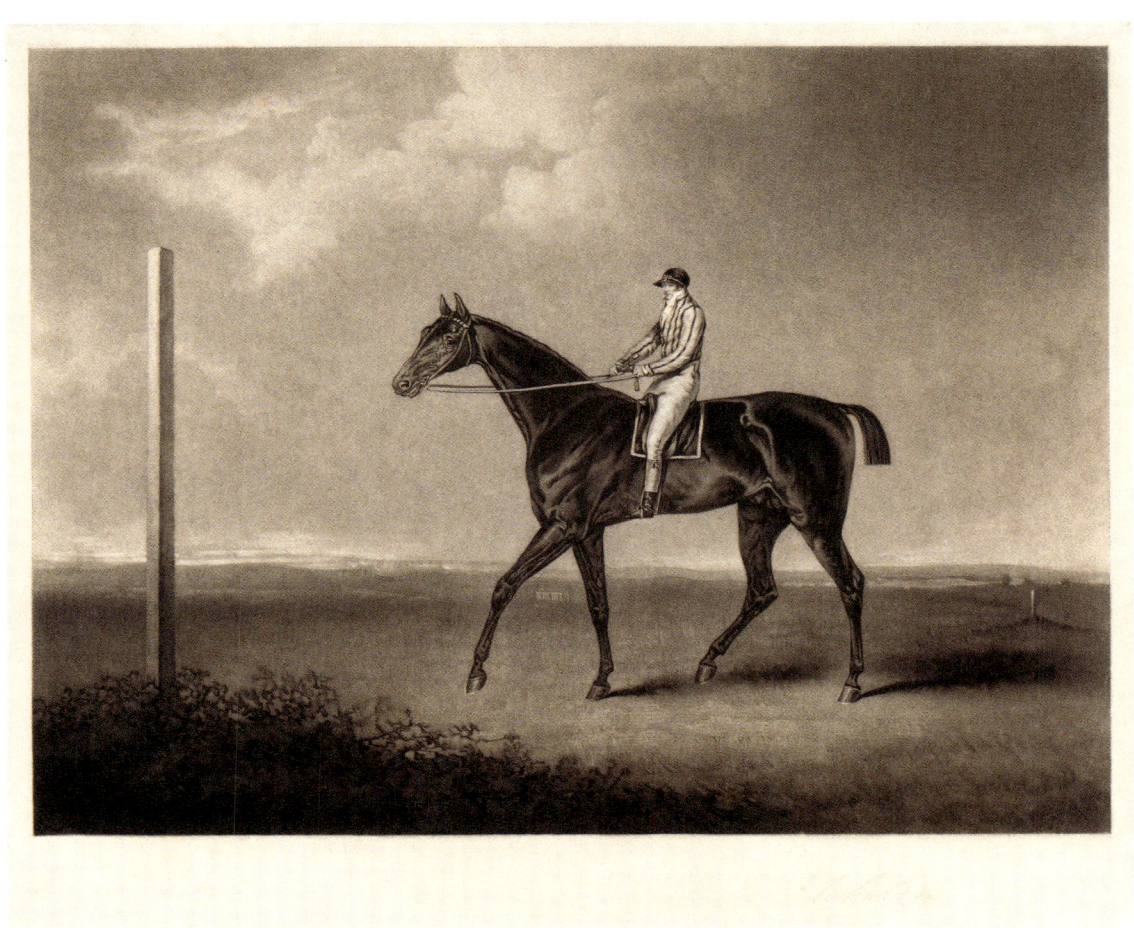

32

33. ISAAC CRUIKSHANK
Scottish, 1786–1811
London Sportsmen Recharging [from a set of four],
ca. 1800
Hand-colored etching, 5 ⅜ x 8 ¹¹⁄₁₆ in.
Paul Mellon Collection, 85.1282.1

Printed and Published by W. Davison Alnwick.

34. ISAAC CRUIKSHANK
Scottish, 1786–1811
London Sportsmen Shooting Flying [from a set of four],
ca. 1800
Hand-colored etching, 5 ⅜ x 8 ¹¹⁄₁₆ in.
Paul Mellon Collection, 85.1282.2

Printed and Published by W. Davison Alnwick.

35. RICHARD BARRETT DAVIS (after)
British, 1782–1854
The King's Harriers in Their Kennel, 1831
Hand-colored lithograph, 10 ¹⁵⁄₁₆ x 16 ⅛ in.
Paul Mellon Collection, 85.1352

*Painted by R. B. Davis, Animal Painter to the King.
Drawn on Stone by I. W. Giles. London: Published by
J. Dickinson, New Bond Stt. Jany. 10th. 1831. Printed
by Engelmann Graf & Coindet, Lithographers to His
Majesty.*

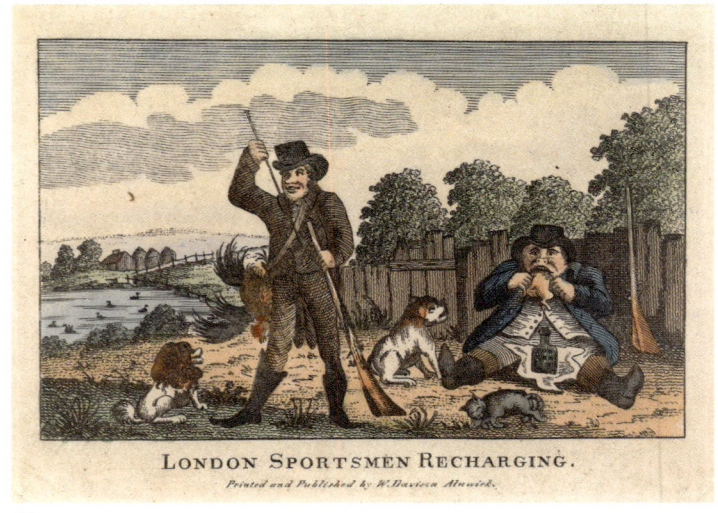

33

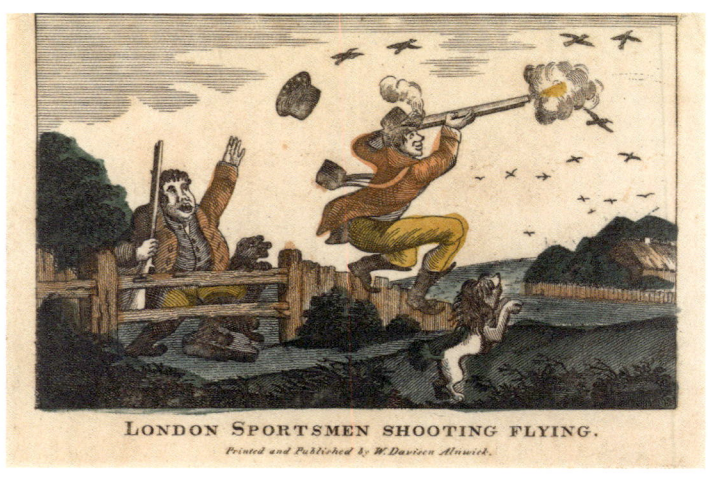

34

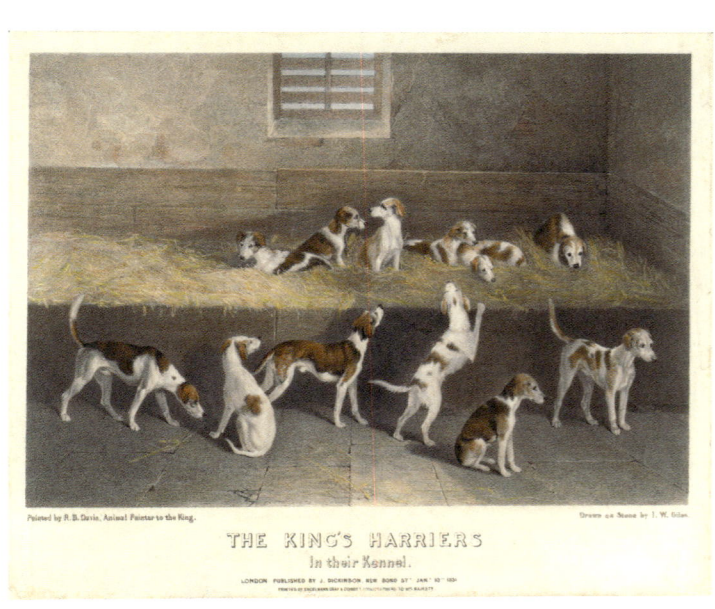

35

36. JOHN DOYLE (after)

Irish, 1797–1868

Mail Coach, Scene — Hyde Park Corner, 1828

Hand-colored aquatint with traces of etching,

17 5/16 x 12 11/16 in.

Paul Mellon Collection, 85.1327

J. Doyle Delt. R. G. Reeve. Sculpt. London. Thomas
McLean. 26 Haymarket, 1828.

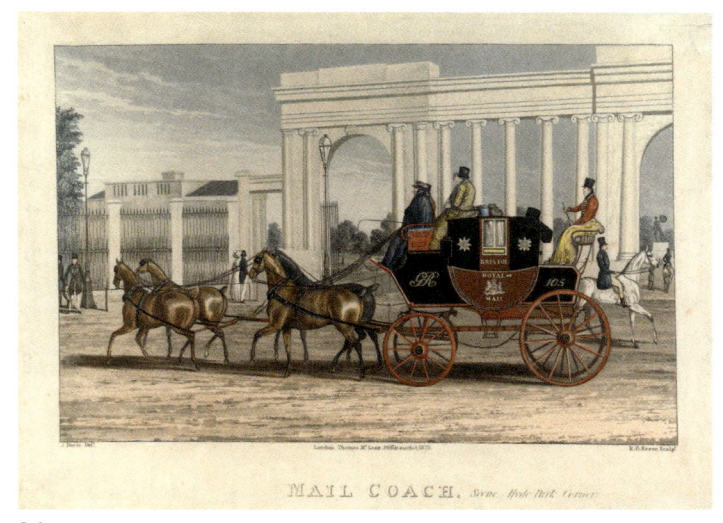

36

37. ROBERT FRANKLAND-RUSSELL

British, 1784–1849

Taking a Lead [from a set of seven], 1813

Hand-colored etching and aquatint, 8 3/16 x 10 11/16 in.

Paul Mellon Collection, 85.1285.5

"Taking a Lead, by which is understood Securing the
Privilege of breaking your neck first, and when / you fall,
of being rode over by a Hundred & Ninety nine of the
best fellows upon earth to a dead certainty."

London, Published July 1st. 1813 by J. Watson. 7. Vere
Street.

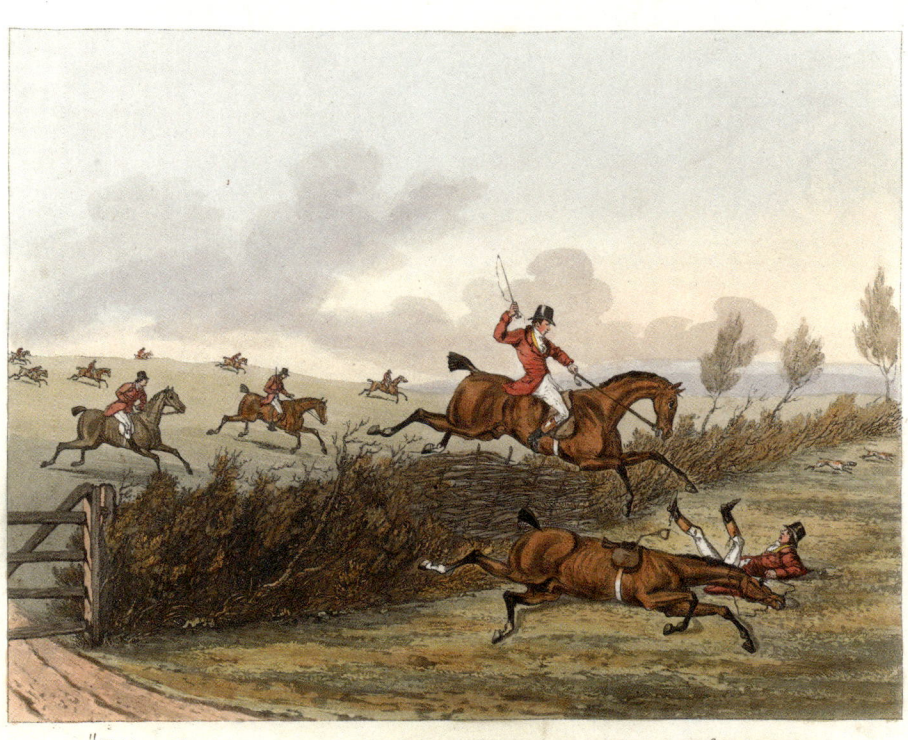

37

38. GEORGE GARRARD (after)
British, 1760–1826
Coach Horses, 1798
Hand-colored mezzotint, 18 ⅝ x 23 ¾ in.
Paul Mellon Collection, 85.1422

To Sir John Leicester Bart. This Plate of / Coach Horses, is respectfully dedicated by his obliged Servant, / John Jeffryes.

G, Garrard Pinxt. J. Young, Sculpt. London, Pubd. 1st. Jany. 1798, by John Jeffryes, Ludgate Hill.

[Coat of arms in center]

39. GEORGE GARRAD (after)
British, 1760–1826
Untitled [*A Blacksmith's Shed in the Yard of an Inn*], 1787
Hand-colored mezzotint, 18 ⅞ x 23 ⅞ in.
Paul Mellon Collection, 85.1421

To his Grace the Duke of Hamilton, Brandon &c. Knight of the most Ancient Order of the Thistle, / this Plate is respectfully Dedicated, by His Grace's much oblig'd and obedient Servant, / G. Garrard.

W. Pether fecit. London, Publish'd May 15th, 1787, by T. Simpson, St. Paul's Church-Yard.

[Coat of arms in center]

40. JOSEPH FRANCIS GILBERT (after)
British, 1792–1855
Priam Winning the Gold Cup in 1831, 1831
Hand-colored aquatint, 19 ⅝ x 28 ½ in.
Paul Mellon Collection, 85.1423

This Plate Representing / Priam Winning the Gold Cup in 1831, on Goodwood Race Course, / Is with permission Inscribed to his Grace, / Charles Duke of Richmond &c. &c. / by his obliged and obedient Servant, J. F. Gilbert.

Engraved by J. Clark. Painted and Published by J. F. Gilbert, Chichester.

[Coat of arms in center]

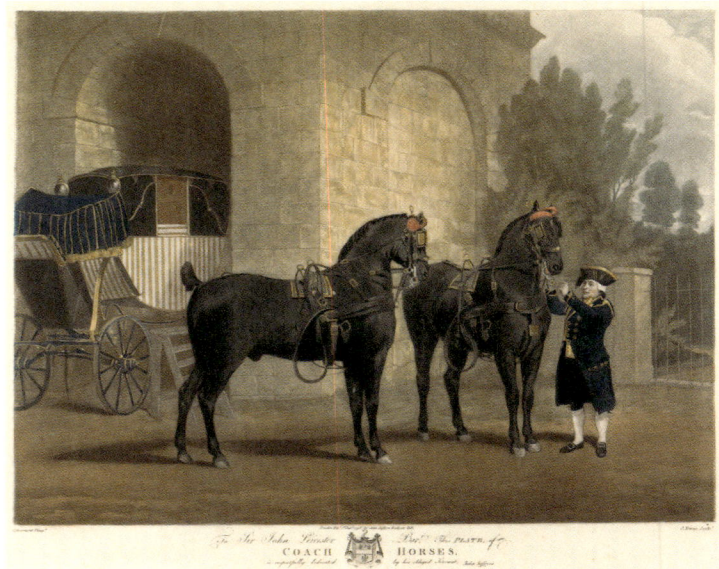

38

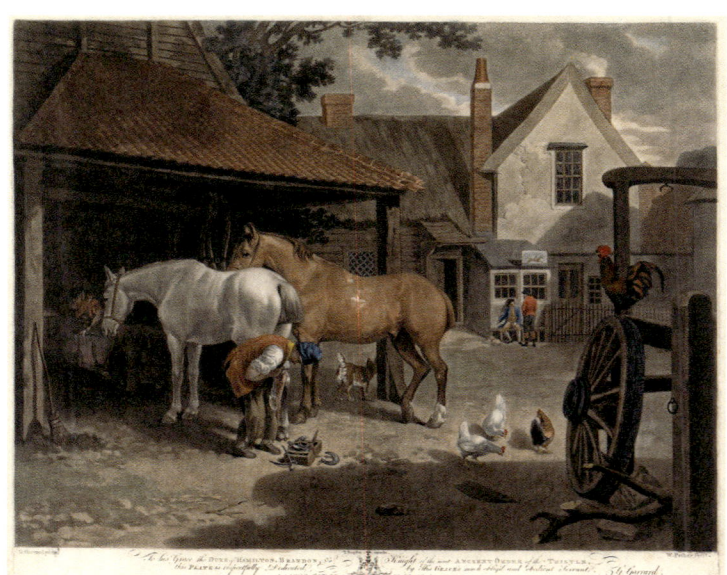

39

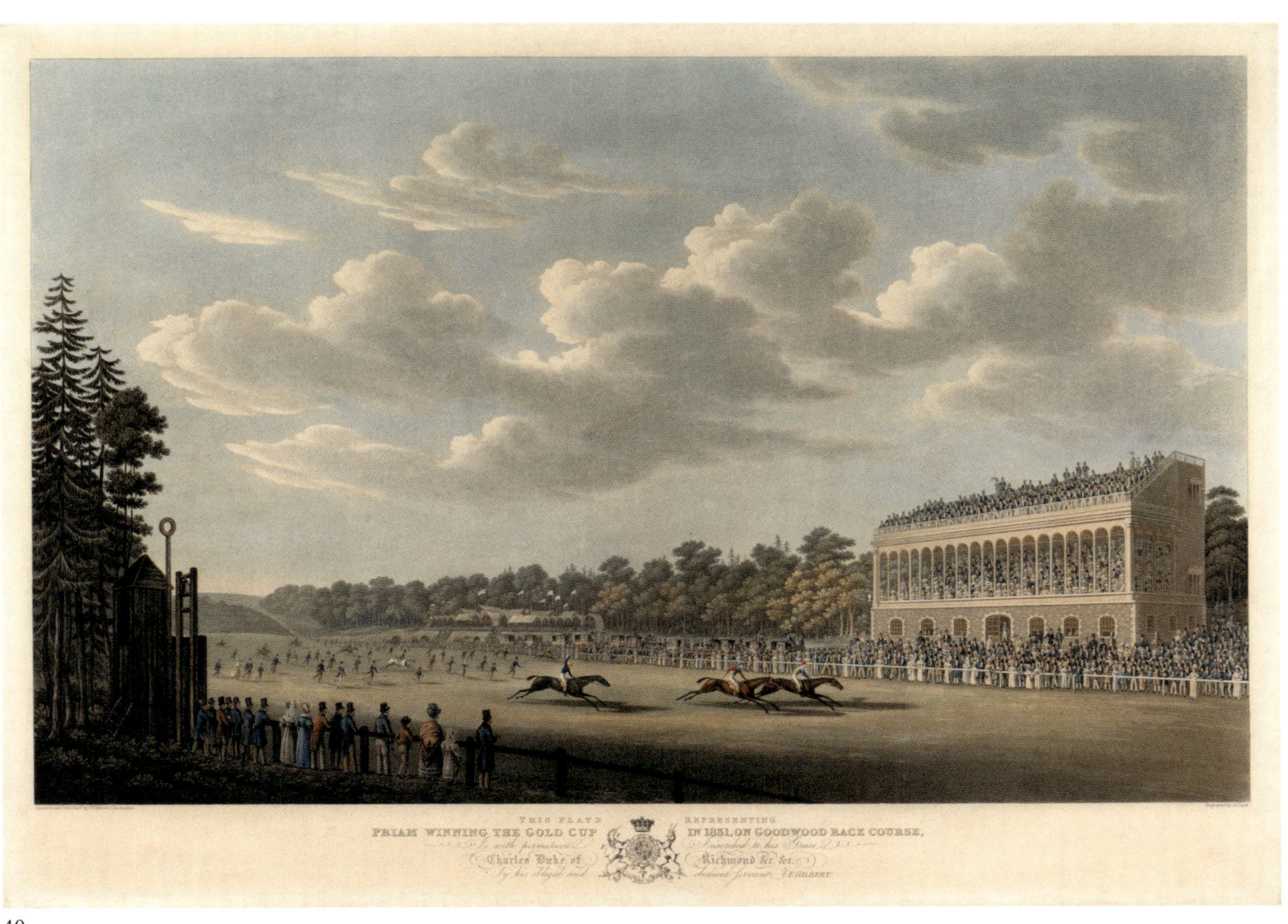

40

41. SAWREY GILPIN
British, 1733–1807
The Managed Horse [from *Characters of Horses*], 1793
Hand-colored etching, 5 9/16 x 6 7/8 in.
Paul Mellon Collection, 85.1287.1

S. Gilpin 1786

With publisher's wrapper: *Characters of horses, / Etched in 1760 / by / S. Gilpin, / Containing / The Managed Horse. The Pad. / The Race Horse. The Coach horse. / The Hunter. The Dray Horse. / The Road Horse. The Cart Horse. / London: published August 1st, 1793, by G. Garrard, Knightsbridge.*

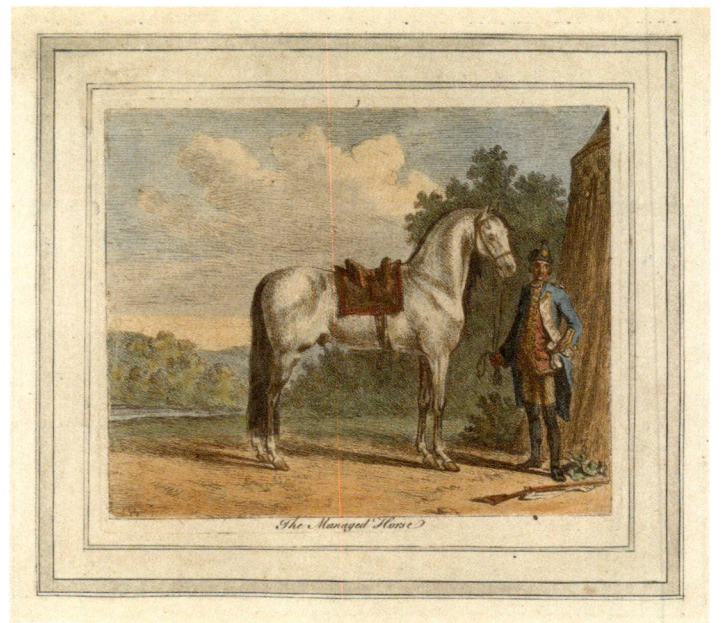

41

42. SAWREY GILPIN
British, 1733–1807
The Pad [from *Characters of Horses*], 1793
Hand-colored etching, 5 9/16 x 6 7/8 in.
Paul Mellon Collection, 85.1287.5

S. Gilpin 17—[86]

[With publisher's wrapper as in cat. no. 41]

43. SAWREY GILPIN
British, 1733–1807
The Cart Horse [from *Characters of Horses*], 1793
Hand-colored etching, 5 5/16 x 6 7/8 in.
Paul Mellon Collection, 85.1287.8

S. Gilpin 1786

[With publisher's wrapper as in cat. no. 41]

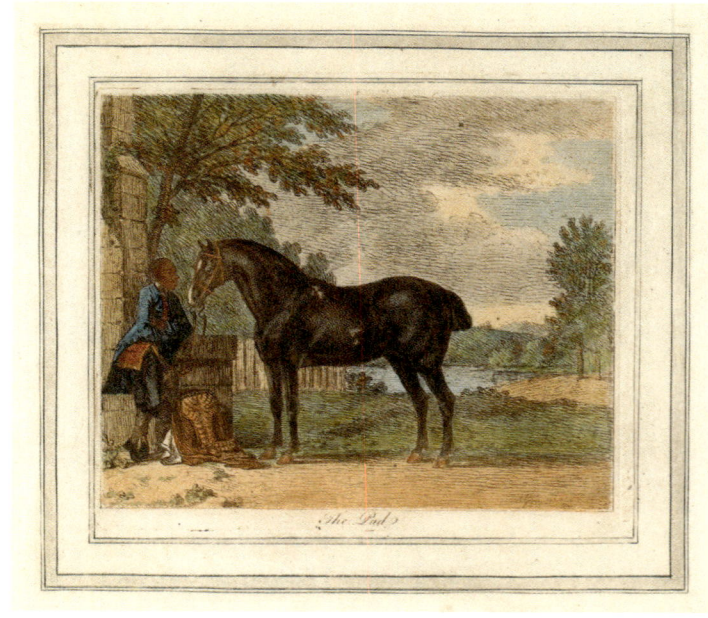

42

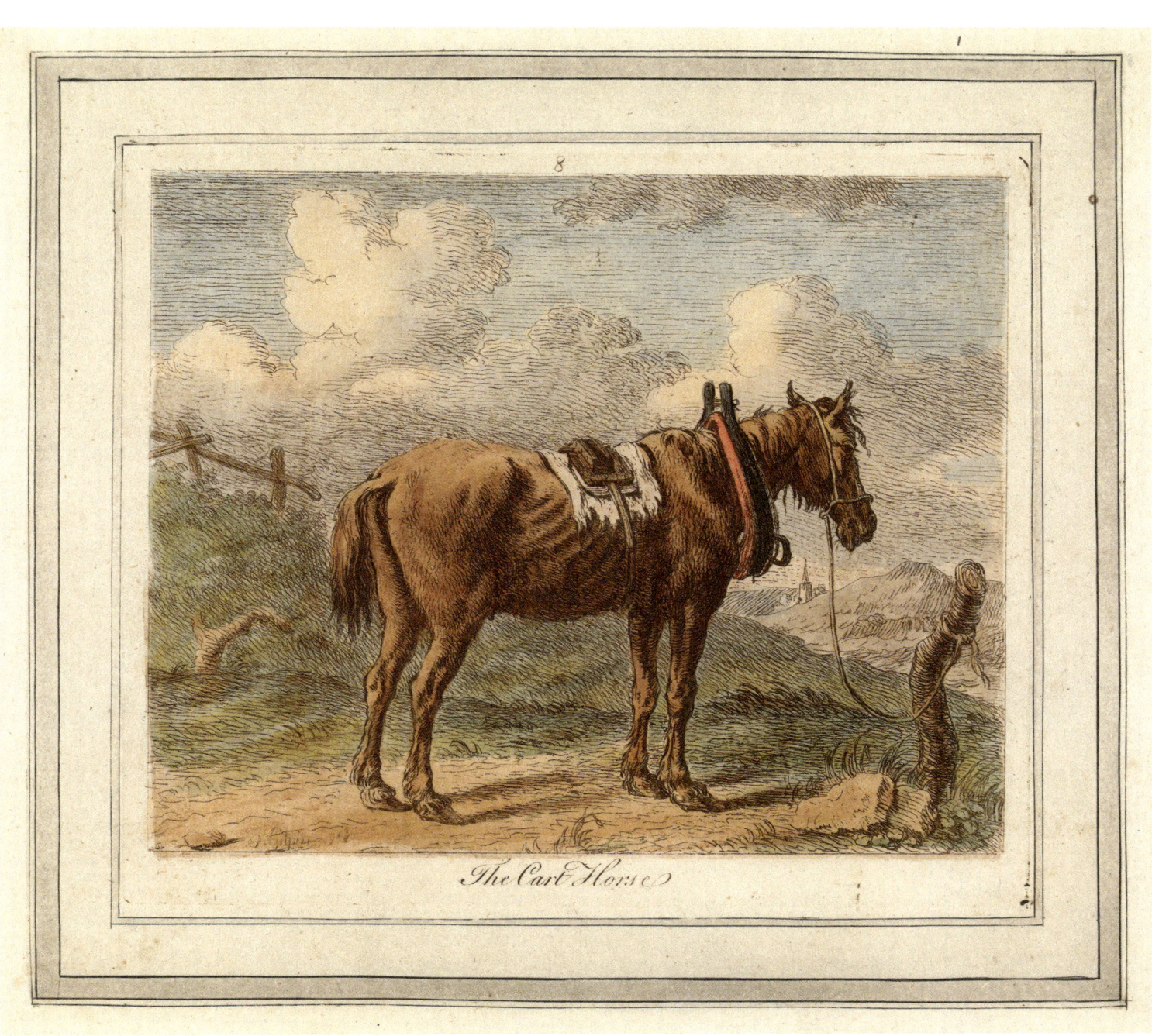

The Cart Horse

43

44. CHARLES COOPER HENDERSON (after)
British, 1803–1877
The Olden Time, Plate V [from *Fores's Coaching
Recollections*], 1846
Hand-colored aquatint, 21 ¼ x 29 ½ in.
Paul Mellon Collection, 85.1448

*From a Picture by C. C. Henderson Esqre. in the
possession of the Publishers.*

*Painted by C. C. Henderson. Engraved by J. Harris.
London: Published October 21st. 1846, by Messrs Fores,
at their Sporting & Fine Print Repository & Frame
Manufactory, 41, Piccadilly, Corner of Sackville St.*

*Publié par Goupil & Vibert 15 Boulevard Montmartre
Deposé a la Direction.*

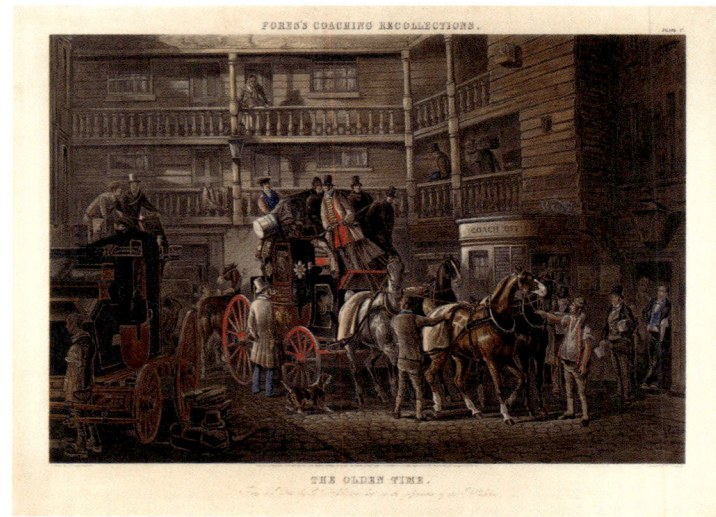

44

45. JOHN FREDERICK HERRING (after)
British, 1795–1865
Mango [proof from a set of thirty], 1837
Color-printed and hand-colored aquatint and etching
with touches of stipple engraving, 12 ⁵⁄₁₆ x 16 ¹¹⁄₁₆ in.
Paul Mellon Collection, 85.1381

*Rose by S. Day. / Mango, / the Winner of the Great St.
Leger Stakes at Doncaster, 1837. / 60 Subscribers — 13
Started. / Bred by Mr. Thornhill in 1834, and is own
Brother to Preserve, Marmalade, Morella, Pickle, and
Perfume. He is got by Emilius out of Mustard (bred by
Mr. Thornhill in 1824) by Merlin, / her Dam Morel, by
Sorcerer, out of Hornby Lass, by Buzzard — Puzzle by
Matchem — Princess by Herod — Blank — Spectator's
Dam. / The Property of C. C. Greville Esqre. / To
whom this Print by permission is most respectfully
dedicated by the Publishers / J. F. Herring and S & J.
Fuller. / London,*

*Painted by J. F Herring. Engraved by C. Hunt.
Published November 1837 by S & J. Fuller, at their
Sporting Gallery, 34, Rathbone Place.*

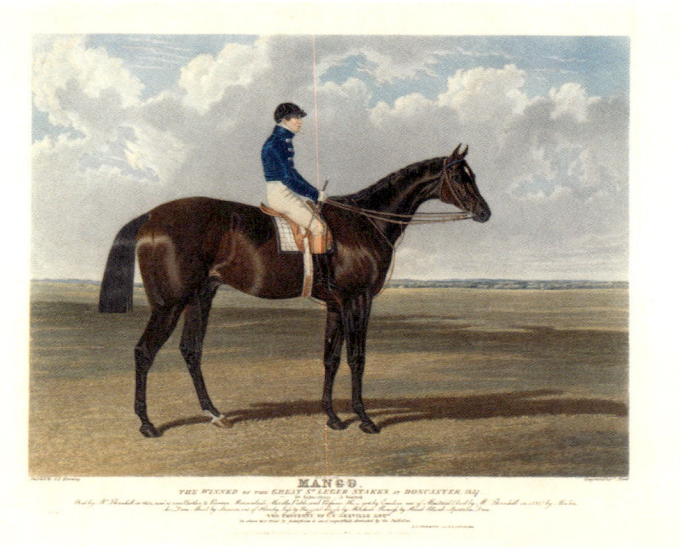

45

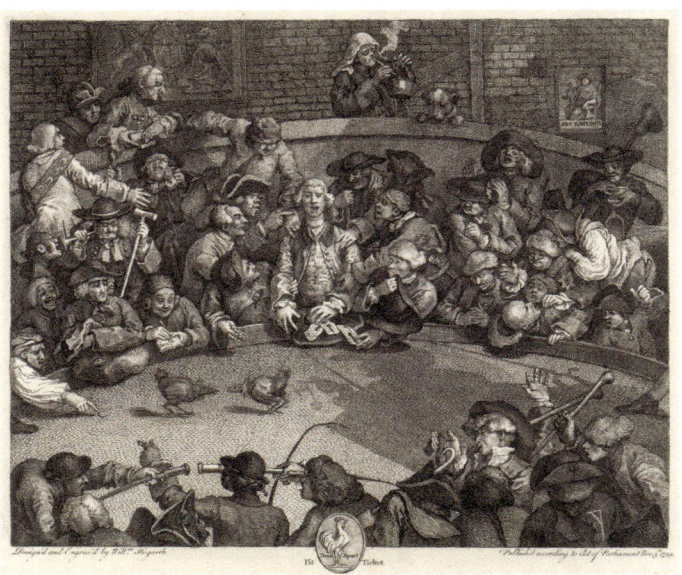

46

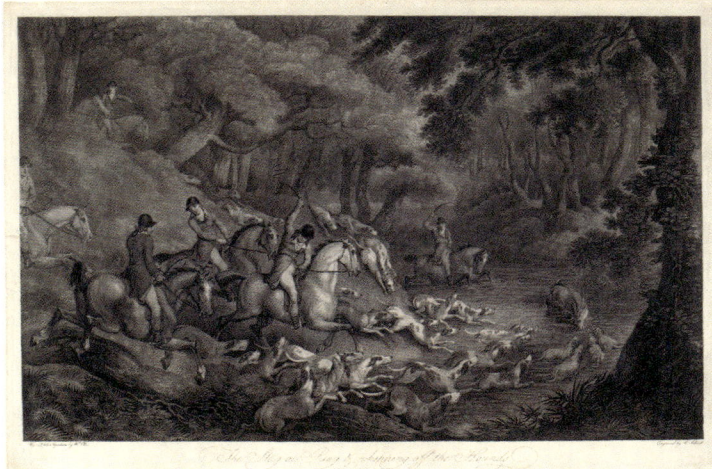

47

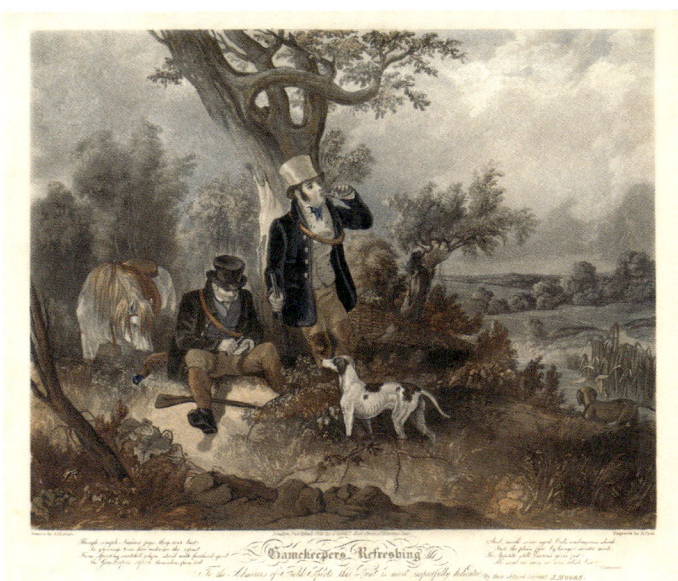

48

46. WILLIAM HOGARTH
British, 1697–1764
The Cock Pit, 1759
Etching and engraving, 12 ⅜ x 15 in.
Gift of Friends of Sporting Art, 2010.90

*Design'd and Engrav'd by Willm Hogarth. Publish'd
according to Act of Parliament Nov. 5th 1759*

47. SAMUEL HOWITT (after)
British, ca. 1765–1822
The Stag at Bay and Whipping Off the Hounds
[from a pair], 1802
Hand-colored aquatint, 18 ⅜ x 27 ¼ in.
Paul Mellon Collection   85.1425.2

*Howitt Del. Aquatint by Wm. Ellis. Engraved by
R. Pollard. Published Augt. 21, 1802, by R. Pollard
Printseller, Spafields London.*

48. SAMUEL JOHN EGBERT JONES (after)
British, 1820–1855
And 'neath Some Aged Oak's Umbrageous Shade
[from *Gamekeepers Refreshing*], 1829
Color-printed and hand-colored aquatint with
touches of stipple engraving and etching,
13 ¹³⁄₁₆ x 17 ⁷⁄₁₆ in.
Paul Mellon Collection, 85.1355

*And, 'neath some aged Oak's umbrageous shade, / Taste
the plain fare, by hunger sweeter made: / To Appetite,
still Exercise gives zest / The meal we earn we ever relish
best. / W. T. Moncrieff.*

Left of title: *Though simple Nature's joys, they ever
last, / In glowing Noon, how welcome the repast / From
Sporting snatch'd, when, stor'd with feather'd spoil, / The
Gamekeepers refresh themselves from toil,*

Below: *To the Admirers of Field Sports this Print is
most respectfully dedicated, / By their obliged Servant, /
J. Moore.*

*Painted by S. J. E. Jones. Engraved by H. Pyall.
London, Published 1829, by J. Moore, West Street, St.
Martin's Lane.*

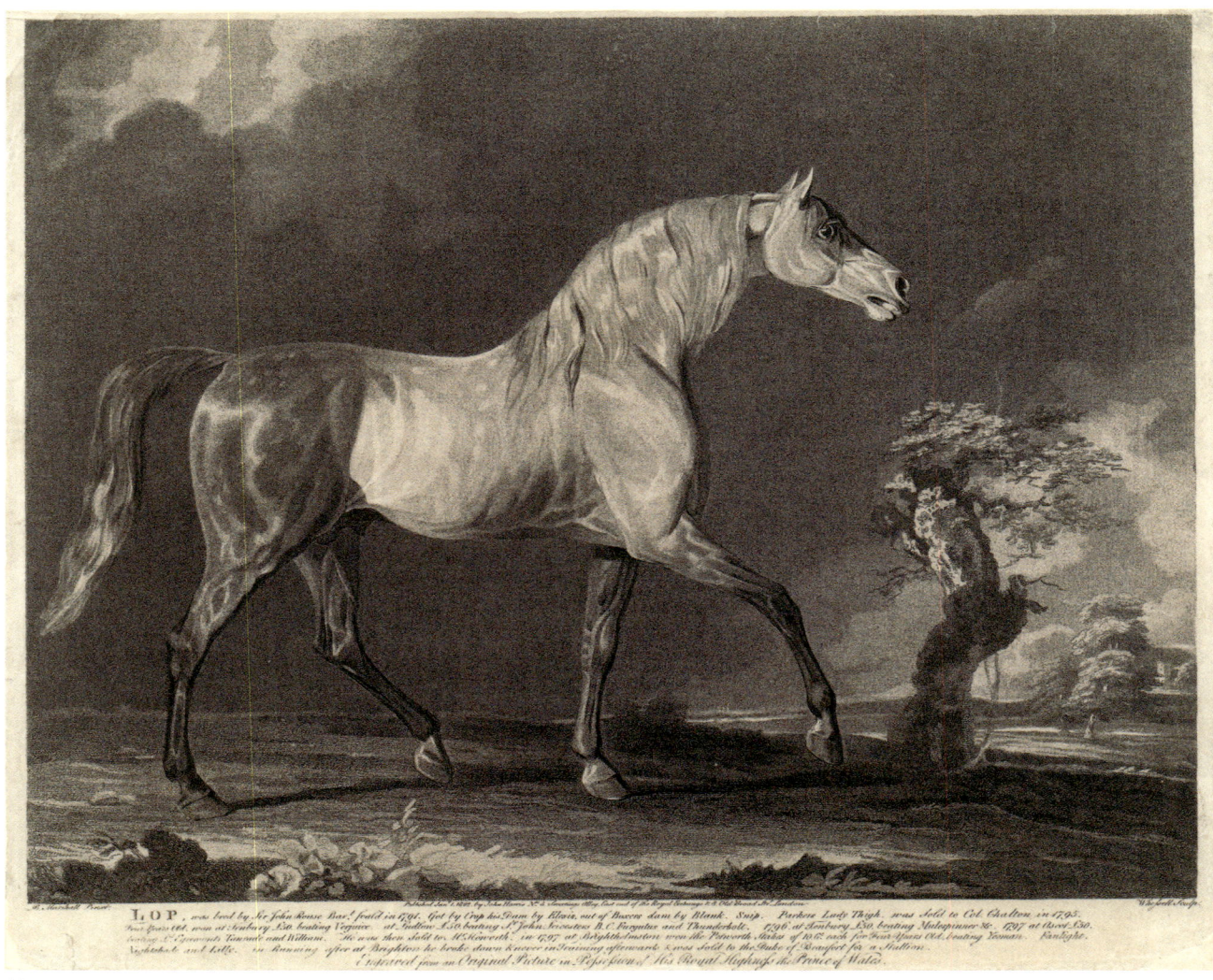

49

49. BENJAMIN MARSHALL (after)
British, 1767–1835
Lop, 1802
Stipple engraving, 15 ¾ x 19 ⅞ in.
Paul Mellon Collection, 85.1404

Lop, was bred by Sir John Rouse Bart. foal'd in 1791. Got by Crop his Dam by Elexis, out of Boxers dam by Blank. Snip. Parkers Lady Thigh. was sold to Col. Chalton in 1795, / Four Years Old, won at Tenbury £50 beating Verjuice. At Ludlon £50 beating Sr. John Leicesters B.C. Furgulus and Thunderbolt. 1796 at Tenbury £50. beating Mulespinner &c. 1797 at Ascot £50. / beating

Ld. Egremonts Tanrade and William. He was then Sold to Mr. Howorth. in 1797 at Brighthelmston won the Petworth Stakes of 10. Gs. each for Four year Old, beating Yeoman. Fanlight. / Nightshade and Lilly. In Running after at Brighton he broke down & Never in Training afterwards & was Sold to the Duke of Beaufort for a Stallion.

Engraved from an Original Picture in Possession of His Royal Highness the Prince of Wales. B. Marshall Pinxt. Whessell Sculp. Published Jany. 1. 1802, by John Harris Nos. 3. Sweetings Alley, East end of the Royal Exchange & 8. Old Broad Strt London.

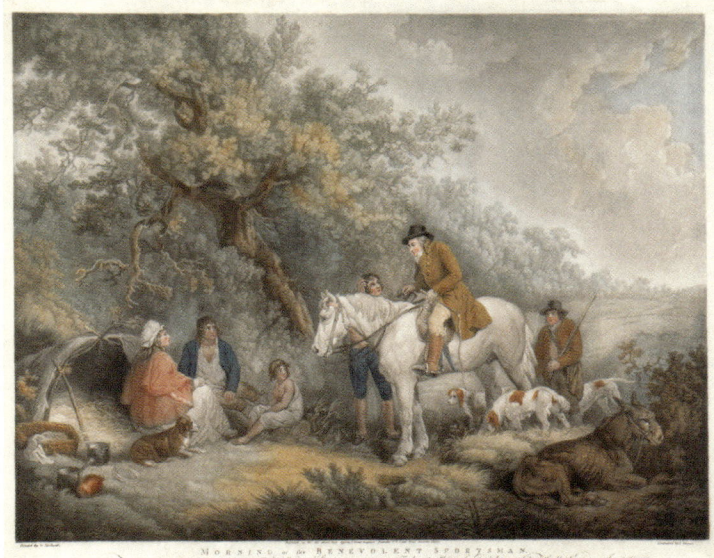

50

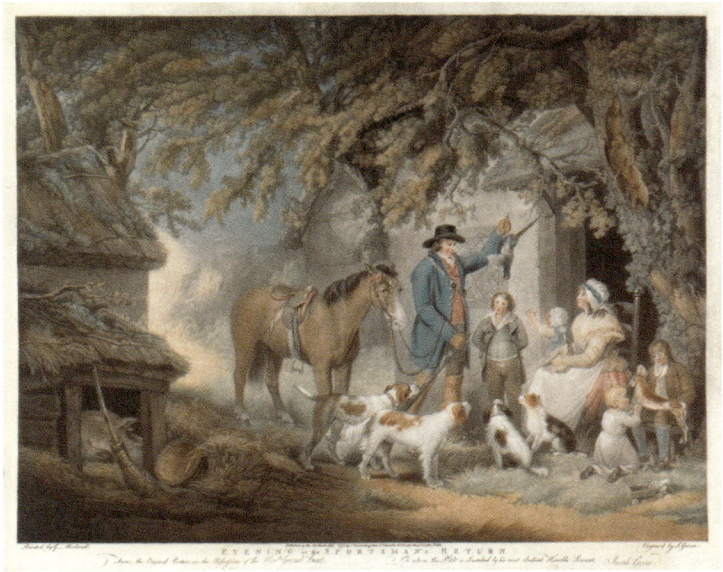

51

50. GEORGE MORLAND (after)
British, 1763–1804
Morning, or the Benevolent Sportsman [from a pair],
1795
Color-printed and hand-colored mezzotint,
19 ¾ x 25 in.
Paul Mellon Collection, 85.1405.1

From the Original Picture in the Possession of the Honble.
General Stuart. To whom this Plate is Inscribed by his
most obedient Humble Servant. / Joseph Grozer.

Painted by G. Morland. Engraved by I. Grozer. Published
as the Act directs May 1795. By I. Grozer Engraver &
Printseller No. 8. Castle Street Leicester Fields.

51. GEORGE MORLAND (after)
British, 1763–1804
Evening, or the Sportsman's Return [from a pair], 1795
Color-printed and hand-colored mezzotint,
19 ⅝ x 25 in.
Paul Mellon Collection, 85.1405.2

From the Original Picture in the Possession of the Honble.
General Stuart. To whom this Plate is Inscribed by his
most obedient Humble Servant. / Joseph Grozer.

Painted by G. Morland. Engraved by I. Grozer. Published
as the Act directs May 1795. by I. Grozer Engraver &
Printseller No. 8. Castle Street Leicester Fields.

52. JAMES NORTHCOTE (after)
British, 1746–1831
Lion and Snake, 1799
Etching and mezzotint, 20 x 25 ⅜ in.
Paul Mellon Collection, 85.1433

J. Northcote R. A. pinxt. S. W. Reynolds sculpt.
London Published Septr. 29. 1799, by James
Daniell & Co. No. 6, Great Charlotte Street,
Black Friars Road.

53. JAMES POLLARD
British, 1792–1867
Cottagers Hospitality to Travellers, or The Coach
Broke Down, 1819
Color-printed and hand-colored aquatint
with traces of etching, 23 ¹³⁄₁₆ x 17 ¹¹⁄₁₆ in.
Paul Mellon Collection, 85.1358

Drawn & Engraved by James Pollard

54. JAMES POLLARD (after)
British, 1792–1867
The Elephant and Castle on the Brighton Road,
1826
Hand-colored aquatint, 23 ⅞ x 31 ¾ in.
Paul Mellon Collection, 85.1434

Painted by James Pollard. Engraved by Theodore
Fielding. London, Published, Feb: 7, 1826, by.
J. Watson, 7. Vere Street.

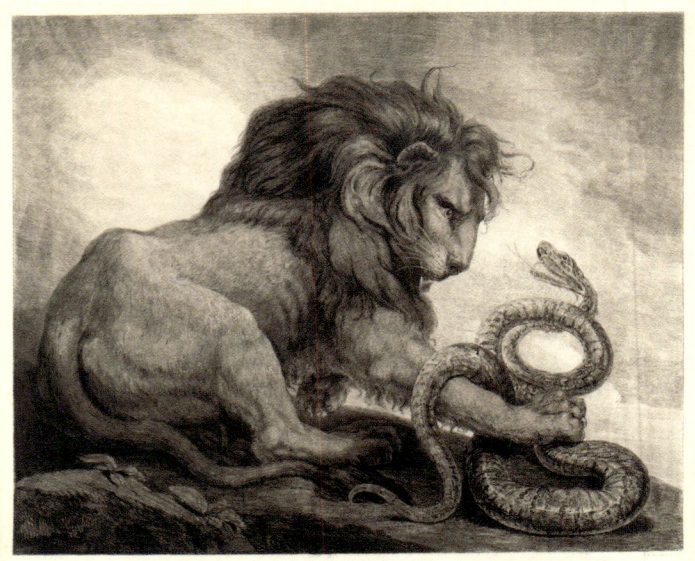

52

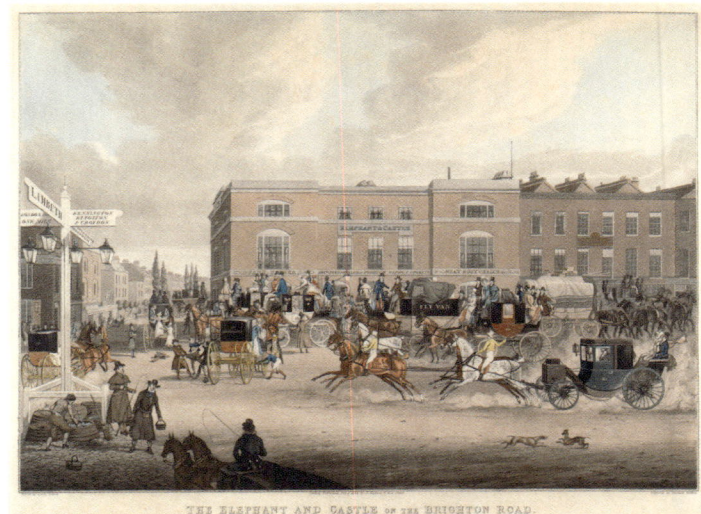

53

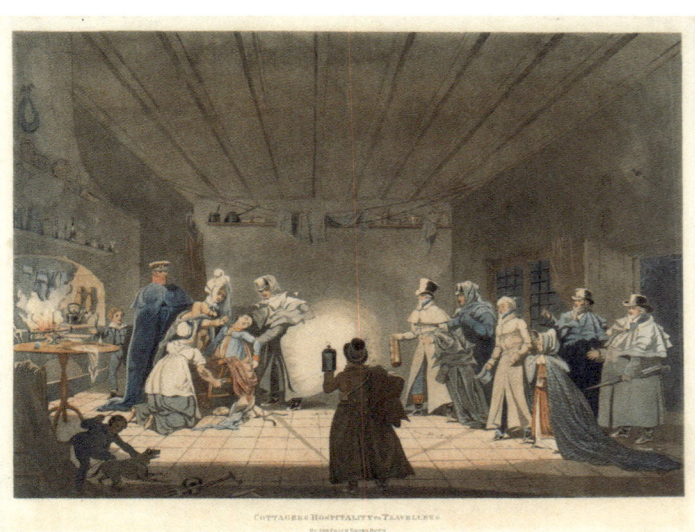

54

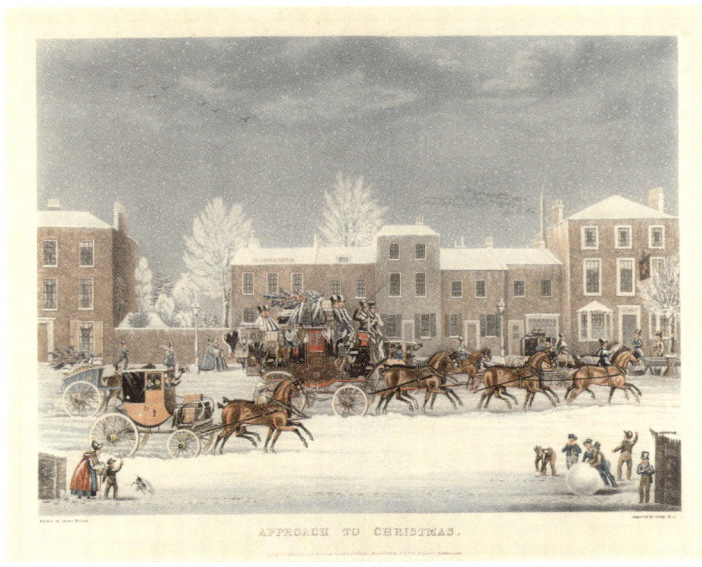

55

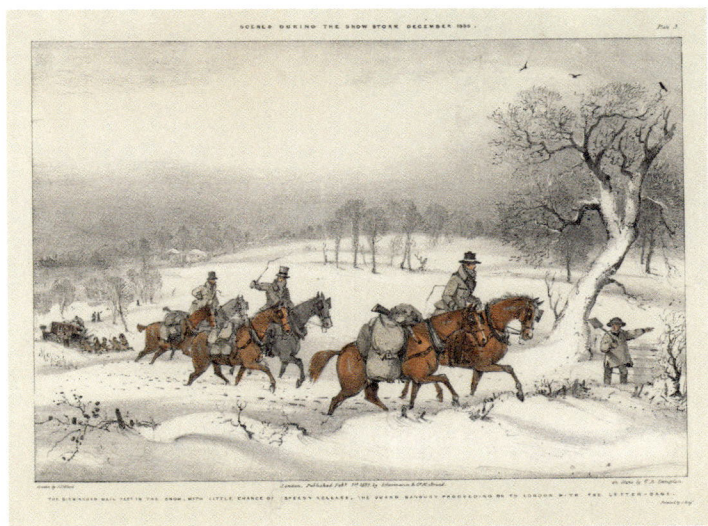

56

55. JAMES POLLARD (after)
British, 1792–1867
Approach to Christmas, 1831
Color-printed and hand-colored etching and aquatint,
15 ⅛ x 20 ½ in.
Paul Mellon Collection, 85.1391

Painted by James Pollard. Engraved by George Hunt.
London, Published by J. Moore at his Picture Frame
Manufactory. No. 1 West St. Upper St. Martins Lane.

56. JAMES POLLARD (after)
British, 1792–1867
The Birmingham Mail Fast in the Snow, Plate 3 [from
Scenes during the Snow Storm, December 1836], 1837
Hand-colored lithograph, 9 ¹³⁄₁₆ x 15 in.
Paul Mellon Collection, 85.1360.3

The Birmingham Mail Fast in the Snow, with Little
Chance of a Speedy Release, The Guard Banbury
Proceeding on to London with the Letter-Bags.

Drawn by J. Pollard., on Stone by G. B. Campion.
Printed by J. Graf. London, Published Feby 1st. 1837, by
Ackermann & Co 96, Strand.

57. PHILIP REINAGLE (after)
British, 1749–1833
Fowling [from a pair], 1810
Mezzotint, 18 x 22 in.
Paul Mellon Collection, 85.1409.2

Painted by P. Reinagle. Engraved by W. W. Barney.
From the Original Picture in the Collection of Lord
Middleton. Published Jany. 1st. 1810, by Thos. Palser,
Surrey Side Westminster Bridge.

58. THOMAS ROWLANDSON
British, 1756 / 57–1827
The Death [from a set of three], 1789
Hand-colored etching and aquatint, 10 ¹¹⁄₁₆ x 14 ⅜ in.
Paul Mellon Collection, 85.1337.3

London, Published Feby. 1st 1789 by S. W. Fores,
No. 3 Piccadilly.

59. THOMAS ROWLANDSON
British, 1756–1827
The Breakfast [from a set of three], 1789
Hand-colored etching and aquatint, 10 ¾ x 14 ½ in.
Paul Mellon Collection, 85.1337.1

London, Published Feby. 1st 1789 by S. W. Fores,
No. 3. Piccadilly.

Inscribed: *Rowlandson. 1789*

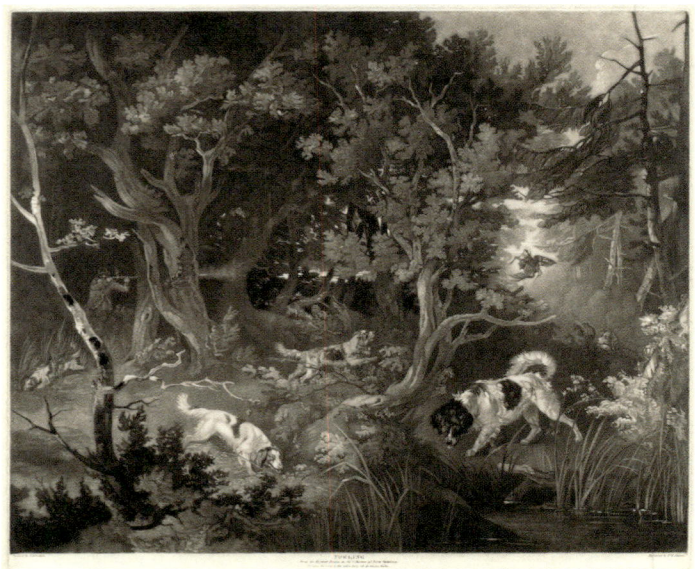

57

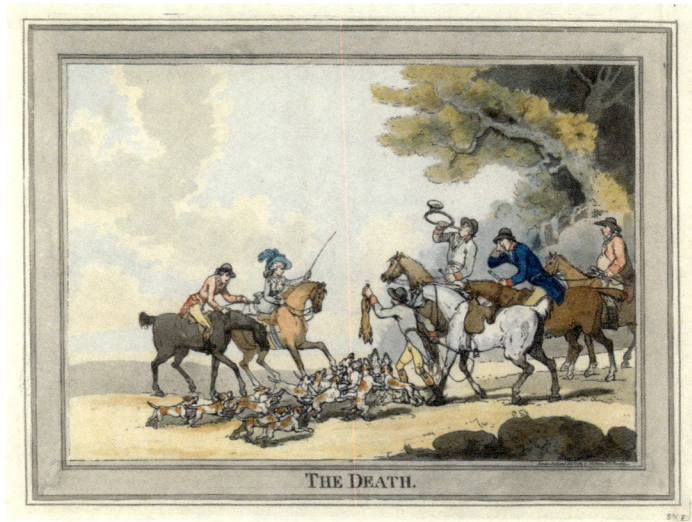

58

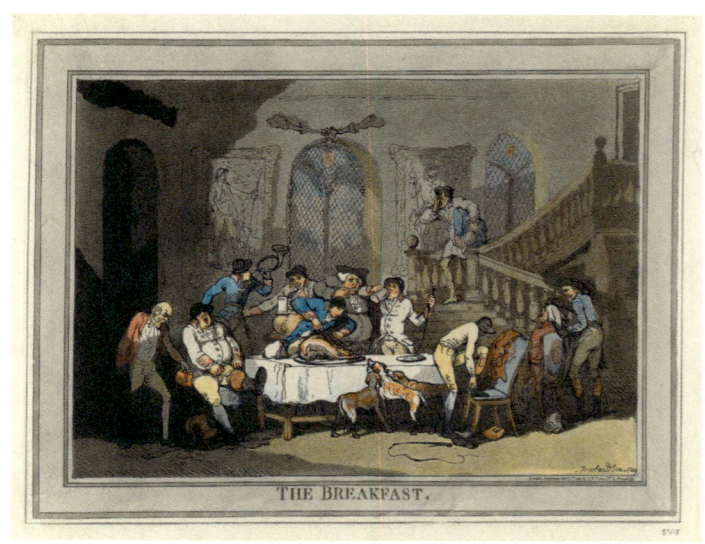

59

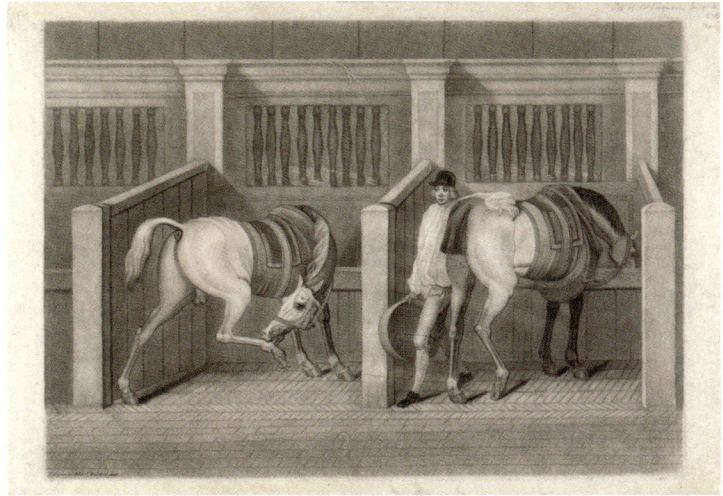

60

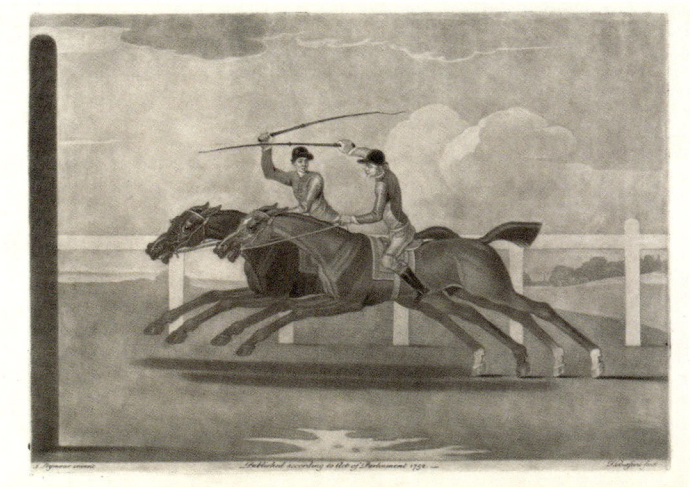

61

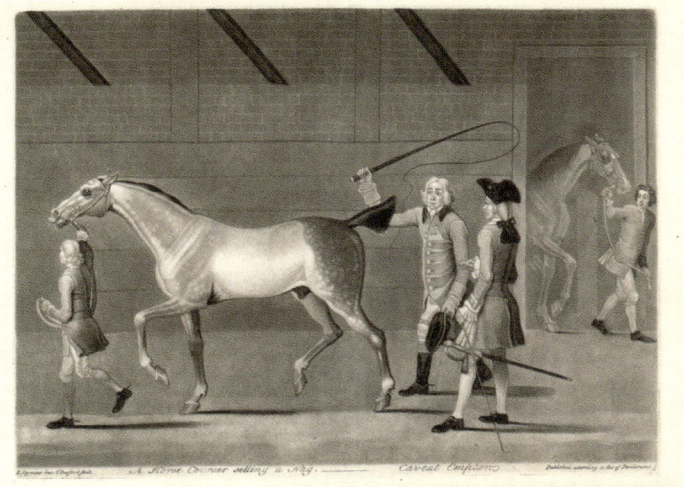

62

60. JAMES SEYMOUR (after)
British, 1702–1752
Two Horses, Rugged in Stalls [from a set of twelve], 1752
Mezzotint, 9 ¹³⁄₁₆ x 13 ¹³⁄₁₆ in.
Paul Mellon Collection, 85.1339.1

J. Seymour delin. T. Burford fecit. [Published by Bowles and Carver]

61. JAMES SEYMOUR (after)
British, 1702–1752
Two Jockeys Racing Neck and Neck to the Winning-Post [from a set of twelve], 1752
Mezzotint, 9 ⅞ x 13 ⅞ in.
Paul Mellon Collection, 85.1339.10

J Seymour invent. Published according to Act of Parliament 5 1752. T. Burford fecit. [Published by Bowles and Carver]

62. JAMES SEYMOUR (after)
British, 1702–1752
A Horse Courser Selling a Nag — Caveat Emptor [from a set of twelve], 1752
Mezzotint, 9 ⅞ x 13 ⅞ in.
Paul Mellon Collection, 85.1339.5

J. Seymour inv. T Burford fecit. Published according to Act of Parliament 5. [Published by Bowles and Carver]

63. JAMES SEYMOUR
British, 1702–1752
*Childers, the Fleetest Horse that Ever Ran at
Newmarket* [from a set of twelve], 1773
Etching, 6 x 10 ⁵⁄₁₆ in.
Paul Mellon Collection, 85.1250

*Printed for Carington Bowles, Map & Printseller,
No. 69 in St. Pauls Church Yard, London. Published
3rd Jany. 1773*

64. JAMES SEYMOUR (after)
British, 1702–1752
*Making a Cast at a Fault; Les Chiens cherchans a
retrouver La Piste* [from a set of four], 1779
Mezzotint, 14 ¼ x 20 in.
Paul Mellon Collection, 85.1394.3

*J. Seymour Pnxt. T. Burford Fecit. Published
according to Act of Parliament by R. Sayer &
J Bennett, Map & Printsellers No. 53 Fleet Street,
1st July 1779*

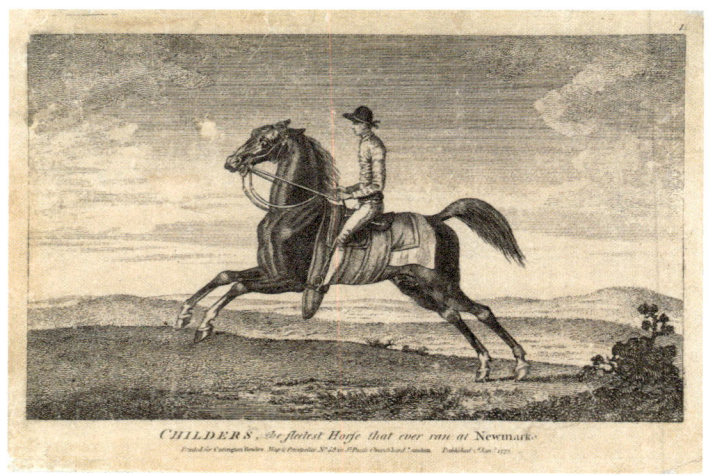

63

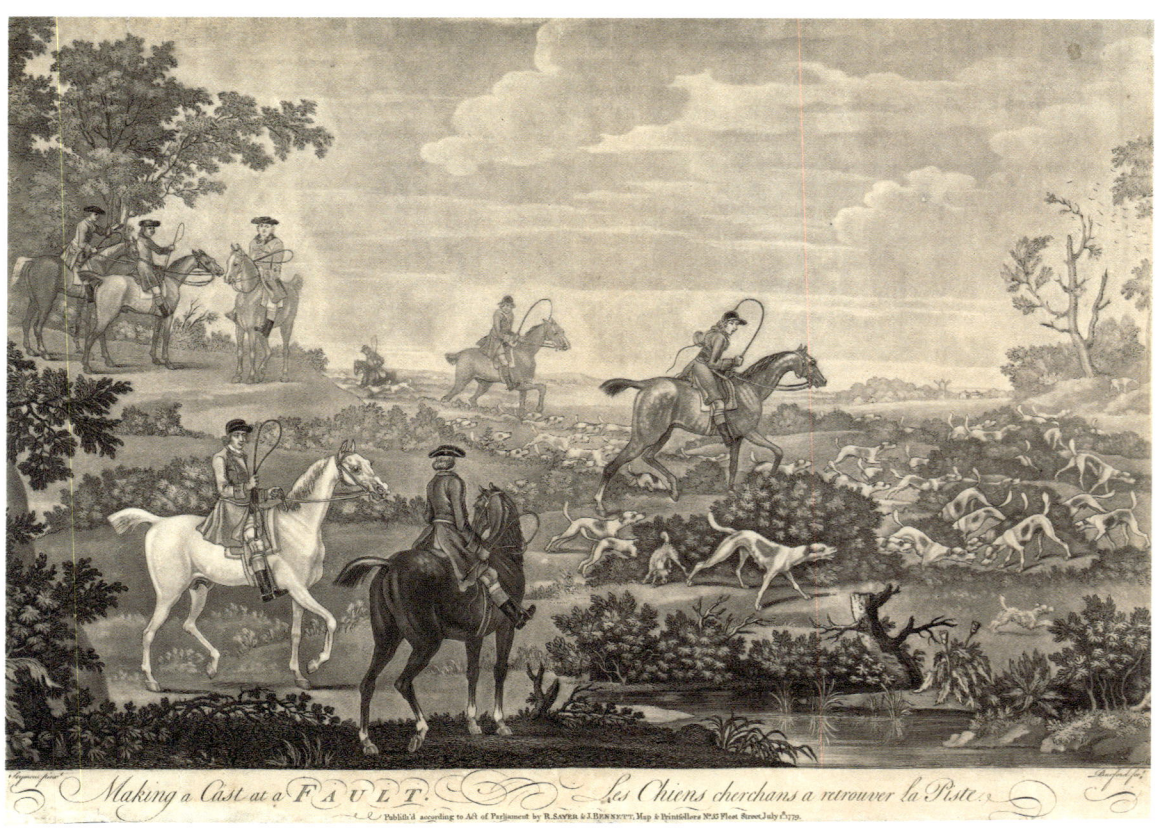

64

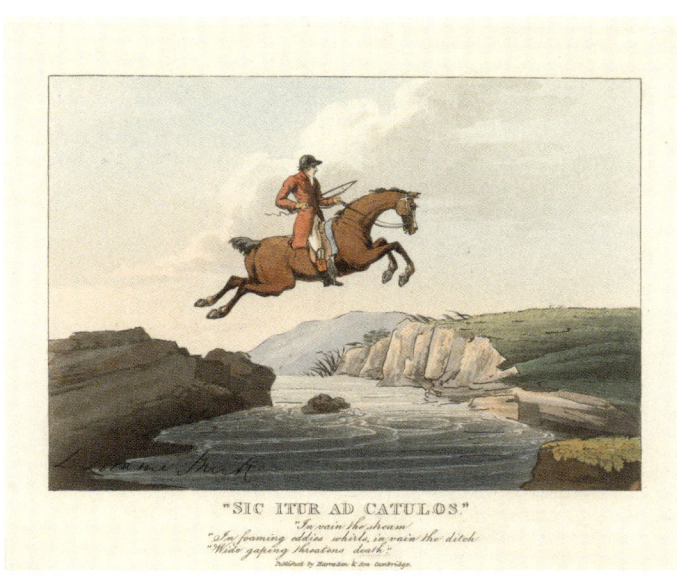

65

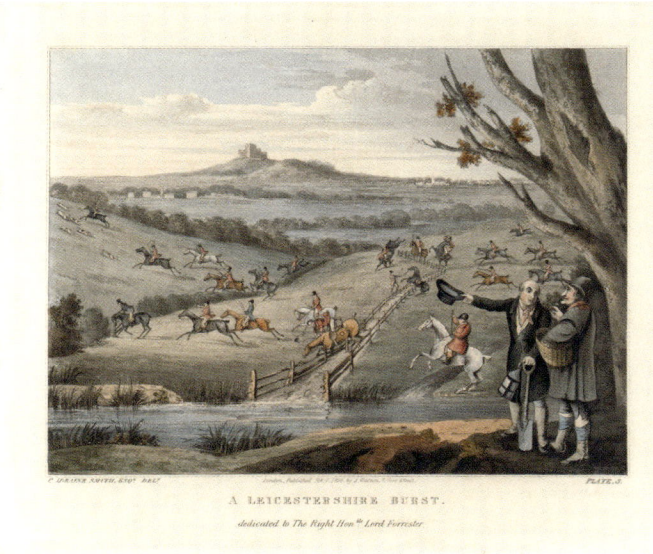

66

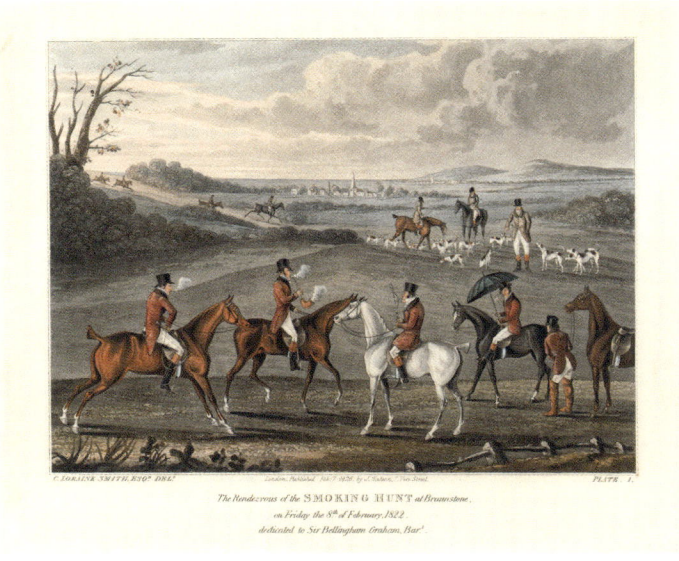

67

65. CHARLES LORAINE SMITH
British, 1751–1835
"Sic Itur ad Catulos" [from *Sketches for College
Rooms*], ca. 1820
Hand-colored etching and aquatint, 5 ¹⁵⁄₁₆ x 8 ½ in.
Paul Mellon Collection, 85.1289.4

"Sic Itur ad Catulos" / *"In vain the stream* / *"In foaming
eddies whirls, in vain the ditch* / *"Wide gaping threatens
death."*

Inscribed: *C. Loraine Smith. Published by Harraden &
Son Cambridge.*

66. CHARLES LORAINE SMITH
British, 1751–1835
A Leicestershire Burst, Plate 3 [from a set of six], 1826
Hand-colored aquatint and etching, 9 ⅝ x 13 in.
Paul Mellon Collection, 85.1341.3

A Leicestershire Burst. / *dedicated to the Right Honble.
Lord Forrester.*

*C. Loraine Smith, Esqr. Delt. London, Published Feb: 7,
1826. by J. Watson, 7, Vere Street.*

67. CHARLES LORAINE SMITH
British, 1751–1835
*The Rendezvous of the Smoking Hunt at Braunstone,
Plate 1.* [from a set of six], 1826
Hand-colored aquatint and etching, 9 ⅝ x 13 in.
Paul Mellon Collection, 85.1341.1

*The Rendezvous of the Smoking Hunt at
Braunstone,* / *on Friday the 8th. of February,
1822.* / *dedicated to Sir Bellingham Graham, Bart.*

*C. Loraine Smith, Esqr. Delt. London, Published Feb: 7.
1826. by J. Watson, 7. Vere Street.*

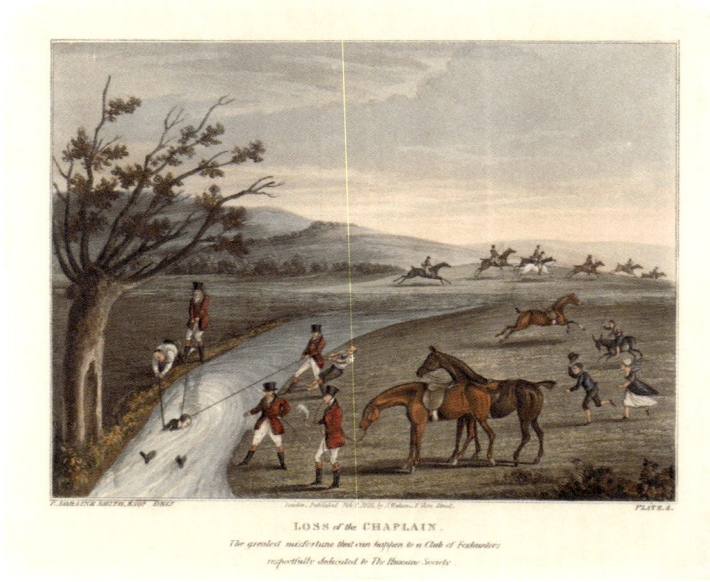

68

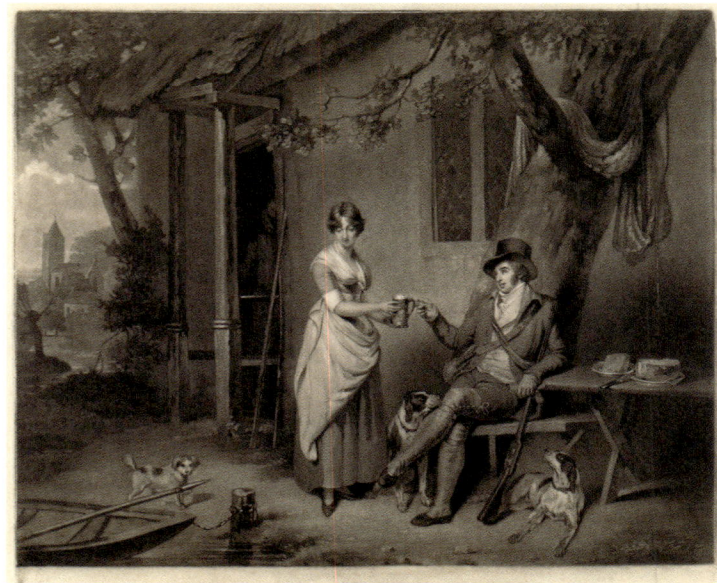

69

68. CHARLES LORAINE SMITH
British, 1751–1835
Loss of the Chaplain, Plate 4 [from a set of six], 1826
Hand-colored aquatint and etching, 9 ½ x 13 in.
Paul Mellon Collection, 85.1341.4

*Loss of the Chaplain. / The greatest misfortune that can
happen to a Club of Foxhunters. / respectfully dedicated
to The Humane Society.*

*C. Loraine Smith, Esqr. Delt. London, Published Feb: 7.
1826, by J. Watson, 7. Vere Street.*

69. JOHN RAPHAEL SMITH
British, 1752–1812
Sportsman's Repast [from a pair], 1801
Mezzotint, proof before letters, 17 x 21 in.
Paul Mellon Collection, 85.1410.2

70. GEORGE STUBBS
British, 1724–1806
Anatomy of the Horse, 1766
Bound book with paper and book binding [plate IX,
opposite page 32], 12 x 14 ¼ in.
Virginia Museum of Fine Arts Library,
Rare Book Collection

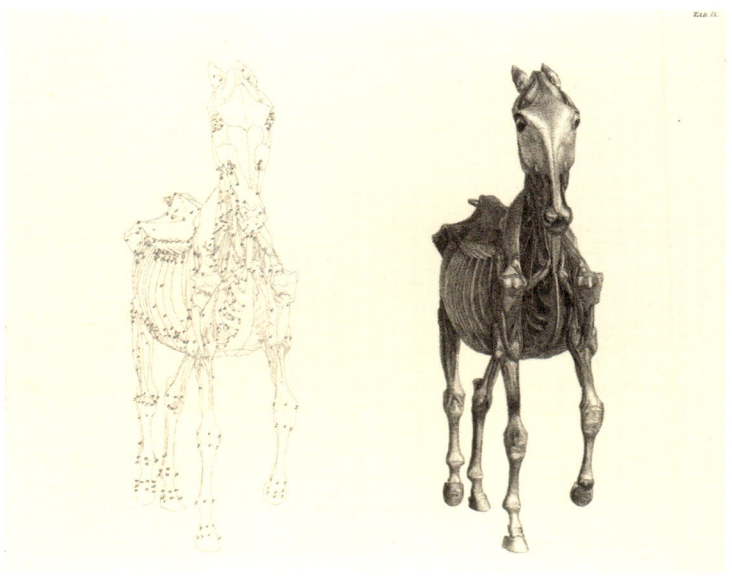

70

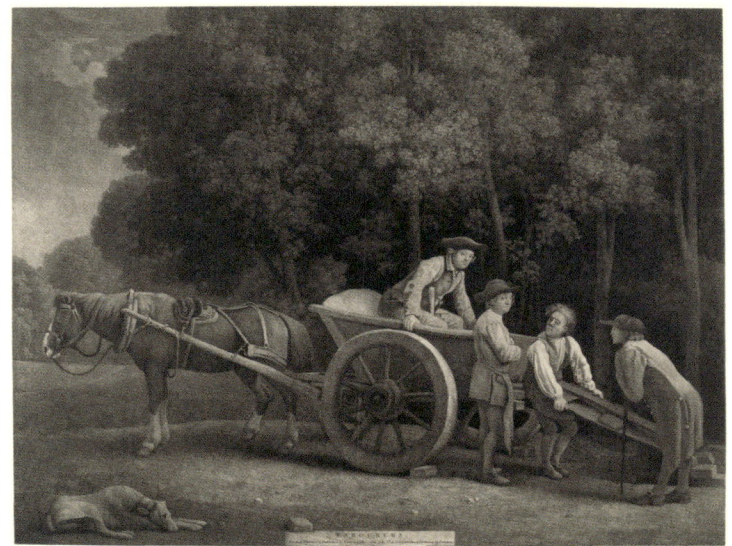

71

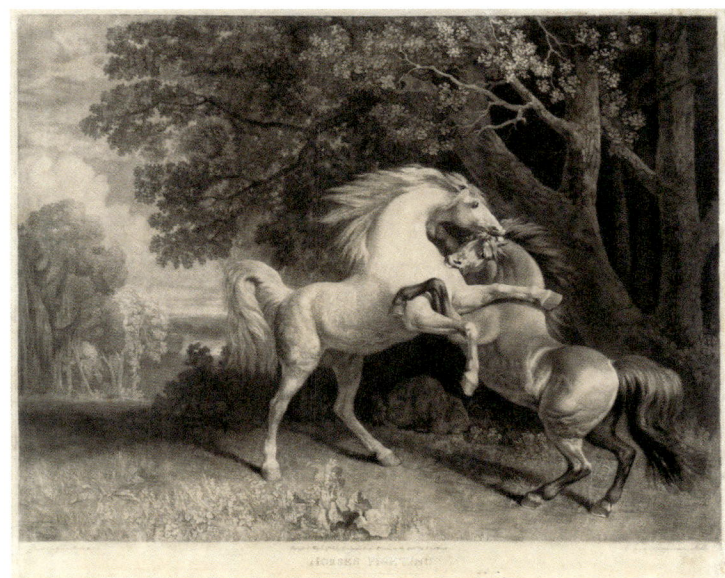

72

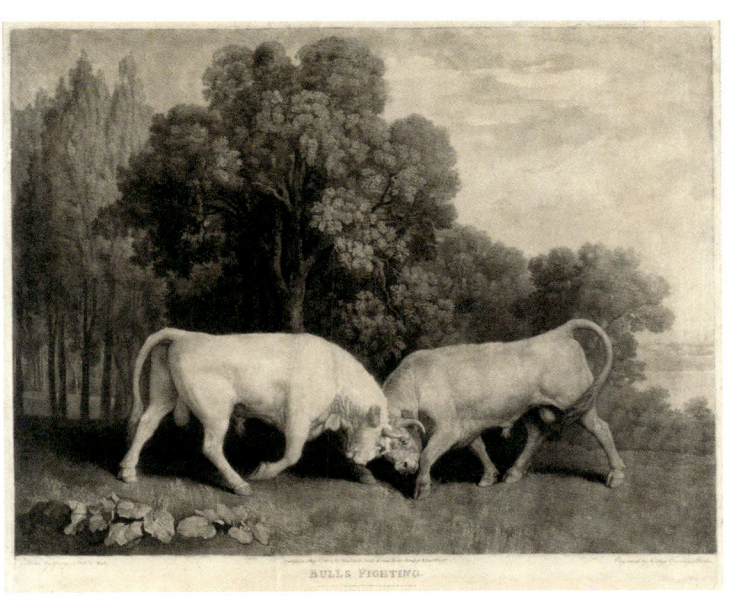

73

71. GEORGE STUBBS
British, 1724–1806
Labourers, 1789
Mezzotint with aquatint, 20 ½ x 27 ⅜ in.
Paul Mellon Collection, 85.1436

Painted, Engraved & Published by Geo. Stubbs. 1 Jany.
1789, No. 24, Somerset Street, Portman Sq. London.

72. GEORGE STUBBS (after)
British, 1724–1806
Horses Fighting [from a pair], 1788
Mezzotint, 19 ⅝ x 24 ⅛ in.
Paul Mellon Collection, 85.1437.2

Painted by George Stubbs R.A. Engraved by
George Townley Stubbs. Published May 1st. 1788,
by Benjamin Beale Evans, in the Poultry, London.

73. GEORGE STUBBS (after)
British, 1724–1806
Bulls Fighting [from a pair], 1788
Mezzotint, 19 ⅝ x 24 ⅛ in.
Paul Mellon Collection, 85.1437.1

Painted by George Stubbs R.A. Engraved by
George Townley Stubbs. Published May 1st. 1788
by Benjamin Beale Evans in the Poultry London.

74. GEORGE STUBBS (after)
British, 1724–1806
Sharke [from a set sixteen], 1794
Color-printed stipple engraving, 16 x 19 in.
Paul Mellon Collection, 85.1413

George Stubbs pinxt. Geo. Townly Stubbs Sculpt.
Engraver to His R.H. the Prince of Wales London,
Published: May 20. 1794, by Messrs. Stubbs, Turf
Gallery, Conduit Street.

75. FRANCIS CALCRAFT TURNER (after)
British, ca. 1782–1846
The Fair [from a pair], 1830
Hand-colored aquatint with touches of etching,
9 ¾ x 11 ¹³⁄₁₆ in.
Paul Mellon Collection, 85.1342.2

Painted by F. C. Turner. Engraved by H. Pyall.
Published 1830. by R. Ackermann & Co. 96,
Strand, London.

76. FRANCIS CALCRAFT TURNER (after)
British, ca. 1782–1846
The Bargain [from a pair], 1830
Hand-colored aquatint with touches of etching,
9 ¾ x 11 ¹³⁄₁₆ in.
Paul Mellon Collection, 85.1342.1

Painted by F. C. Turner. Engraved by H. Pyall.
Published 1830. by R. Ackermann & Co. 96,
Strand, London.

77. FRANCIS CALCRAFT TURNER (after)
British, ca. 1782–1846
The Death, 1842
Hand-colored aquatint, 22 ⅜ x 33 ½ in.
Paul Mellon Collection, 85.1450

Published by W. Stevens, Engraver & Printer,
Cheltenham.

[Engraved by John E. Ferneley]

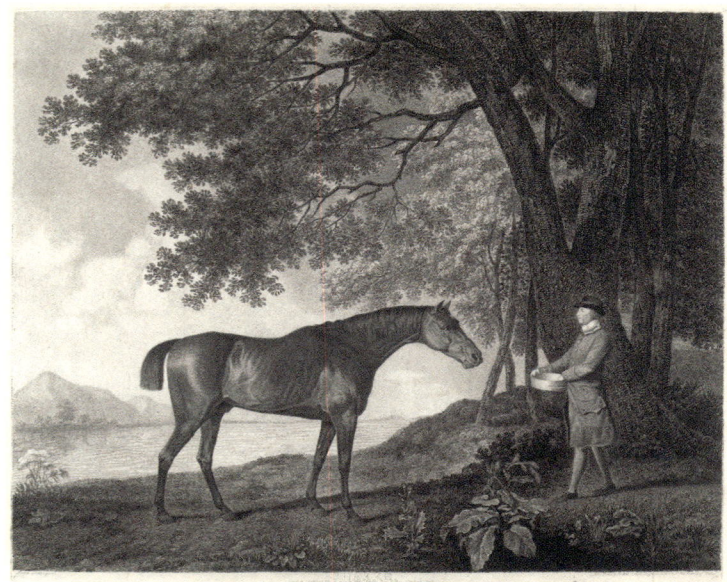

74

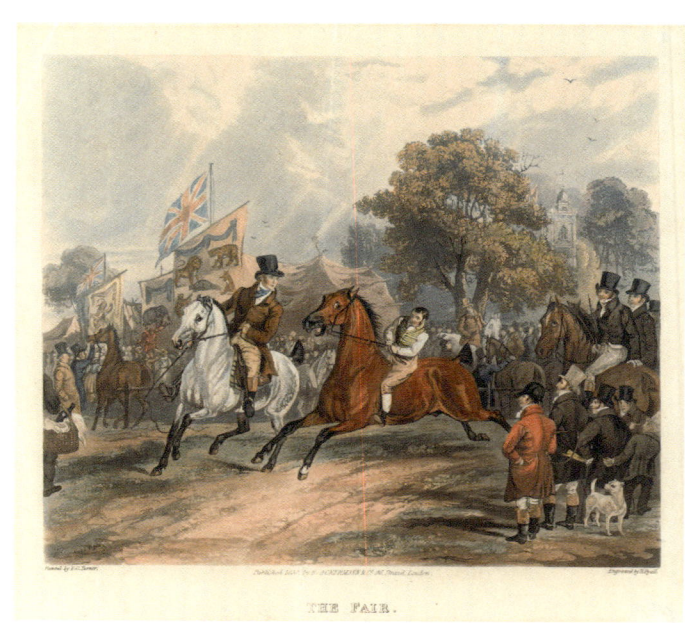

75

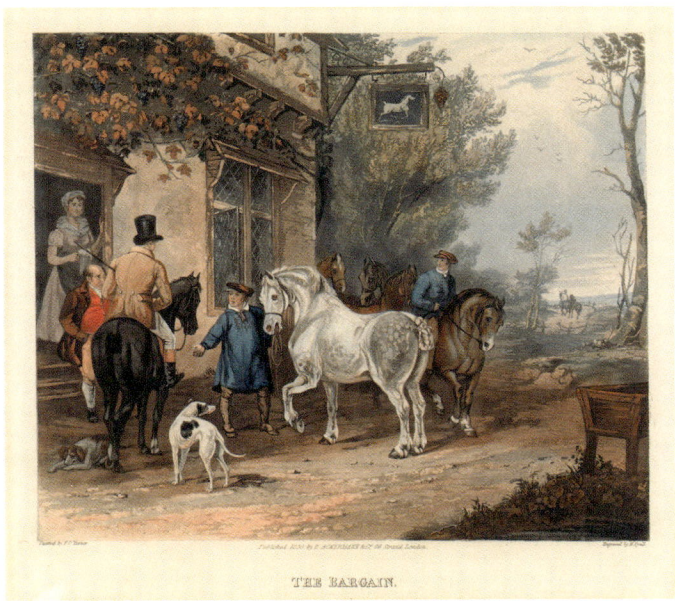

THE BARGAIN.

76

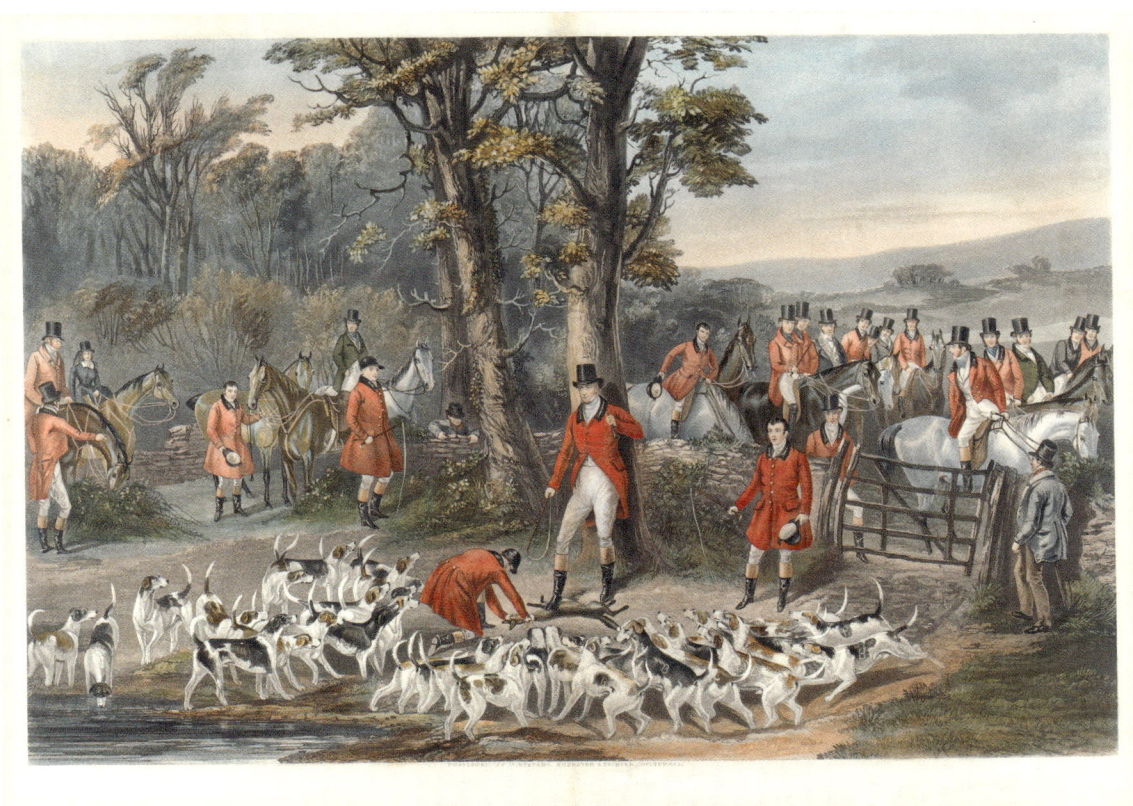

77

78. UNKNOWN
English
The Old Free Method of Rouzing a Brother Sportsman,
ca. 1780
Mezzotint with touches of etching, 12 ¾ x 9 in.
Paul Mellon Collection, 85.1292

*266 Printed for Carington Bowles, Map & Printseller,
No. 69 in St. Pauls Church Yard, London. Publish'd as
the Act directs.*

79. FRANCIS WHEATLEY (after)
British, 1747–1801
The Amorous Sportsman, 1786
Hand-colored mezzotint, 17 x 22 in.
Paul Mellon Collection, 85.1396

*Painted by F. Wheatly [sic] Engraved by C. H.
Hodges. London Publish'd, October 30th 1786: by J. R.
Smith No. 31: King Street Covent Garden*

80. DEAN WOLSTENHOLME, THE ELDER
British, 1757–1837
Dog and Badger [from a pair], ca. 1820–30
Hand-colored aquatint and etching, 11 ½ x 14 ¾ in.
Paul Mellon Collection, 85.1369.1

*Painted by Wolstenholme. Published by T. Palser,
Surry side, Westminster Bridge.*

81. DEAN WOLSTENHOLME, THE ELDER (after)
British, 1757–1837
Returning [from a set of four], ca. 1820–30
Hand-colored aquatint, 16 ½ x 21 ¼ in.
Paul Mellon Collection, 85.1415.4

*Painted by D. Wolstenholme. Engraved by D.
Wolstenholme, Junr. Published by T. Truman. No. 6
Wellington Terrace. Waterloo Bridge.*

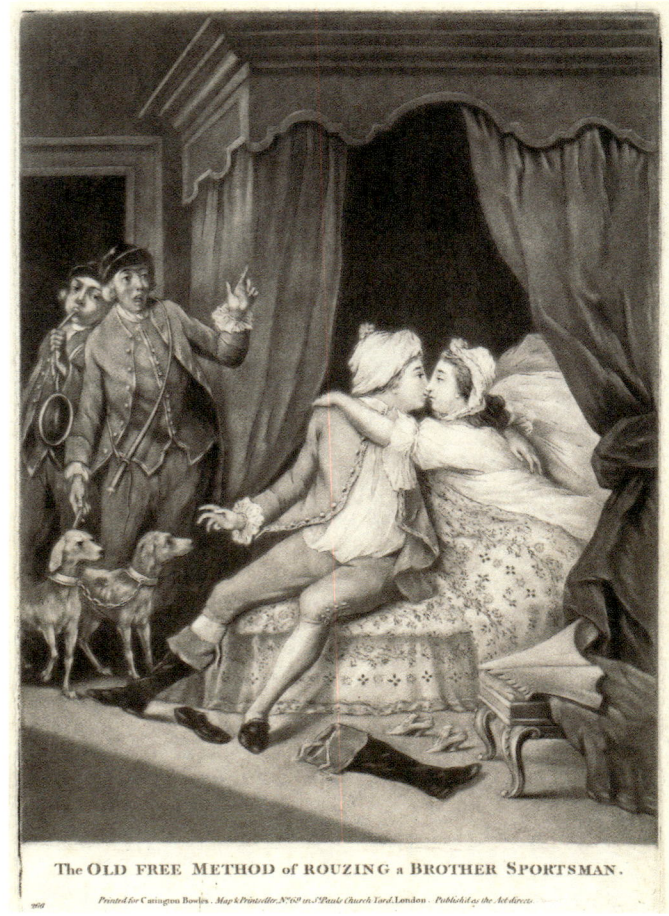

78

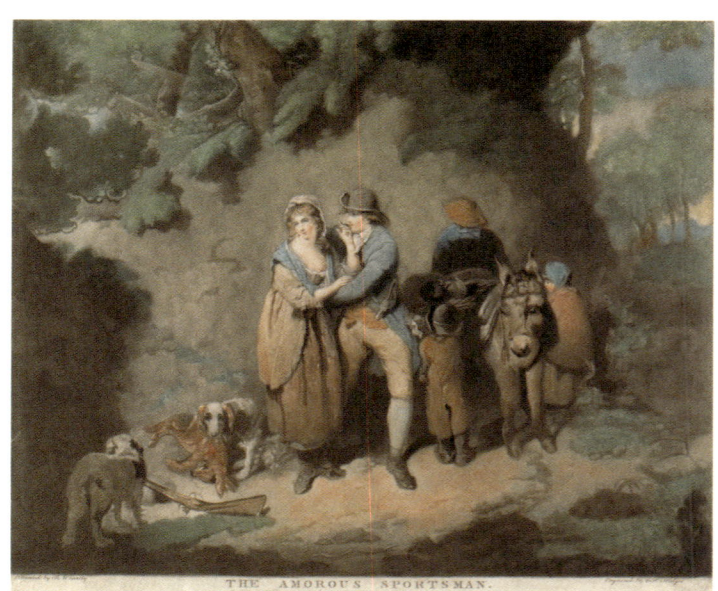

79

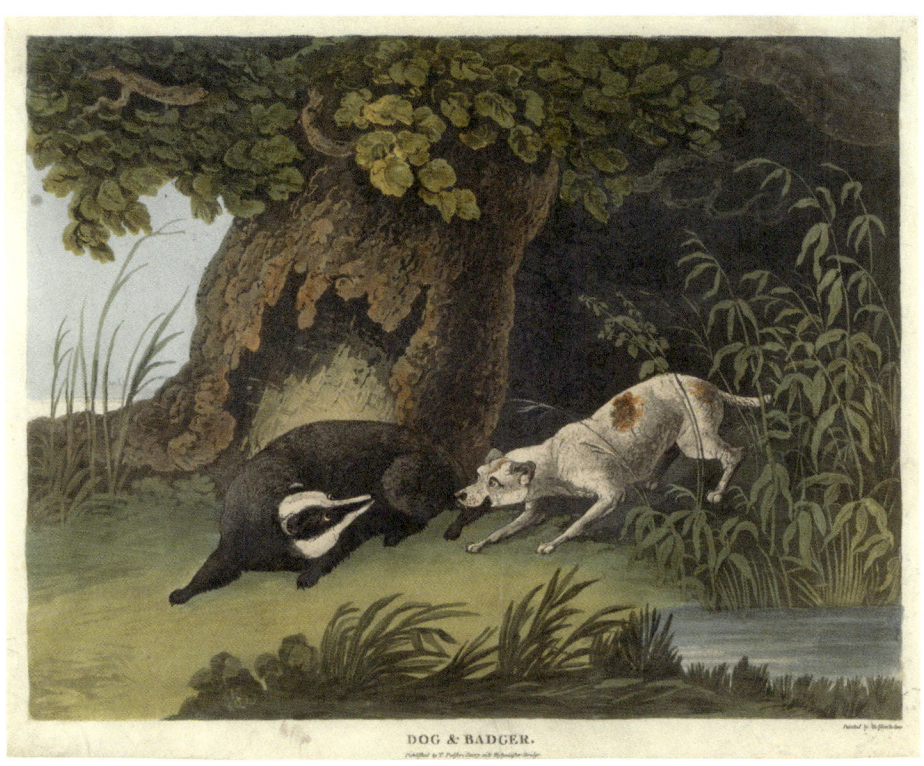

80

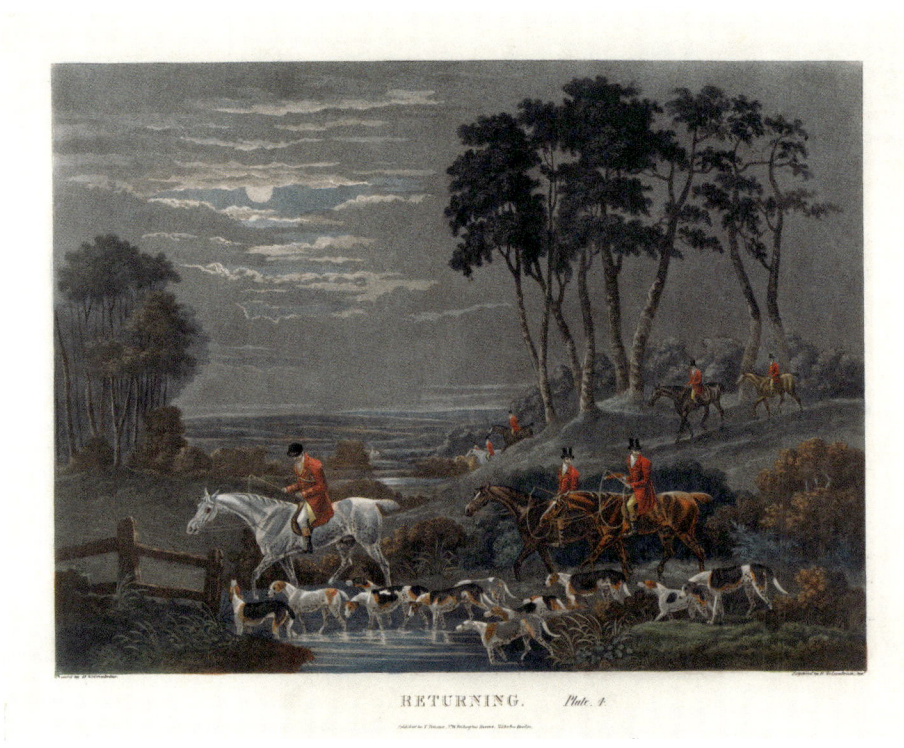

81

82. JOHN WOOTTON (after)
English, ca. 1683–1764
The Father of the Turf, Tregonwell Frampton Esqre.
of Moreton, in Dorsetshire — Keeper of the Running
Horses at Newmarket, to their Majesties William the
Third, Queen Anne, George the First, & George the
Second; Died 12th. of March 1727 — Aged 86 years, 1791
Mezzotint, 17 ¾ x 14 in.
Gift of Friends of Sporting Art, 2011.91

Engraved (from an Original Painting by Mr. Wootton)
by John Jones Engraver Extraordinary to H.R.H. the
Prince of Wales, & Principal Engraver to H.R.H. the
Duke of York.

The Father of the Turf, Tregonwell Frampton Esqre.
of Moreton, in Dorsetshire — Keeper of the Running
Horses at Newmarket, to their Majesties William the
Third, Queen Anne, George the First, & George the
Second; Died 12th. of March 1727 — Aged 86 years / This
extraordinary Character was born in the Reign of King
Charles the First, when the Sports of Horse Racing
commenced at Newmarket, and he was owner of the
celebrated Horse DRAGON, whose Portrait appears / in
a Frame in the Back Ground. — The most remarkable
event in the lives of this Gentleman & his Horse Dragon,
is most pathetically depicted by Dr. John Hawkesworth
(in No. 37 of the Adventurer) in the following words,
supposed to be spoken by the / Horse in the Elysium of
Beasts and Birds. — "It is true," replied the STEED "I
was a favourite: but what avails it to be the favourite
of caprice, avarice, and barbarity; My tyrant was a
Man who had gained a considerable fortune by play,
particularly by racing. — I had / "won him many large
sums, but being at length excepted out of every match,
as having no equal, he regarded even my excellence
with malignity, when it was no longer subservient to
his interest. Yet I still lived in ease and plenty; and as
he was able to sell even my plea- / "sures, though my
labour was become useless, I had a seraglio in which
there was a perpetual succession of new beauties. At
last, however, another competitor, appeared: I enjoyed
a new triumph by anticipation; I rushed into the field,
panting for the conquest; and the first heat / "I put my
master in possession of the stakes, which amounted to
1000 Guineas. Mr. _____ the proprietor of the mare that
I had distanced not withstanding this disgrace, declared

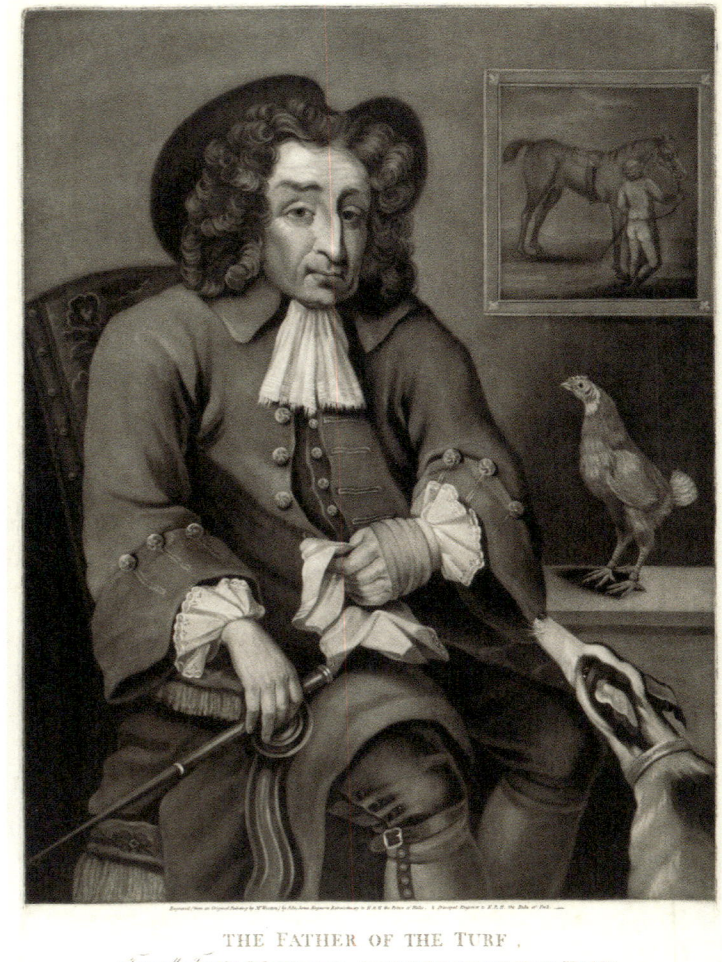

82

with great zeal, that she should run the next day against
any gelding in the world for / "double the sum: my master
immediately accepted the challenge, and told him, that
he would the next day produce a gelding that should beat
her: but what was my astonishment and indignation,
when I discovered that he most cruelly and fraudulently
intended to / "qualify me for this match upon the spot:
and to sacrifice my life at the very moment in which
every nerve should be strained in his service. As I knew
it would be in vain to resist, I suffered myself to be
bound: the operation was performed, and I was instantly
mount- / ed and spurred on the the goal. Injured as I was,
the love of glory was still superior to the desire of revenge:
I determined to die as I had lived, without an equal; and
having again won the race, I sank down at the post in an
agony, which soon after put an end to my life."

*When I had heard this horrid narrative, which indeed
I remembered to be true, I turned about in honest
confusion, and blushed that I was a man.*

*Publish'd as the Act directs, [4 June 1791, effaced] &
sold by the Proprietor J. Bodger, Land Surveyor, Stilton,
Hunts. & at No. 53 High Holborn. Mr. Weatherby,
Racing Calendar Office No. 7 Oxendon Street
Haymarket. & at Messrs. Tattersalls, London. at the
Coffee Room, Newmarket: Also at all the Principal
Towns in England. _____ See the Seven Companion
Prints in Racing Calendar Book 1790, last Page*

83. JOSEPH WRIGHT (of Derby)
British, 1734–1797
A Farrier's Shop, 1771
Mezzotint, black ink, 19 ¾ x 13 in.
Paul Mellon Collection, 85.1398

Josh. Wright Prinxt. W. Pether. Publish'd Decr. 1t. 1771.

84. JOHANN ZOFFANY (after)
German, active in Britain, 1733–1810
Portrait of Master Sayer Fishing, 1772
Mezzotint, 18 ³⁄₁₆ x 14 in.
Paul Mellon Collection, 85.1370

*J. Zoffany Pinxt. 1770. Richd. Houston fecit 1772.
Published as the Act directs 25 March 1772. by R. Sayer
No. 53 Fleet Street.*

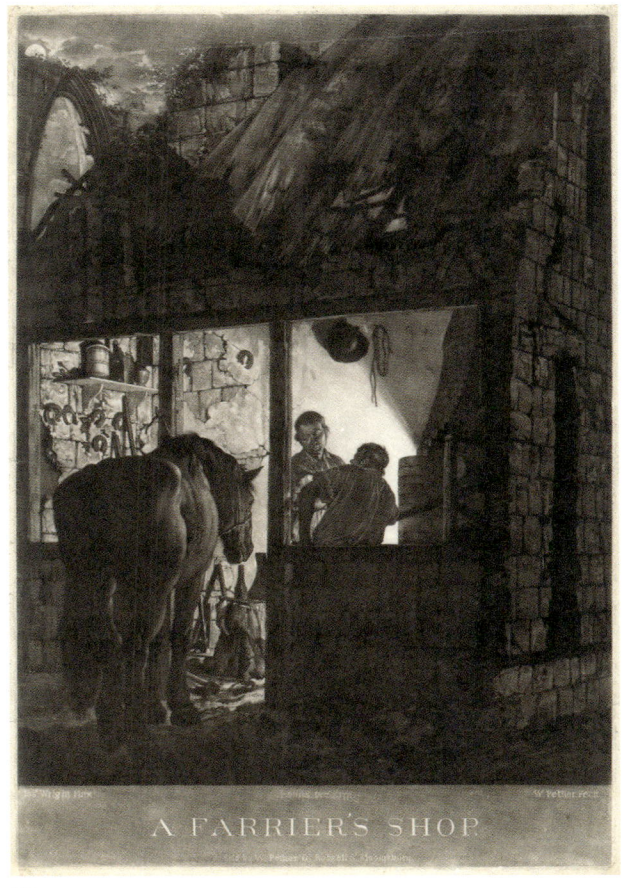

83

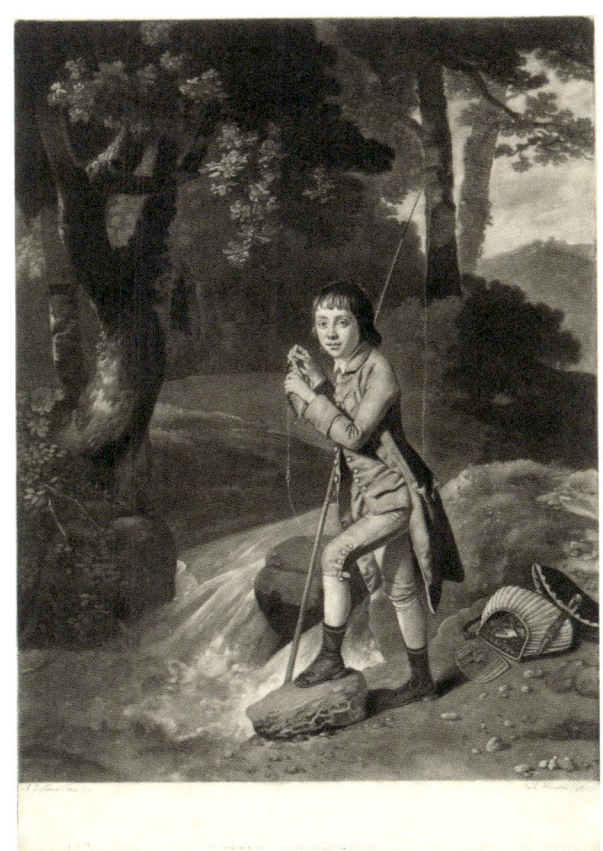

84

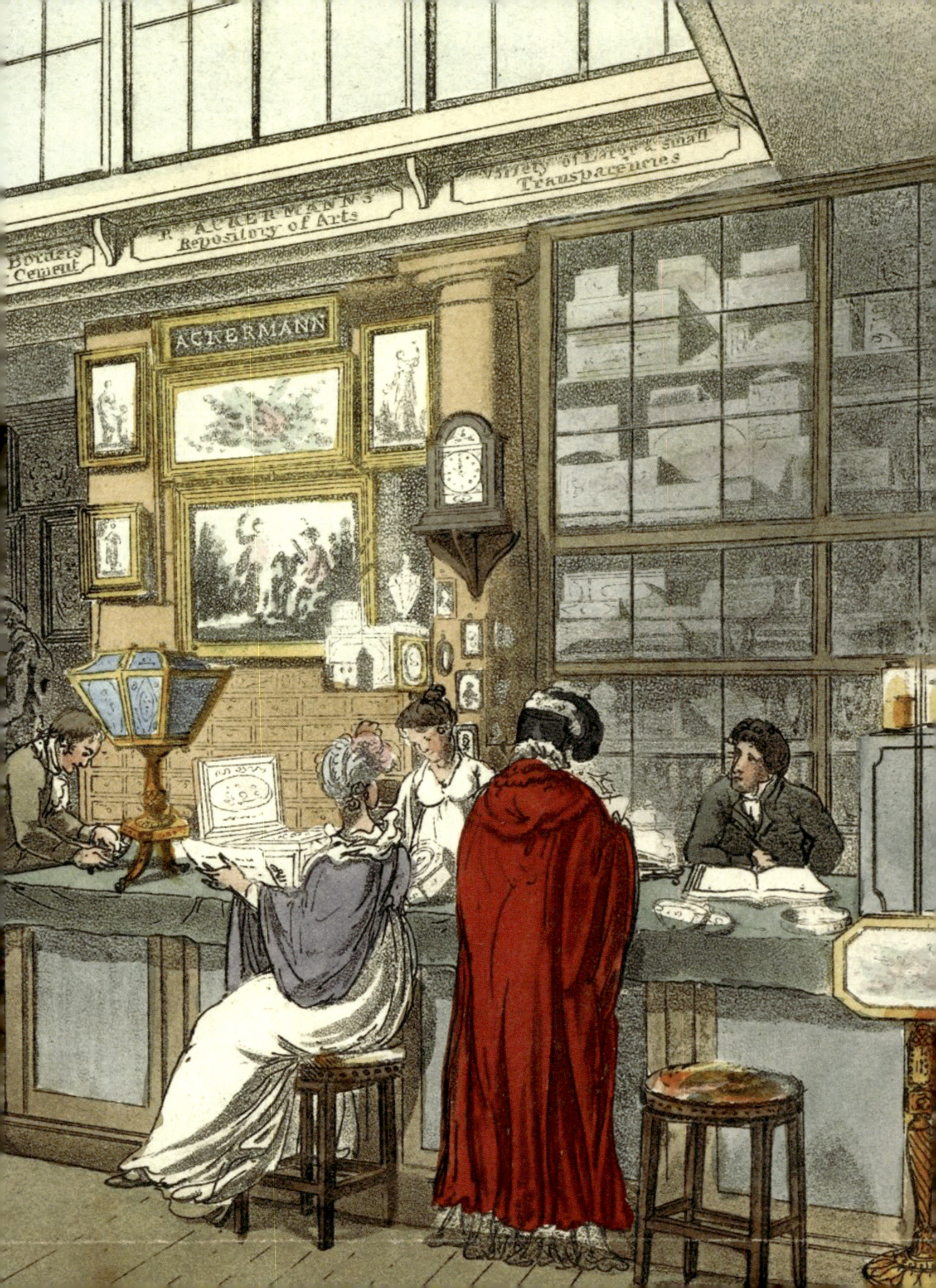

Appendix

Paul Mellon's collection of British sporting prints at VMFA is remarkable not only for its quantity and quality but also for its inclusion of several important earlier holdings — namely those of the connoisseur and historian C.F.G.R. Schwerdt and of the royal collector Henry, Duke of Gloucester. Paul Mellon (who significantly referred to himself as "a collector of collections") purchased the prints from a source unknown to the museum. They have historically resided in specially made color-coded cloth- and leather-bound boxes, and thus were carefully maintained and preserved, free of the fading, foxing, and other conservation problems endemic to a genre that was served largely as wall decorations in college rooms, dining rooms, taverns, and inns.

A comprehensive review of VMFA's entire collection of works on paper in 2004–5 led to the discovery of a number of the outer covers in which the prints were originally sold by firms such as Ackermann's and Fores's. These "wrappers" provide much additional information about the prints as well as their production and marketing. They are therefore reproduced here with the hope that future researchers will find them, along with the essays, a useful starting point for the reconsideration of this understudied genre of British art.

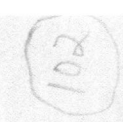

No 3

RUDIMENTS

FOR

DRAWING

THE HORSE.

ENGRAVED BY J. C. ZEITTER,

FROM DESIGNS BY H. ALKEN, AND J. C. ZEITTER.

London:

R. ACKERMANN, 191, REGENT STREET,

AT THE

ECLIPSE SPORTING GALLERY AND NEW SPORTING MAGAZINE OFFICE.

1837.

A CATALOGUE
OF
SPORTING AND OTHER PRINTS,
PUBLISHED BY
RUDOLPH ACKERMANN.
191, REGENT STREET.

N.B. *The Measurement given is the size of each Print, exclusive of either Blank Margin or Inscription.*

MEMOIRS
OF THE LIFE OF THE LATE
JOHN MYTTON, Esq.
OF HALSTON, SHROPSHIRE.
Wit Notices of his Hunting, Shooting, Driving, Racing, Eccentric and Extravagant Exploits.
BY NIMROD,
WITH NUMEROUS ILLUSTRATIONS,
BY H. ALKEN, AND T. J. RAWLINS.
Second Edition, reprinted with considerable additions, from the *New Sporting Magazine.*
Royal 8vo. Price 25s. Handsomely bound in Cloth.

THE QUORN HUNT,
IN A SERIES OF EIGHT PLATES BEAUTIFULLY COLOURED
FROM DRAWINGS BY HENRY ALKEN, ILLUSTRATING
NIMROD'S
Celebrated Article on English FOX HUNTING, in the "Quarterly Review,"
Size of Prints, 20½ inches by 12⅞. Price 4*l.* 14*s.* 6*d.*

THE PIRATE DEFEATED,
Representing a gallant Action, between Mr. R. B. Crawford, of H. M. S. Esk, with one gun and five men, in the Bight of Benin, March 20, 1826, beating off the Spanish Pirate Carolina, carrying ten guns and ninety men, commanded by Capt. Antonio Soumath, from an original Picture in the possession of Rear Admiral Sir Charles Bullen, C. B., K. C. H. &c. &c. to whom this Plate is with permission most respectfully dedicated.
Size of Print 17⅞ by 11⅞. Price 10*s.* 6*d.* beautifully coloured, from the original Picture by W. Joy.

JUST PUBLISHED,
A SPLENDID MEZZOTINT ENGRAVING,
THE FORESTER,
FROM A PICTURE BY Mr. C. HANCOCK, ENGRAVED BY H. C. BECKWITH.
Size 16¼ inches by 11⅝.

PORTRAIT OF HIS GRACE THE LATE DUKE OF GORDON'S BLACK TROTTING MARE,
WINNER OF THE NORTHAMPTON TROTTING SWEEPSTAKES, MARCH, 1836.
DRAWN ON STONE BY T. FAIRLAND, FROM THE ORIGINAL PICTURE BY W. BARRAUD.
Size of Print 14 inches by 11¼. Price 12*s.* coloured; 8*s.* plain.

THE HUNTING EXPLOITS OF COUNT SANDOR,
IN TEN HIGHLY COLOURED PLATES,
FROM PAINTINGS BY J. FERNELEY, ENGRAVED BY E. DUNCAN.
13¾ inches by 10¼. Price 3*l.* 3*s.* the set.

THE WATERFORD LINE SCHOONERS,
A fine coloured Print representing the Schooners "Alexander, Capt. Nicholls," "Martha, Capt. Dwyre," and "Rapid, Capt. Miller."
FROM A PAINTING BY JOHN LYNN.
Size of Print, 21 inches by 12⅞. Price 21*s.*

THE GRAND LEICESTERSHIRE STEEPLE-CHASE.
IN A SERIES OF EIGHT PLATES, BEAUTIFULLY COLOURED,
FROM PAINTINGS BY HENRY ALKEN, ENGRAVED BY BENTLY, WITH PORTRAITS OF THE HORSES AND RIDERS, AND REMARKS BY NIMROD.
18 inches by 14. Price 3*l.* 3*s.* the set.

MR. DELME RADCLIFFE AND HIS HARRIERS,
10½ inches by 8¼. Price 7*s.* 6*d.* coloured.

THE FOX AND PARTRIDGE,
A VERY SPIRITED COLOURED LITHOGRAPHIC PRINT,
FROM A PAINTING, BY R. R. RENAGLE, R. A.
Dedicated by Special Permission to the Right Honourable the Earl of Kintore.
Price 7s. 6d. each, col. Size of Print, 14 inches by 11½.

TALLY-HO!
FROM A PAINTING, BY Mr. CHARLES HANCOCK.
Price 7s. 6d. coloured. Size, 15 inches by 10⅝.

THE RIGHT AND THE WRONG SORT,
A PAIR OF HUMOUROUS SPORTING PRINTS,
FROM DRAWINGS, BY H. ALKEN,
Price 25s. the pair. Size of Prints, 18½ inches by 11½

THE SOUTHERN WHALE FISHERY,
Two Prints representing the above Fishery in the South Seas. The mode of attacking the Whale and boiling it down on board; in which also is displayed the hazardous mode of pursuing the Whale.
Price 15s. each highly coloured. Size of Prints, 20½ inches by 13½.
ALSO LATELY PUBLISHED,
A fine mezzotint Portrait of that celebrated Sportsman,
GEORGE BAKER, ESQ.
OF DURHAM,
Price 15s. Print; 21s. Proofs; 31s. 6d. Proofs before Letters.

T. GOOSEY,
A large Lithographic Print, with a Portrait of the above famous Huntsman to Lord Forester; and part of the Belvoir Hounds.
Price 30s. print; and 42s. coloured. Size of print, 22 inches by 17.

BEAUTY AND GENERAL
FROM A PAINTING BY SCHWANFELDER, ENGRAVED BY E. DUNCAN.
19 inches by 15, highly coloured. Price 1*l.* 1*s.*

A large Lithographic
HEAD OF A BLOOD-HOUND,
Coloured,
FROM A PAINTING BY AGASSE.
Price 10s. 6d. Size, 15¼ inches by 13½

GROUSE SHOOTING, OTTER HUNTING, SALMON FISHING, AND DEER SHOOTING.
FROM DRAWINGS, BY W. HEATH.
Price 20s. the Four Plates. Size, 12½ inches by 8¾

A Portrait of
JOHN WARD ON HIS FAVOURITE HUNTER BLUE RUIN
FROM THE ORIGINAL PICTURE, BY BARRAUD.
Price 12s. plain; 21s. coloured. Size, 18¾ inches by 14½

HUNTING QUALIFICATIONS,
IN SIX PLATES.
BY HENRY ALKEN,
ACCOMPANIED WITH A HUMOUROUS DESCRIPTION OF EACH PLATE.
10 inches by 6¼. Price, 1*l.* 10*s.* the set, highly coloured

HUNTING RECOLLECTIONS,
IN SIX PLATES, HIGHLY COLOURED,
BY HENRY ALKEN.
10¾ inches by 8¼. Price 1*l.* 1*s.* the set.

MY STUD,
IN SIX COLOURED PLATES,
BY HENRY ALKEN.
10½ inches by 8¼. Price 1*l.* 1*s.* the set.

DEER STALKING,
IN TWO HIGHLY COLOURED PLATES,
FROM PAINTINGS BY J. FERNELEY, ENGRAVED BY E. DUNCAN.
24 inches by 18¾. Price 1*l.* 5*s.* each plate.

HEADS OF SPORTING ANIMALS,
Viz. the Fox, Bloodhound, and Newfoundland Dog.
FROM PAINTINGS BY C. HANCOCK ENGRAVED BY BECKWITH.
6⅜ inches by 5¼. Price coloured, 12*s.*, proofs 10*s.* 6*d.*, plain 7*s.* 6*d.* the set.

PORTRAITS OF THE WINNING HORSES OF THE GREAT ST. LEGER STAKES AT DONCASTER, AND THE DERBY STAKES AT EPSOM,

FROM PAINTINGS BY MR. J. FERNELEY, OF MELTON MOWBRAY, AND MR. C. HANCOCK, AT MESSRS. TATTERSALL'S GROSVENOR PLACE.

ROWTON	ST. GILES	GLENCOE
PRIAM	DANGEROUS	MUNDIG
VELOCIPEDE	CADLAND	QUEEN OF TRUMPS
SPANIEL	CHORISTER	BAY MIDDLETON
RIDDLESWORTH	SULTAN	ELIS.

16½ inches by 19½ highly coloured. Price 15s. each.

A PANORAMIC VIEW OF A FOX-CHASE,
BY H. ALKEN.
Coloured, and fitted into a Roll-up Case. Price 1l. 11s. 6d.

FOX HOUNDS RUNNING IN COVERT,
FROM A PAINTING BY R. B. DAVIS.
15¾ inches by 11½. Price 15s. coloured, 12s. plain.

SHOT,
A CELEBRATED POINTER,
FROM A PAINTING BY A. COOPER, R. A.
24½ inches by 19½ highly coloured. Price 1l. 4s.

DASH,
A CELEBRATED SETTER,
FROM A PAINTING BY AGASSE.
24½ inches by 19, highly coloured. Price 1l. 4s.

TOM TRUMB,
THE CELEBRATED AMERICAN TROTTER,
19½ inches by 15, coloured, Price 1l.

BADGERS,
AFTER A PAINTING BY BENNET.
18½ inches by 18¾, coloured. Price 1l. 1s.

HARES,
AFTER A PAINTING BY BENNET,
19½ inches by 15, coloured. Price 1l. 1s.

FOXES AND CUBS,
FROM A PAINTING BY BENNET,
20½ inches by 16½, coloured. Price 1l. 4s.

SPORTING DOGS,
IN TWO SMALL BOOKS,
BY H. ALKEN.
Price 5s. each, coloured; 2s. plain.

ALKEN'S RUDIMENTS FOR DRAWING THE HORSE AND OTHER ANIMALS,
In Six Numbers, at 2s. 6d. each, or the Six Numbers, neatly half-bound, 20s.

FANCY BALL COSTUMES,
IN SIX PLATES,
DRAWN AND ETCHED BY WILLIAM HEATH.
Price coloured, 2s. 6d. each.

THE DESTRUCTION OF THE HOUSES OF PARLIAMENT, BY FIRE,
DRAWN AND LITHOGRAPHED BY WILLIAM HEATH.
14½ inches by 10½. Price 7s. 6d. coloured; 5s. proofs.

SPORTING ANECDOTES,

THE SPORTING SWEEP—or, To tell you the truth, gemmen, I can't vote for you, 'cause I runs with the Duke.

THE SPORTING MILLER—or, Half-a-crown you don't clear it.

THE COACH—or three Blind uns and a Bolter.

JORROCKS'S HUNT BREAKFAST—or, a Terrible Surprise.

THE SPORTING BUTCHER—or, Lord Marrowbones and his Man.

SWELL AND THE SURREY, two plates—Hounds at Fault, and Full Cry.

THE HUNTING TAILOR—Hastings and Lord Segrave—Push him sharp at it, My Lord.

THE HUNTED TAILOR—or, the Double Fracture, breaking the Sabbath and breaking the Window.

THE SPORTING PARSON'S HUNTING LECTURE—Hold hard! gentlemen, for the love of Mercy, Hold Hard!

THE SPORTING GRAZIER—Fox-hunting versus Politics—I always Vote for the Gentleman wot hunts the County.

THE SPORTING BISHOP—The Clerical View Holloa! or the Hounds at fault.

Also just Published,

A NEW ANECDOTE.

FOX-HUNTING IN CANADA—Put Morris on York, and what will stop them? Mungo for a Hundred.
FROM DRAWINGS BY H. ALKEN.
13 inches by 8½. Price 3s. 6d. each, highly coloured.
N.B. These Anecdotes are to be continued occasionally.

FIGHTING COCKS,
IN A SERIES OF SIX PLATES,
FROM DRAWINGS BY NEWTON FIELDING.
7½ inches by 6½, highly coloured. Price 1l 1s. the set.

KNIGHTS IN ARMOUR,
IN A SERIES OF TWELVE PLATES,
BY H. ALKEN.
Price, coloured, 18s.; plain, 9s.

GAME COCKS,
IN TWO SMALL PRINTS.
Neatly mounted and coloured. Price 5s. the pair.

FOUR SMALL HUNTING MEDALLIONS,
BY H. ALKEN.
Highly coloured. Price 8s. the four.

SIX SMALL HUNTING MEDALLIONS,
BY H. ALKEN.
Highly coloured. Price 10s. 6d. the six.

FOUR SMALL SHOOTING MEDALLIONS,
BY H. ALKEN.
Highly coloured. Price 8s. the four.

FOUR SMALL RACING MEDALLIONS,
BY H. ALKEN.
Highly coloured. Price 8s. the four.

SIX SMALL MEDALLIONS OF MAMALUKES AND COSSACKS,
BY H. ALKEN.
Highly coloured. Price 8s. the six.

MAMALUKES AND COSSACKS,
IN TWO PLATES,
Highly coloured. Price 10s. 6d. the pair. Plain, on tinted paper, 7s.

A PORTRAIT OF "CHANCE," THE FIREMEN'S DOG,
DRAWN AND LITHOGRAPHED BY WILLIAM HEATH.
9½ inches by 7½. Price 4s. coloured; 2s. 6d. proofs.

PORTRAITS OF IBRAHIM AND DRAMA PACHA,
LITHOGRAPHED BY GAUCI.
Price, each, 3s. coloured; 1s. 6d. plain.

PORTRAITS OF GENERAL CHASSE AND MARSHALL GERARD.
Price 5s. the pair coloured; 2s. 6d. plain.

G. HARLEY'S RUDIMENTS OF LANDSCAPE DRAWING,
Complete. Price 1l. 16s.; the coloured part alone, 1l.; the sepia part, half-bound, or Three Numbers 10s. 6d. The pencil part, half-bound, 10s.; or Six Nos. at 1s. each.

G. HARLEY'S JUVENILE DRAWING-BOOK,
In Twelve Numbers at 8d. each.

G. HARLEY'S LESSONS ON DRAWING TREES
Four Numbers, at 2s. 6d. each.

R. ACKERMANN,
Printseller, Publisher, Fancy Stationer,
MANUFACTURER OF SUPERFINE WATER-COLOURS,
To their Majesties, and the Royal Family.

Begs leave to recommend his Colours to the Nobility and Gentry, as being prepared with the utmost care, and approved by the most Eminent Artists of the United Kingdom.

SOLD IN CAKES OR BOXES AT THE FOLLOWING PRICES:—

	£.	s.	d.
In Boxes of Yew-Tree, Rosewood, &c. ornamented and highly varnished, from £2. 2s. to	10	10	0
In Mahogany Boxes, 45 Cakes, Palettes, Marble Slab, Pencils, &c.	3	13	6
Ditto, ditto, 36 Cakes, ditto	3	3	0
Ditto, ditto, 32 ditto, ditto	2	12	6
Ditto, ditto, 24 ditto, ditto	2	2	0
Ditto, ditto, 18 ditto, ditto	1	11	6
Ditto, ditto, 12 ditto, ditto	1	1	0
Ditto, 12 Cakes, Lock and Drawer	0	15	0
Neat Mahogany Boxes, with a sliding Top, 30 Cakes	1	16	0

	£.	s.	d.
Highly-finished Mahogany Brass-capp'd, &c. from 52s. 6d. to	7	0	
Boxes of Velvet Colours complete, with directions	2	2	0
Ditto, ditto, ditto	1	4	0
Boxes of Body Colours	2	2	0
Ditto of Colours for painting on glass	2	2	0
Ditto of Chalks, complete 5s., 63s., and	2	2	0
Handsome Rose-wood, Inlaid Brass, ornamented 12 Cakes, fitted up complete	2	12	6

		£.	s.	d.
				Small Cakes.
Ditto, ditto, ditto 18 Cakes, ditto	3	3	0
Ditto, ditto, ditto 24 ditto, ditto	4	4	0
Ditto, ditto, ditto 32 ditto, ditto	5	5	0
Ditto, ditto, ditto 30 ditto, larger	5	15	6
Box and Extras	6	7	0
Ditto, ditto, ditto 40 ditto, ditto	10	10	0

	£.	s.	
Ditto, ditto	32 ditto	1 8 0	Cakes.
Ditto, ditto	24 ditto	1 0—0 14 0	
Ditto, ditto	18 ditto	0 15 0—0 10 6	
Ditto, ditto	12 ditto	0 10 6—0 7 0	
Ditto, ditto	6 ditto	0 6 0—0 4 6	

SUPERFINE WATER-COLOURS, PER CAKE.

	s. d.		s. d.		s. d.
Ultramarine	1 1	Smalt	5	Permanent White	1 6
Ultramarine, Ash	5	Extra Madder Lake	5	Prout's Black	1 6
Guinet's Ultramarine	0 3	Intense Blue	3	Prepared Black for Inlaying	1 6
Scarlet	0 6	Rose Madder	3	Ultramarine in Saucers,	2 6
Burnt Carmine	0 7	Pink Madder	3	5s. and	1 0
Imperial Permanent Blue, equal to Ultramarine in tint	0 5	Burnt Lac Lake	2	Scarlet in Saucers	1 0
Platena Yellow	0 5	Permanent Green	2	Fine Chinese Gold, in Saucers, 10s. 6d. and	2 0
French Blue	0 3	Cobalt	1	Ditto in Shells	1 6
Carmine	0 3	Lake, Crimson	1	Gold, Silver, and Copper Bronze, in Pockets	2 0
Permanent Crimson	0 5	Lake, Scarlet	1	Carmine in Powder	1 0
Purple Madder	0 5	Lake, Purple	1	Permanent White Liquid in Cups	2 6
Orange Vermillion	0 5	Brown Madder	1		
Gallstone	0 5	Indian Yellow	1		
		Indian Black	1	Sepia	1 6

Ladies' Chess-Boards and Work-Boxes, varnished and fitted up in the neatest manner.

An elegant assortment of ALBUMS, SCRAP BOOKS, &c.

ACKERMANN'S LIQUID CEMENT, FOR FIXING DRAWINGS AND PRINTS IN DITTO.

Price one Shilling per Bottle.

A LARGE ASSORTMENT OF THE MOST BRILLIANT-COLOURED

RICE PAPER,

SUPERIOR TO ANY YET OFFERED FOR SALE, AND STAINED TO ANY PATTERN.

A GREAT ASSORTMENT OF BERLIN AND WORSTED PATTERNS.

DRAWINGS LENT OUT TO COPY.

R. ACKERMANN solicits the attention of the Amateurs of the Art of Drawing to his CIRCULATING PORTFOLIOS, which comprise a very extensive Collection of Drawings and Prints of Figures, Landscapes, Flowers, Fruits, &c. The following are the Terms of Subscription.

Four Guineas per year; Two Guineas the Half Year; and One Guinea the Quarter.

The money to be paid at the time of Subscribing.

Weekly Subscribers to pay Two Shillings and Sixpence per Week; taking at a time Drawings or Prints not exceeding Two Guineas; for which a Deposit is to be made until the Drawings or Prints are returned.

Subscribers are not to take, at one time, Drawings or Prints to a greater amount than their subscriptions; but they may exchange them as often as agreeable. It will be needless to recommend care to be taken of the Drawings and Prints in their possession, as they can only be received back in a reasonably good state. Such as have been creased, received oil, ink, or colour spots, or are torn or cut, must be paid for.

A large assortment of White-Wood Articles of every description for TRANSFERRING, by means of ACKERMANN'S TRANSFER VARNISH.

GOLD, FANCY WOOD, AND MINIATURE FRAMES OF EVERY DESCRIPTION MADE TO ORDER.

H. Ackermann's prepared genuine Cumberland Black Lead Pencils,

OF DIFFERENT DEGREES OF HARDNESS AND DEPTH OF SHADE.

H A degree harder than the genuine Cumberland Lead, and used generally by Artists for Outlines

HH Two degrees harder, and used by Architects

HHH Three degrees harder, and used by Architects, Engineers, Surveyors, &c. &c.

F Fine Pencils for Drawing, used by Artists, Drawing-Masters, and Pupils

EBB Extra Black and double thick in Lead, for very bold Drawing

FF Fine Pencils for Drawing, used by Artists, Drawing-Masters, &c. (double thick in Lead)

B Black for Shading, used by the same

BB A deeper Black for Shading than B

HB Hard and Black for Shading

EHB Extra Hard and Black, and thick in Lead.

ACKERMANN'S Fine Genuine Cumberland Black-lead Pencils (not prepared) have been known for many years as the best Pencils for Sketching and general use. They are particularly adapted for Young Students to copy from LITHOGRAPHIC STUDIES.

The Prepared Pencils FF, F, and BB, serve for the deep Shades and finishing Touches.

Also Burgess's Pencils for Bold Drawing.

N.B. Drawing Materials of every Description, and the greatest Variety of Drawing Books and Rudiments in Lithography, &c. &c.

N. B.—*Subscribers' Names received for the NEW SPORTING MAGAZINE, at 30s. the Year; the Subscription to be paid in advance.*

There are Eleven Volumes and Two Numbers Published, at 15s. the Volume; or 2s. 6d. per Number Proof Impression of the Plates 2s. each, and 2s. 6d. Coloured.

WALTER SPIERS, PRINTER, 399, OXFORD STREET, LONDON.

ALL AT ONE SHILLING PER CAKE.

Ackermann's Yellow	Dragon's Blood	Transparent Yellow
Antwerp Green	Dutch Pink	Ochre
Antwerp Blue	Emerald Green 1 & 2	Varley's Grey
Bistre	French Green	—— Warm Grey
Blue Black	Full Red	—— Purple Grey
Blue Verditer	Gamboge	—— Dark Green
Brown Ochre	Green Bice	—— Warm Green
Brown Pink	Green Verditer	Prussian Blue
Bronze	Hooker's Green, 1 and 2	Prussian Green
Burnt Indian Earth	Indigo	—— Neutral Tint
Burnt Roman Ochre	Indian Red	Vandyke Brown
Burnt Sienna	Indian Pink	Venetian Red
Burnt Umber	Ivory Black	Vermillion, Chinese
Chrome Yellow, Nos. 1, 2, and 3	King's Yellow	White
Orange Chrome	Lac Lake	Yellow Lake
Cologne Earth	Lamp Black	Yellow Ochre
		Yellow Orpiment
		York Brown

Light Red	Saturnine Red
Mineral Blue	
Naples Yellow	
Neutral Tint	
Olive Green	
Payne's Neutral Tint	
Purple	
Red Ochre	
Red Orpiment	
Raw Sienna	
Raw Umber	
Roman Ochre	
Sap Green	

All these Colours may be had in Half-Cakes, at Half-Price.

COLOURS FOR ORIENTAL AND POONAH TINTING, BRONZES, VARNISHED PAPER, AND BRUSHES FOR DITTO.

Macpherson's Permanent Tints for Miniature Painting, 31s. 6d. & 20s. per box, containing 12 Tints;

Or per Cake, Shade-Tint, Dark Complexion, Half-Tint, Flesh-Tint, Auburn, Yellow, Blue, Maroon Crimson, Deep Blue, Light Hair, and Intense Sepia. 2s. each;

Carnation, 3s.—Half-Cakes at Half-Price.

Macpherson's Opaque Back-Ground, for ditto, 2s. 6d. per Bottle.—*Frost's Brown*, at 2s. per Bottle.

ACKERMANN'S Colours for Flower Painting, 24s. and 21s. per Box.

ALSO THE NUMEROUS REQUISITES FOR DRAWING AS FOLLOWS :—

DRAWING PAPERS.

Demy	20 inches by 15½
Medium	22½ ditto 17½
Royal	24 ditto 19
Super-royal	27½ ditto 19½
Imperial	30 ditto 22
Elephant	23 ditto 23
Columbier	35 ditto 23½
Atlas	34 ditto 26
Double Elephant	40 ditto 27
Grand Emperor	65½ ditto 47
Antiquarian	53 ditto 31
Antiquarian, extra large	56 ditto 38

Guard-Books and Albums

Sketching-Books, plain, various sizes and Bindings

Portfolios of all sizes

Ivory for Miniatures

Black-Lead Pencils, prepared

Black Italian, French, and German Chalks

Conté à Paris, glazed

Conté à Paris, square

Leather and Paper Stumps

Steel and Brass Port Crayons

Drawing-Boards, on a variety of Plans

Sketching-Boards and Portable Stools

Tin Japanned Sketching Colour Boxes of various sizes

Bristol Drawing Paper and Card Boards

Vellum

Wove Cartridge for Landscapes

Rough-grained Cartridge

Tinted Drawing Papers for Crayons

Writing Papers

Transparent Tracing Paper

Tissue Paper, Demy and Double Crown

Ditto ditto, Tinted

Fine White Velvet for Painting

Marble and Earthenware Slabs

Ivory and Earthenware Pencil-Racks

Ivory Palettes

Earthenware ditto

Ditto Saucers

Ditto ditto in Cabinets

Indian Glue

A CHOICE COLLECTION OF ENGLISH AND FOREIGN PRINTS; LIKEWISE A GREAT VARIETY OF WATER-COLOUR DRAWINGS, ETC. FOR SCRAP-BOOKS.

Drawings of Flowers, Fruit, Shells

Ditto Landscapes and Shipping

Paper Painted in Imitation of Satin and other Woods and Marbles

Ditto, ditto of Morocco, various colours

Ditto, ditto Embossed

Embellished Writing Paper and Cards

Gold and Silver Paper of various sorts

Gold Borders

Fire Screens, with or without Poles, ornamented or plain

Card Racks, ditto ditto

Hand Screens, ornamented or plain

Handles for ditto, ditto ditto

Pasteboard for Ladies' Fancy Works, plain or coloured

Work Tables

Gold Size, with printed Directions

Varnishing Brushes, of all sizes

Liquid Colours for Maps

Indian Ink of various Qualities

Indian Rubber, Solid and in Bottles

Sable Pencils

Camel-Hair Pencils, for Water-Colour drawings, of superior Quality

Scrubs for Velvet Painting

Mathematical Instruments, in complete Sets

Pink and Blue Saucers

Prepared Black, for Imitation of Inlaid Work

Bramah's Patent Pens, &c.

Palmer's Portable Pens

Prepared Ox-Gall

Colourless Ox-Gall

Black and White Patterns

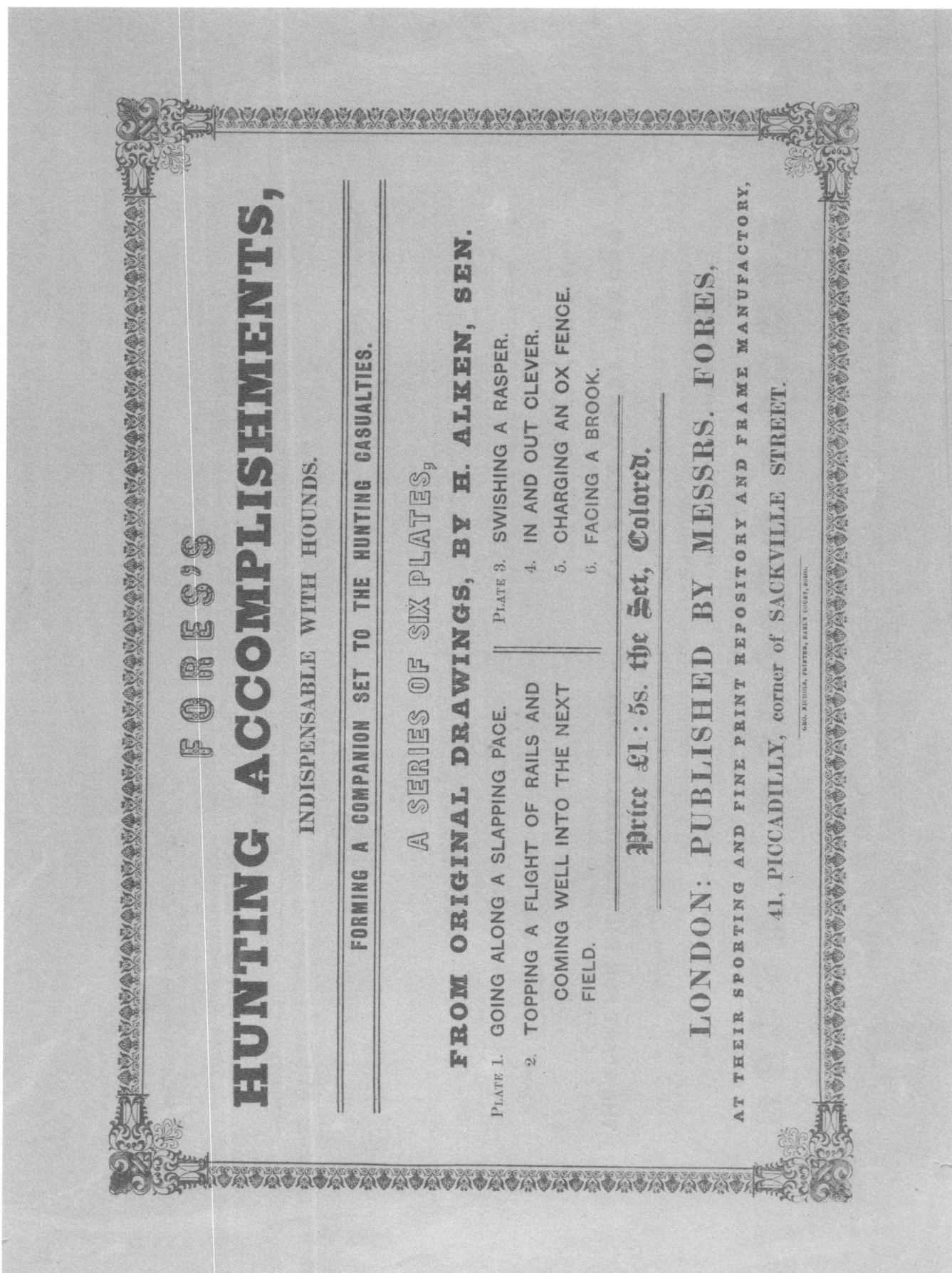

FORES'S

HUNTING ACCOMPLISHMENTS,

INDISPENSABLE WITH HOUNDS.

FORMING A COMPANION SET TO THE HUNTING CASUALTIES.

A SERIES OF SIX PLATES,

FROM ORIGINAL DRAWINGS, BY H. ALKEN, SEN.

PLATE 1. GOING ALONG A SLAPPING PACE.   PLATE 3. SWISHING A RASPER.

2. TOPPING A FLIGHT OF RAILS AND   4. IN AND OUT CLEVER.

    COMING WELL INTO THE NEXT   5. CHARGING AN OX FENCE.

    FIELD.   6. FACING A BROOK.

Price £1 : 5s. the Set, Colored.

LONDON: PUBLISHED BY MESSRS. FORES,

AT THEIR SPORTING AND FINE PRINT REPOSITORY AND FRAME MANUFACTORY,

41, PICCADILLY, corner of SACKVILLE STREET.

GEO. NICHOLS, PRINTER, EARL'S COURT, SOHO.

FORES'S SPORTING AND FINE ENGRAVINGS,

Published at 41, PICCADILLY, corner of SACKVILLE STREET, LONDON.

THE CHASE, THE TURF, THE ROAD, AND THE SEA.

FORES'S SPORTING SCRAPS,

Sheets, containing Four Subjects, Colored, Price 7s., adapted for Framing, Scrap Books, or Screens.

STEEPLE CHASING, HUNTING, RACING, COURSING, SHOOTING, YATCHING, ROWING, &c.

LEFT AT HOME,

REPRESENTS A FINE STAMP OF HUNTER AND HOUNDS, OF PERFECT FORM, EXCITED BY THE SOUND OF THE HUNTSMAN'S HORN.

Price, Proofs .... £3 : 2 : 0   Prints, Colored .... £1 : 11 : 6

A subject full of life, and possessed of inexpressible charms for a True Sportsman.

FORES'S STEEPLE CHASE SCENES,

Price £2 : 12 : 6 the Set of Six Plates, Colored, from Original Drawings, by H. Alken, Sen.

Plate 1. THE STARTING FIELD
  A picked lot possessed of judgment and confidence.

2. WATTLE FENCE, WITH A DEEP DROP
  Skill and nerve brought into play.

Plate 3. IN AND OUT OF THE LANE
  Science and a firm seat put to the test.

4. THE WARREN WALL
  A quick eye and steady hand often save a fall.

Plate 5. THE BROOK
  The pace and pluck clear it gallantly.

6. THE RUN IN
  A good finisher, backed by luck, lands him a winner.

FORES'S HUNTING CASUALTIES,

THAT MAY OCCUR WITH HOUNDS.

A Series of Six Plates, from Original Drawings, by H. Alken, Sen. Price £1. 5s. the Set, Colored.

Plate 1. A TURN OF SPEED OVER THE FLAT
  The result of being Broke in a Grazing Country.

2. A STRANGE COUNTRY
  Only give him his Head, and he'll bring you in at the Death.

Plate 3. DISPATCHED TO HEAD QUARTERS
  Taking it with a Military Seat.

4. UP TO SIXTEEN STONE
  Master of My Weight, but would rather My Weight was Master of him.

Plate 5. A RARE SORT FOR THE DOWNS
  They told me he'd leave Every Thing behind him.

6. A MUTUAL DETERMINATION
  If he goes on this Rate, I am afraid I must Part with him.

FORES'S MARINE SKETCHES.

A COLLECTION OF MARINE SUBJECTS, COLORED, BY SUPERIOR ARTISTS.

THE CUTTER YACHT, CYNTHIA, 50 Tons .... Price, Colored .... 10s.
THE LEDA, R.W.Y.C. a Pair .... Ditto ...... 20s.
THE WYVERN, PRIDE AND GRIEF, R.Y.S. a Pair . Ditto ...... 20s.

THE KESTREL, R.Y.S. .... Price, Colored .... 21s.
THE DOLPHIN, R.T.Y.C. .... Ditto ...... 21s.
H. M. S. DIDO, 18 Guns, a Pair .... Ditto ...... 14s.

Plain .... 5s.
Ditto .... 10s.
Ditto .... 10s.

FORES'S HUNTING DIARY,

Price 5s.

TO RECORD THE SPORT OF THE SEASON,

Arranged for the followers of Fox Hounds, Stag Hounds, and Harriers.

FORES'S HUNTING RACK,

Price 10s. Colored.

A RECEPTACLE FOR THE APPOINTMENT CARDS,

Arranged for the Meets of Three Packs.

THE HORSE'S MOUTH,

SHOWING THE AGE BY THE FORM OF THE TEETH.

BY E. MAYHEW, M.R.C.V.S.
Colored Plates, Price 10s. 6d.

THE AGE, exhibited by the Tables of the Teeth.

FORES'S CELEBRATED WINNERS.

THE FLYING DUTCHMAN,

Winner of the Derby and St. Leger, 1849.

WITH PORTRAITS OF J. FOBERT, THE TRAINER, AND C. MARLOW, THE JOCKEY.

THE HERO,

WITH PORTRAITS OF JOHN DAY, SEN. AND ALFRED DAY.

Price, Colored from the Original Pictures, £1 : 1s. each.

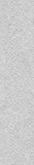

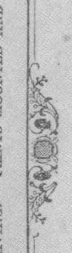

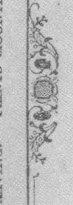

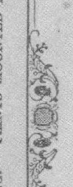

FORES'S GUIDE

TO THE

FOX HOUNDS & STAG HOUNDS OF ENGLAND,

BY GELERT.   Price 5s.

THREE INSTRUCTIVE ANATOMICAL PLATES OF THE HORSE,

Price 4s. each plate, coloured, or 5s. each mounted in a case, pocket size.

THE STRUCTURE OF THE FOOT clearly defined.

THE STRUCTURE OF THE FOOT clearly defined.

THE MUSCLES accurately delineated.

A COLLECTION OF ORIGINAL PICTURES BY HERRING, HENDERSON, SHAYER, DAVIS, CUNLIFFE, ALKEN, SEN. &c., AND A SELECTION OF WATER-COLOR DRAWINGS BY VARIOUS ARTISTS.

CHOICE ARTISTS' PROOFS OF ALL THE FINE ENGRAVINGS FROM PICTURES BY EDWIN LANDSEER, AND OTHERS.

MANUFACTURERS OF FANCY WOOD, ORNAMENTAL GOLD, AND IMITATION CARVED OAK FRAMES, OF NEW AND DURABLE PATTERNS, SUITABLE FOR PICTURES, DRAWINGS, AND THE DIFFERENT STYLES OF ENGRAVING.   PRINTS MOUNTED AND VARNISHED.

GEO. NICHOLS, PRINTER,   EARL'S COURT, SOHO.

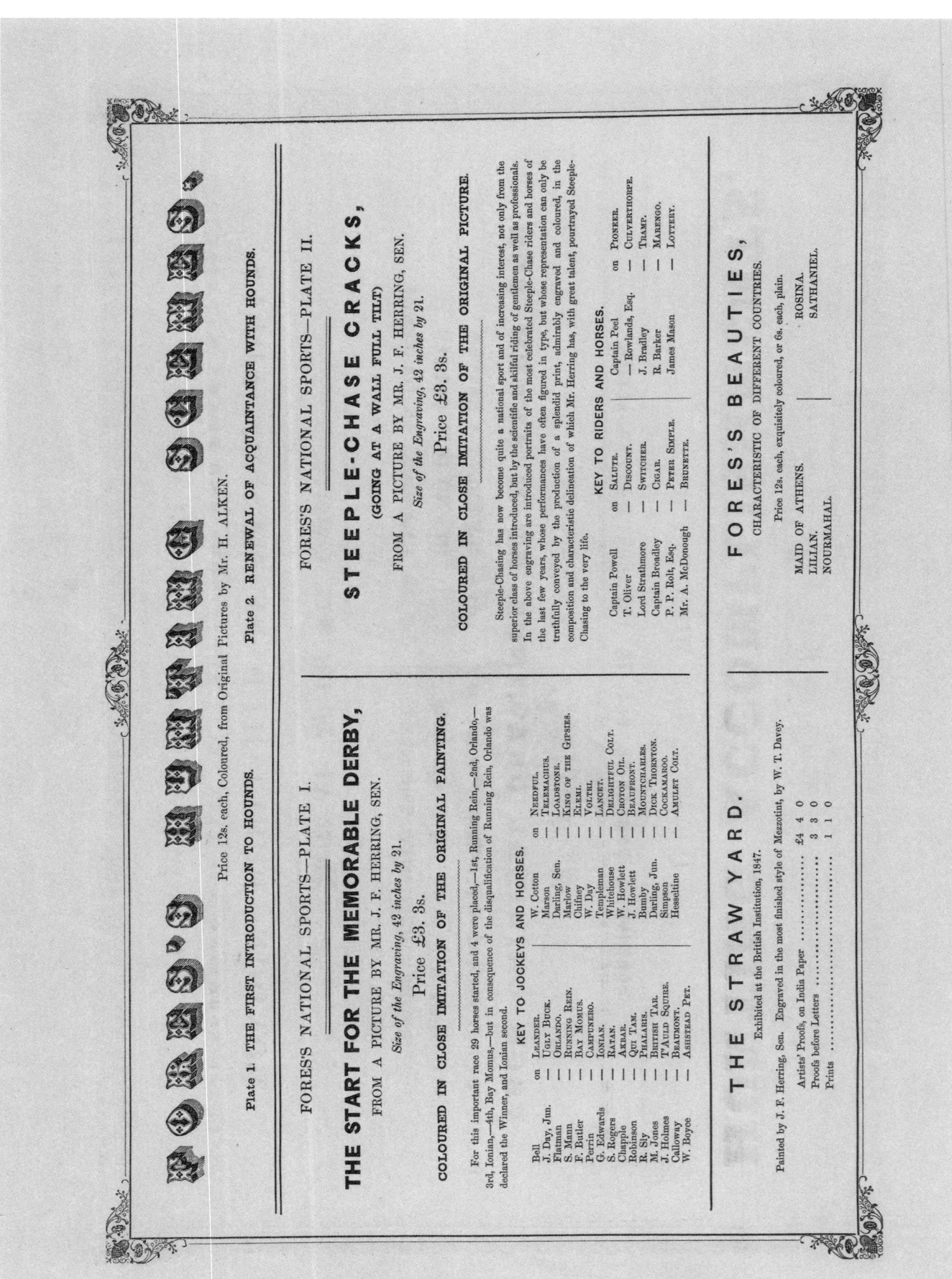

FORES'S COACHING RECOLLECTIONS.
The Set of Five, Coloured, price £5. 5s. By Henderson.

1. CHANGING HORSES.
2. ALL RIGHT.
3. PULLING UP TO UNSKID.
4. WAKING UP.
5. THE OLDEN TIME.

FORES'S STABLE SCENES.
The Set of Four, Coloured, price £4. 4s. By Herring, Sen.

1. THE MAIL CHANGE.
2. THE HUNTING STUD.
3. THOROUGH BREDS.
4. THE TEAM.

FORES'S SPORTING TRAPS.
From the original Pictures by C. C. Henderson, Esq. Price 21s. each, Coloured. To range with the Stable Scenes and Coaching Recollections.

Plate 1. GOING TO THE MOORS.   Plate 2. GOING TO COVER.

FORES'S SERIES OF THE BRITISH STUD.
Comprising Portraits of the most celebrated Thorough-bred Stallions and Mares.

1. SIR HERCULES and BEESWING.
2. TOUCHSTONE and EMMA.
3. PANTALOON and LANGUISH.
4. CAMEL and BANTER.
5. MULEY MOLOCH and REBECCA.
6. LANERCOST and CRUCIFIX.

Price £1 1s. each Plate, Coloured in close imitation of the original Pictures, painted expressly by Mr. J. F. Herring, Sen. for this Work.

FORES'S STEEPLE-CHASE WINNERS.
BRUNETTE,
The celebrated Steeple-Chase Mare.

An admirable PORTRAIT of this extraordinary animal. Beautifully Coloured and Engraved, price £1. 1s.
From the original picture by Herring, Sen.

FORES'S ROAD SCENES.
HORSES GOING TO A FAIR.

1. HUNTERS and HACKS.   2. CART HORSES.

A Pair, price £1. 10s. Coloured, from Pictures by C. G. Henderson, Esq.

FORES'S COACHING INCIDENTS.

Plate 1. KNEE DEEP.
Getting into a snow drift.

Plate 3. FLOODED.
Going it by water above and below.

Plate 5. IN TIME FOR THE COACH.
Box Seat occupied.

2. STUCK FAST.
Snowed up and getting out.

4. THE ROAD versus RAIL.
Beating the Train.

6. LATE FOR THE MAIL.
The Guard asleep.

Price 15s. each, Coloured from the original Pictures by C. C. Henderson, Esq.

FORES'S OPERA SKETCHES.
Price 10s. 6d. each, Coloured.

JENNY LIND, in LA FIGLIA DEL REGGIMENTO.
MARIE PAUL TAGLIONI, in the POSNANIA.
CAROLINA ROSATI, in THEA; OU, LA FEE AU FLEURS.
EMMA HARDING, in THE PHANTOM DANCERS.
LUCILE GRAHN, in LA FILLE DU BANDITTE.
FLORA FABBRI, in the DEVIL TO PAY.
MISS FAIRBROTHER, in THE FORTY THIEVES.
MISS FAIRBROTHER, in VALENTINE AND ORSON.

FORES'S YEOMANRY COSTUMES.
Price 5s. each, Coloured.

1. BUCKS ARTILLERY CORPS.
2. BUCKS HUSSARS.
3. SUFFOLK (PRIVATES).
4. YORKSHIRE HUSSARS.
5. SOUTH SALOPIAN.
6. SECOND WEST YORK.
7. WEST ESSEX.
8. SUFFOLK (OFFICERS).

THE ROADSTER'S ALBUM.
A Pictorial Remembrancer of Travelling Scenes, 17 Coloured Engravings. Price £2. 12s. 6d., bound in Cloth, imperial 4to.

BIBLIOGRAPHY

Alexander, David, and Richard T. Godfrey. *Painters and Engraving: The Reproductive Print from Hogarth to Wilkie.* Exh. cat. New Haven and London: Yale Center for British Art, 1980.

Alken, Henry. *The National Sports of Great Britain.* 1825. Reprint, New York: D. Appleton, 1903.

Annals of Sporting. "Portrait of a Modern Game-Keeper, With Remarks on his general character and Qualifications." *Annals of Sporting* 1 (March 1, 1822).

Bayard, Jane, and Ellen D'Oench. *Darkness into Light: The Early Mezzotint.* Exh. cat. New Haven: Yale University Art Gallery, 1975.

Barrell, John. *The Dark Side of Landscape: The Rural Poor in English Painting 1730–1840.* Cambridge: Cambridge University Press, 1980. Reprint, 2006.

Beckett, J. V. *The Agricultural Revolution.* Oxford: Basil Blackwell, 1990.

Beckford, Peter. *Thoughts on Hunting, In a Series of Familiar Letters to a Friend.* London: E. Easton, 1781.

Berkeley, Grantley. *A Pamphlet in Defence of the Game Laws, In Reply to the Assailants; and on their Effects upon the Morals of the Poor.* London: Longman, Brown, Green, and Longmans, 1845.

Bermingham, Ann. *Landscape and Ideology: The English Rustic Tradition, 1740–1860.* Berkeley: University of California Press, 1986.

Blaine, Delabere P. *An Encylopaedia of Rural Sports.* London: Longman, Orme, Brown, Green and Longmans, 1841.

Boalch, D. H. *Prints and Drawings of British Farm Livestock, 1780–1910: A Record of the Rothamsted Collection.* Harpenden, 1958.

Bok-van Kammen, Welmoet. *Stradanus and the Hunt.* PhD diss., Johns Hopkins University, 1977.

Bovill, E. W. *The England of Nimrod and Surtees, 1815–1854.* London: Oxford University Press, 1959.

Burke, Joseph, ed. *The Analysis of Beauty, with the Rejected Passages from the Manuscript Drafts and Autobiographical Notes.* Oxford: Clarendon Press, 1955.

Clayton, Timothy. *The English Print, 1688–1802.* New Haven and London: Yale University Press for the Paul Mellon Centre for Studies in British Art, 1997.

Chambers, J. D., and G. E. Mingay. The Agricultural Revolution, 1750–1880. New York: Schocken Books, 1968.

Coombs, David. "The English Sporting Print." in British Sporting Painting, 1650–1850. Exh. cat. London: Hayward Gallery, 1975.

——. *Sport and the Countryside in English Paintings, Watercolours and Prints.* Oxford: Phaidon, 1978.

Cormack, Malcolm. *Constable.* Oxford and New York: Phaidon, 1983.

——. *The Paintings of Thomas Gainsborough.* Cambridge: Cambridge University Press, 1991.

——. *Country Pursuits: British, American, and French Sporting Art from the Mellon Collections in the Virginia Museum of Fine Arts.* Richmond: Virginia Museum of Fine Arts in association with University of Virginia Press, 2007.

De Quincey, Thomas. *The English Mail Coach,* 1849. Reprint, London: J. M. Dent; New York: Dutton, 1961.

Delteil, Loys. *Théodore Géricault: The Graphic Work.* 1924. Rev. ed., San Francisco: Alan Wofsy Fine Arts, 2010.

Deuchar, Stephen. *Noble Exercise: The Sporting Ideal in Eighteenth Century British Art.* Exh. cat. New Haven and London: Yale Center for British Art, 1982.

——. *Sporting Art in Eighteenth Century England: A Social and Political History.* New Haven and London: Yale University Press for the Paul Mellon Centre for Studies in British Art, 1988.

Donald, Diana. *The Age of Caricature: Satirical Prints in the Reign of George III.* New Haven and London: Yale University Press for the Paul Mellon Centre for Studies in British Art, 1996.

——. *Picturing Animals in Britain, 1750–1850.* New Haven and London: Yale University Press for the Paul Mellon Centre for Studies in British Art, 2007.

Egerton, Judy. *The Paul Mellon Collection: British Sporting and Animal Paintings, 1655–1867.* London: Tate Gallery for the Yale Center for British Art, 1978.

——. *Wright of Derby.* Exh. cat. New York: Metropolitan Museum of Art, 1990.

——. *George Stubbs, Painter.* New Haven and London: Yale University Press for the Paul Mellon Centre for Studies in British Art, 2007.

Egerton, Judy, and Dudley Snelgrove. *The Paul Mellon Collection: British Sporting and Animal Drawings, ca. 1500–1850.* London: Tate Gallery for the Yale Center for British Art, 1978.

Elsee, John. *A Statement of Facts with Observations on the Propriety of Inclosing Waltham Forest.* London: J. Bailey, 1818.

Ford, John. *Ackermann, 1783–1983: The Business of Art.* London: Ackermann, 1983.

George, Mary Dorothy. *Catalogue of Political and Personal Satires in the British Museum, 1771–1852.* London: British Museum, 1935–49.

Gilbey, Sir Walter. A*nimal Painters of England.* 3 vols. London: Vinton, 1900–11.

Gilmour, Pat. "Lithography." In *Grove Art Online.* Oxford Art Online. Dec. 16, 2011. http://www.oxfordartonline.com/subscriber/article/grove/art/T051371

Godfrey, Richard T. *Wenceslaus Hollar: A Bohemian Artist in England.* Exh. cat. New Haven and London: Yale Center for British Art, 1994.

Goldman, Paul. *Sporting Life: An Anthology of British Sporting Prints.* Exh. cat. London: British Museum, 1983.

Griffin, Emma. *Blood Sport: Hunting in Britain since 1066.* New Haven and London: Yale University Press, 2007.

Grundy, C. Reginald. *James Ward, R.A.: His Life and Works.* London: Otto Limited, 1909.

Hind, Arthur M. *A History of Engraving and Etching, From the 15th Century to the Year 1914.* 1923. Reprint, New York: Dover, 1963.

Hopkins, Harry. *The Long Affray: The Poaching Wars in Britain, 1760–1914.* London: Secker and Warburg, 1985.

Hyland, Ann. "The Horse at War." In *The Essential Horse.* Hilary Bracegirdle and Patricia Connor, eds. London: Wilson, Philip, 2003.

Jones, Malcolm. *The Print in Early Modern England: An Historical Oversight.* New Haven and London: Yale University Press for the Paul Mellon Centre for Studies in British Art, 2010.

Kendall, George E. "Notes on the Life of John Wootton with a List of Engravings after his Pictures." *The Walpole Society* 21 (1932–33).

Kendall, Richard. *Degas: Beyond Impressionism.* Exh. cat. London: National Gallery Publications in association with the Art Institute of Chicago, 1966.

Lane, Charles. *Sporting Aquatints and Their Engravers.* 2 vols. Leigh-on-Sea: F. Lewis Publishers, 1978–79.

——. British *Racing Prints, 1700–1940.* London: Sportsman's Press, 1990.

Laver, James. *English Sporting Prints.* London and Sydney: Ward Lock, 1970.

Lawley, Francis. "Introduction." *Index of Engravings with the Names of the Artists in the Sporting Magazine from the Year 1792 to 1870.* London: Vinton and Company for Walter Gilby, 1892.

Lennox-Boyd, Christopher, C. R. Dixon, and T. Clayton. *George Stubbs: The Complete Engraved Works.* London and New York: Stipple Publishing, 1989.

Lodge, Susan. "Géricault in England." *Burlington Magazine* CVII, no. 753 (December 1965).

Maas, Jeremy. *Gambart, Prince of the Victorian Art World.* London: Barrie and Jenkins, 1975.

Maidment, B. E. *Reading Popular Prints, 1790–1870.* Manchester: Manchester University Press, 1996.

Man, Felix. *150 Years of Artists' Lithographs, 1803–1953.* London: Heinemann, 1953.

Meyer, Arline. J*ohn Wootton, 1682–1764: Landscapes and Sporting Art in Early Georgian England.* Exh. cat. London: Iveagh Bequest, Kenwood, Greater London Council, 1984.

Muir, J. B. *A Descriptive Catalogue of the Engraved Works of J. F. Herring,* Senior. London, 1893.

Munsche, P. B. *Gentlemen and Poachers: The Game Laws, 1671–1831.* Cambridge: Cambridge University Press, 1981.

Nevill, Ralph. *Old English Sporting Prints and Their History.* London: The Studio, 1923.

Nimrod [Charles James Apperley]. "Nimrod's Tour." *The Sporting Magazine* 16 (August 1825).

——. Nimrod's *Hunting Reminiscences Comprising Memoirs of Masters of Hounds, Notices of Crack Riders and Characteristics of the Hunting Countries of England.* London: Lane, 1926. Rev. ed., 1843.

Noakes, Aubrey. *The World of Henry Alken.* London: Witherby, 1953.

——. *Ben Marshall, 1768–1835.* Leigh-on-Sea: F. Lewis Publishers, 1978.

Noon, Patrick J. *Crossing the Channel: British and French Painting in the Age of Romanticism.* Exh. cat. London: Tate Publishing, 2003.

O'Connell, Sheila. *The Popular Print in England, 1550–1850.* London: British Museum Press, 1999.

O'Donaghue, F., and H. M. O'Donaghue. *Catalogue of Engraved British Portraits in the British Museum.* London: British Museum, 1908–25.

Overton, Mark. *Agricultural Revolution in England: The Transformation of the Agrarian Economy, 1500–1850.* Cambridge: Cambridge University Press, 1996.

Parris, Leslie. *Constable and David Lucas.* Exh. cat. New York: Salander-O'Reilly Galleries, 1993.

Paulson, Ronald. *Hogarth's Graphic Works.* 2 vols. Rev. ed., New Haven and London: Yale University Press, 1970.

——. *Hogarth, His Life, Art, and Times.* 3 vols. New Haven and London: Yale University Press for the Paul Mellon Centre for the Studies in British Art, 1971.

——. *Emblem and Expression: Meaning in English Art of the Eighteenth Century.* Cambridge: Harvard University Press, 1975.

Paviere, Sydney H. *A Dictionary of British Sporting Painters.* Leigh-on-Sea: F. Lewis Publishers, 1965.

Pennington, Richard. *A Descriptive Catalogue of the Etched Work of Wenceslaus Hollar, 1607–1677.* Cambridge: Cambridge University Press, 1982.

Penny, Nicholas, ed. *Reynolds.* Exh. cat. New York: Abrams, 1986.

Prideaux, S. T. *Aquatint Engraving.* London: Duckworth and Company, 1909.

Podeschi, John B. *Books on the Horse and Horsemanship, 1400–1941.* London and New Haven: Tate Gallery for the Yale Center for British Art, 1981.

Postle, Martin, ed. *Johann Zoffany RA: Society Observed.* Exh. cat. New Haven and London: Yale University Press, 2011.

Reff, Theodore. *Degas: The Artist's Mind.* New York: Metropolitan Museum of Art and Harper and Row, 1976.

Rix, Brenda D. *Pictures for the Parlour: The English Reproductive Print from 1775 to 1900.* Exh. cat. Toronto: Art Gallery of Ontario, 1983.

Robertson, David. *Sir Charles Eastlake and the Victorian Art World.* Princeton: Princeton University Press, 1978.

Selway, N. C. *The Regency Road.* London: Faber and Faber, 1957.

——. *James Pollard, 1792–1867.* Leigh-on-Sea: F. Lewis Publishers, 1965.

——. *The Golden Age of Coaching and Sport.* Leigh-on Sea: F. Lewis Publishers, 1972.

Schwerdt, C. F. G. R. *Hunting, Hawking, Shooting, Illustrated in a Catalogue of Books, Manuscripts, Prints, and Drawings.* 4 vols. Privately printed, 1928–37.

Siltzer, Frank. *The Story of British Sporting Prints.* London: Halton and Truscott Smith, 1929.

Smith, John Chalenor. *British Mezzotint Portraits.* 4 vols. London: H. Southeran, 1883.

Smith, Thomas. *Extracts from the Diary of a Huntsman.* 2nd ed. London: Whittaker and Company, 1841.

Snelgrove, Dudley, *The Paul Mellon Collection of British Sporting and Animal Prints, 1658–1874.* London: Tate Gallery for the Yale Center for British Art, 1981.

Sparrow, Walter Shaw. *British Sporting Artists from Barlow to Herring.* London: John Lane, The Bodley Head, 1922.

——. *Henry Alken.* London: Williams and Norgate, 1927.

Sporting Magazine. "A Singular Trial." *The Sporting Magazine* 10 (July 1797).

——. "Journal of Modern Characters, A Bon Vivant." *The Sporting Magazine* 17 (November 1800).

——. "Convictions *for Offences against the Game Laws.*" *The Sporting Magazine* 37 (January 1811).

——. "Notices about Hunting." *The Sporting Magazine* 37 (February 1811).

——. "Slight Sketch of the Late Hunting Season in Leicestershire, &c." *The Sporting Magazine,* M.S., 11 (June 1835).

Taylor, Basil. *Sport and the Horse.* Exh. cat. Richmond: Virginia Museum of Fine Arts, 1960.

——. *The Prints of George Stubbs.* Exh. cat. London: Victoria and Albert Museum, 1969.

——. *Animal Painting in England from Barlow to Landseer.* London: Penguin Books, 1970.

Tooley, R. V. *English Books with Coloured Plates, 1790–1860.* London: Batsford, 1954.

Twyman, Michael. *Lithography, 1800–1850.* London: Oxford University Press, 1970.

Virginia Museum of Fine Arts. *Painting in England, 1700–1850: Collection of Mr. and Mrs. Paul Mellon.* Exh. cat. Richmond: Virginia Museum of Fine Arts, 1963.

Walker, Stella A. *Sporting Art, England, 1700–1900.* New York: Clarkson N. Potter, 1972.

Warner, Malcolm, and Blake, Robin. *Stubbs and the Horse.* Exh. cat. New Haven and London: Yale University Press in association with Kimbell Art Museum, Fort Worth, 2004.

Webster, Mary. *Francis Wheatley.* London: Paul Mellon Foundation for British Art, 1970.

Wilder, F. L. *English Sporting Prints.* London: Thames and Hudson, 1974.

Williamson, Tom. *The Transformation of Rural England, Farming and the Landscape, 1700–1870.* Exeter: Exeter University Press, 2002.

Zouch, Henry. *An Account of the Present Daring Practices of Night-Hunters and Poachers, with some Hints upon which to Form a Law, as well for Restraining these Offenders as for the Preservation of Game throughout the Kingdom.* London: J. Stocksdale, 1783.

This catalogue sheds new light on a common but often overlooked contribution of British art: the sporting print. Highly sought after during the eighteenth and nineteenth centuries, these prints endure today as vivid, direct, and even witty symbols of English culture. *Catching Sight* features more than eighty prints and three essays that go beyond the symbolism to examine these works from both art-historical and social perspectives.

Malcolm Cormack details the production and sale of sporting prints; Mitchell Merling explores the aesthetic implications of the sophisticated visual languages employed by sporting artists; and Corey Piper analyzes the meaning of the prints in the larger context of late eighteenth- and nineteenth-century rural society. The essays are followed by a checklist of works in the exhibition and an appendix reproducing source materials for understanding the production and marketing of these works.

124 PAGES

84 CATALOGUE ENTRIES AND

164 FULL-COLOR REPRODUCTIONS

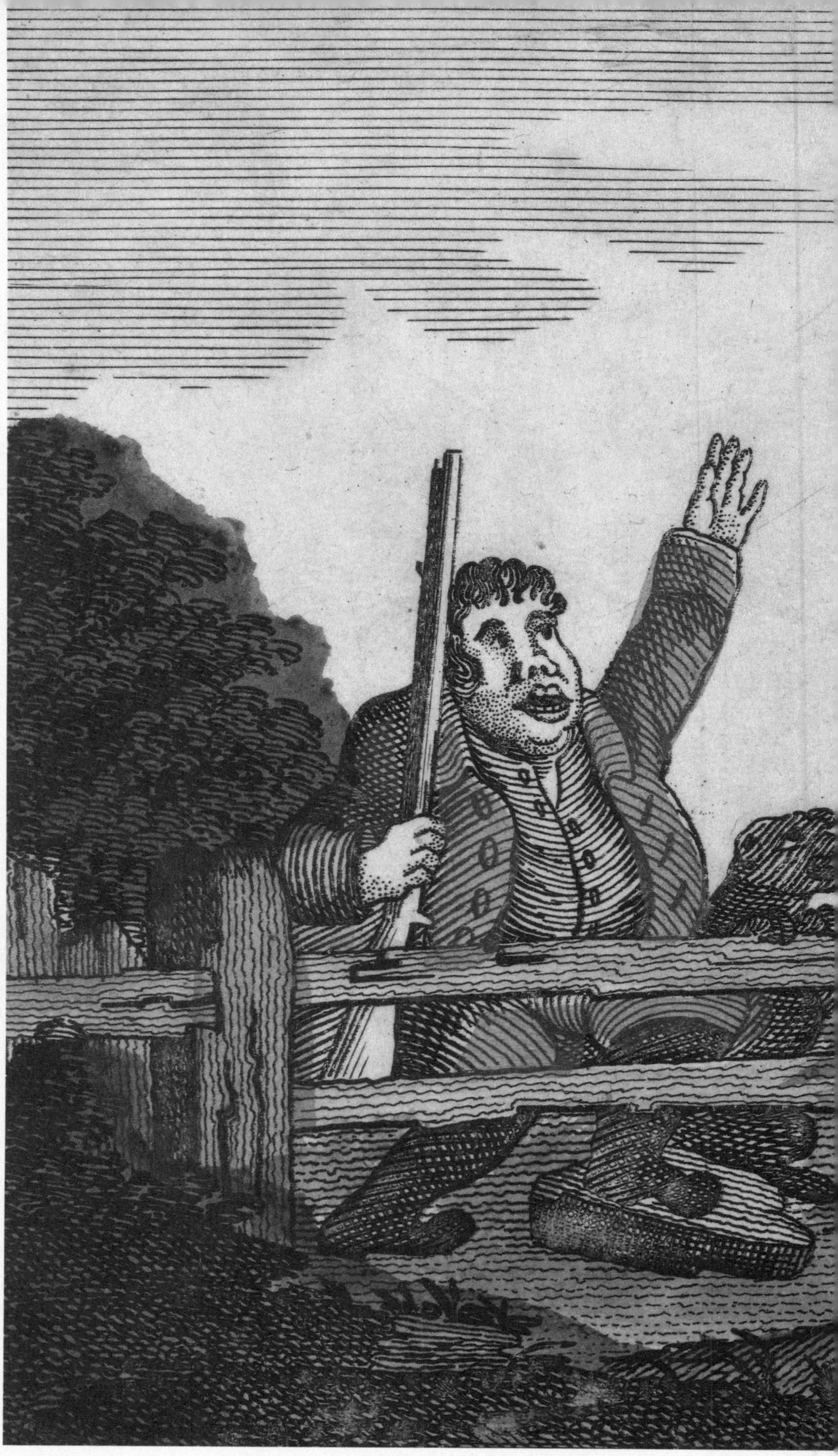

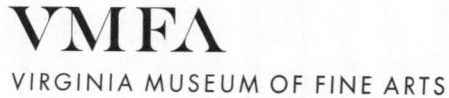

VMFA

VIRGINIA MUSEUM OF FINE ARTS

ISBN 978-193435103-1

9 781934 351031